TOEFL® MAP
ACTUAL TEST

New TOEFL® Edition

Listening 1

DARAKWON

TOEFL® MAP
ACTUAL TEST New TOEFL® Edition
Listening 1

Publisher Chung Kyudo
Editors Cho Sangik, Zong Ziin
Authors Michael A. Putlack, Stephen Poirier, Angela Maas, Maximilian Tolochko
Designers Park Narae, Chung Kyuok

First published in April 2022
By Darakwon, Inc.
Darakwon Bldg., 211, Munbal-ro, Paju-si, Gyeonggi-do 10881
Republic of Korea
Tel: 82-2-736-2031 (Ext. 250)
Fax: 82-2-732-2037

ISBN 978-89-277-8010-6 14740
978-89-277-8007-6 14740 (set)

www.darakwon.co.kr

Photo Credits
Shutterstock.com

Components Main Book / Translation Book
9 8 7 6 5 4 3 24 25 26 27 28

TOEFL® MAP ACTUAL TEST

New TOEFL® Edition

Listening 1

INTRODUCTION

Studying for the TOEFL® iBT is no easy task and is not one that is to be undertaken lightly. It requires a great deal of effort as well as dedication on the part of the student. It is our hope that, by using *TOEFL Map Actual Test Listening* as either a textbook or a study guide, the task of studying for the TOEFL® iBT will become somewhat easier for the student and less of a burden.

Students who wish to excel on the TOEFL® iBT must attain a solid grasp of the four important skills in the English language: reading, listening, speaking, and writing. The Darakwon *TOEFL Map* series covers all four of these skills in separate books. There are three different levels in all four topics. In addition, there are *TOEFL Map Actual Test* books that contain a number of actual tests that students can use to prepare themselves for the TOEFL® iBT. This book, *TOEFL Map Actual Test Listening*, covers the listening aspect of the test by providing conversations and lectures in the TOEFL® iBT actual test format.

TOEFL Map Actual Test Listening has been designed for use both in a classroom setting and as a study guide for individual learners. It contains a total of seven full-length listening actual tests. Each test contains a varying number of conversations and lectures. Every conversation and lecture are the same length as those found on the TOEFL® iBT. The conversations and lectures also have the same numbers and types of questions that appear on actual TOEFL® iBT listening section passages. In addition, the changes that were made to the TOEFL® iBT in August 2019 have been incorporated into this book. By studying these conversations and lectures, learners should be able to prepare themselves to take and, more importantly, to excel on the TOEFL® iBT.

TOEFL Map Actual Test Listening has a great amount of information and should prove to be invaluable as a study guide for learners who are preparing for the TOEFL® iBT. However, while this book is comprehensive, it is up to each person to do the actual work. In order for *TOEFL Map Actual Test Listening* to be of any use, the individual learner must dedicate him or herself to studying the information found within its pages. While we have strived to make this book as user friendly and as full of crucial information as possible, ultimately, it is up to each person to make the best of the material in the book. We wish you luck in your study of both English and the TOEFL® iBT, and we hope that you are able to use *TOEFL Map Actual Test Listening* to improve your abilities in both of them.

Michael A. Putlack
Stephen Poirier
Angela Maas
Maximilian Tolochko

TABLE OF CONTENTS

HOW IS THIS BOOK DIFFERENT

CONTAINS CONVERSATIONS AND LECTURES MOST RECENTLY PRESENTED

- Has 18 conversations and 25 lectures in total
- Reconstructs the most frequently asked questions after analyzing real TOEFL® iBT questions
- Reflects the changes made to the TOEFL® iBT in August 2019

CONSISTS OF VARIOUS TOPICS

- Deals with academic topics such as the humanities, sciences, and arts
- Handles all types of conversations regarding campus life

PROVIDES AN EXPLANATION FOR EVERY QUESTION

- Shows the question types and provides detailed explanations
- Presents tips for getting a higher score

PRESENTS TRANSLATIONS OF THE CONVERSATIONS AND LECTURES

- Contains translations for all conversations and lectures

OFFERS FREE MP3 FILES

- Provides MP3 files for free at www.darakwon.co.kr
- Includes QR codes for listening to the MP3 files instantly

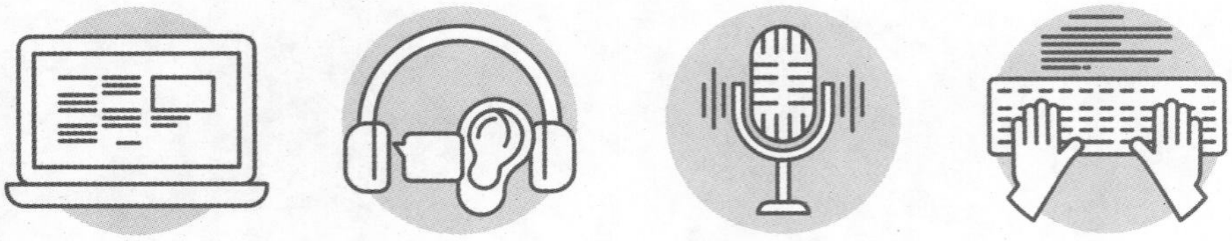

HOW TO USE THIS BOOK

QUESTION

This book contains every type of question that appears on the TOEFL® iBT. The difficulty level of the questions is the same as those on the actual TOEFL® iBT.

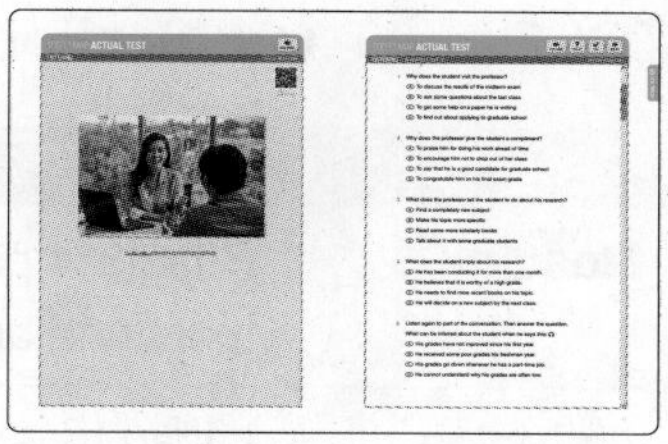

SCRIPT AND EXPLANATION

Every question has its own detailed explanation, so readers can learn why some answer choices are correct while others are not. Readers can also check their listening ability by consulting the scripts. The scripts are word-for-word reproductions of the recordings of the conversations and lectures.

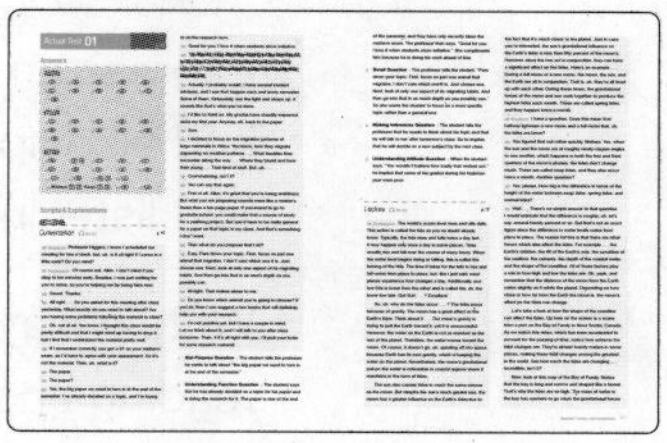

TRANSLATION

In case some Korean readers cannot fully understand the script, a translation section has been attached to the book. This section can help readers grasp the meanings of certain conversations and lectures.

WORD REMINDER

Words and expressions that frequently appear on the actual TOEFL® iBT are listed in this section. In addition, readers can learn key words related to specific topics.

ABOUT THE TOEFL® iBT

TOEFL® iBT Test Sections

Section	Tasks	Time Limit	Questions
Reading	Read 3-4 passages from academic texts and answer questions.	54 – 72 minutes	30 – 40 questions
Listening	Listen to lectures, classroom discussions, and conversations and then answer questions.	41 – 57 minutes	28 – 39 questions
	Break 10 minutes		
Speaking	Express an opinion on a familiar topic and also speak based on reading and listening tasks.	17 minutes	4 tasks
Writing	Write essay responses based on reading and listening tasks and support an opinion in writing.	50 minutes	2 tasks

TOEFL® iBT Test Contents

The TOEFL® iBT test is a test given in English on an Internet-based format. The TOEFL® iBT has four sections: reading, listening, speaking, and writing. The test requires approximately three and a half hours to take.

Combining All Four Skills: Reading, Listening, Speaking, and Writing

During the test, learners must use more than one of the four basic skills at the same time. For instance, learners may have to:

- listen to a question and then speak a response
- read and listen and then speak a response to a question
- read and listen and then write a response to a question

What Is the TOEFL® iBT Test?

The TOEFL® iBT test measures how well learners understand university-level English. The test requires students to use a combination of their reading, listening, speaking, and writing skills to do various academic tasks.

Which Learners Take the TOEFL® iBT Test?

Around one million people take the TOEFL® iBT test every year. The English abilities of most people taking the test are anywhere from intermediate to advanced. The following types of people most commonly take the TOEFL® iBT test:

- students who will study at institutes of higher learning
- students who wish to gain admission to English education programs
- individuals who are applying for scholarships or certificates
- learners who want to determine the level of their English ability
- students and other individuals who are applying for visas

Who Accepts TOEFL® iBT Test Scores?

In more than 130 countries around the world, over 8,000 colleges, universities, agencies, and other institutions accept TOEFL® iBT scores. In addition, the following places utilize TOEFL® iBT scores:

- immigration departments that use the scores when issuing visas
- medical and licensing agencies that award various certificates
- individuals who are trying to determine the level of their English ability

ABOUT THE LISENING QUESTION TYPES

Type 1 Gist-Content Questions

Gist-Content questions cover the test taker's basic comprehension of the listening passage. While they are typically asked after lectures, they are sometimes asked after conversations as well. These questions check to see if the test taker has understood the gist of the passage. They focus on the passage as a whole, so it is important to recognize what the main point of the lecture is or why the two people in the conversation are having a particular discussion. The test taker should therefore be able to recognize the theme of the lecture or conversation in order to answer this question correctly. On occasion, the test taker is asked to identify two correct answers to a single question.

Type 2 Gist-Purpose Questions

Gist-Purpose questions cover the underlying theme of the passage. While they are typically asked after conversations, they are sometimes asked after lectures as well. Because these questions focus on the purpose or theme of the conversation or lecture, they begin with the word "why." They focus on the conversation or lecture as a whole, but they are not concerned with details; instead, they are concerned with why the student is speaking with the professor or employee or why the professor is covering a specific topic.

Type 3 Detail Questions

Detail questions cover the test taker's ability to understand facts and data that are mentioned in the listening passage. There questions most commonly appear after lectures; however, they also come after conversations, especially when the conversations are about academic topics. Detail questions require the test taker to listen for and remember details from the passage. The majority of these questions concern major details that are related to the main topic of the lecture or conversation rather than minor ones. However, in some cases when there is a long digression that is not clearly related to the main idea, there may be a question about the details of the digression. On occasion, the test taker is asked to identify two correct answers to a single question. These questions may also appear as charts.

Type 4 Understanding the Function of What Is Said Questions

Understanding the Function of What Is Said questions cover the test taker's ability to determine the underlying meaning of what has been said in the passage. This question type often involves replaying a portion of the listening passage. There are two types of these questions. Some ask the test taker to infer the meaning of a phrase or a sentence. Thus the test taker needs to determine the implication—not the literal meaning—of the sentence. Other questions ask the test taker to infer the purpose of a statement made by one of the speakers. These questions specifically ask about the intended effect of a particular statement on the listener.

Type 5 Understanding the Speaker's Attitude Questions

Understanding Attitude questions cover the speaker's attitude or opinion toward something. These questions may appear after both lectures and conversations. This question type often involves replaying a portion of the listening passage. There are two types of these questions. Some ask about one of the speaker's feelings concerning something. These questions may check to see whether the test taker understands how a speaker feels about a particular topic, if a speaker likes or dislikes something, or why a speaker might feel anxiety or amusement. The other category asks about one of the speaker's opinions. These questions may inquire about a speaker's degree of certainty. Others may ask what a speaker thinks or implies about a topic, person, thing, or idea.

Type 6 Understanding Organization Questions

Understanding Organization questions cover the test taker's ability to determine the overall organization of the passage. These questions almost always appear after lectures. They rarely appear after conversations. These questions require the test taker to pay attention to two factors. The first is the way that the professor has organized the lecture and how the professor presents the information to the class. The second is how individual information given in the lecture relates to the lectures as a whole. To answer these questions correctly, the test taker should focus more on the presentation and the professor's purpose in mentioning the facts rather than the facts themselves.

Type 7 Connecting Content Questions

Connecting Content questions almost exclusively appear after lectures, not after conversations. These questions measure the test taker's ability to understand how the ideas in the lecture relate to one another. These relationships may be explicitly stated, or the test taker may have to infer them from the words that are spoken. The majority of these questions concern major relationships in the passage. These questions also commonly appear in passages in which a number of different themes, ideas, objects, or individuals are being discussed.

Type 8 Making Inference Questions

Making Inferences questions cover the test taker's ability to understand implications made in the passage and to come to a conclusion about what these implications mean. These questions appear after both conversations and lectures. These questions require the test taker to hear the information being presented and then to make conclusions about what the information means or what is going to happen as a result of that information.

TOEFL® MAP

ACTUAL TEST

Listening 1

01

CONTINUE

VOLUME

00-01

Listening Section Directions

This section measures your ability to understand conversations and lectures in English.

The Listening section is divided into separately timed parts. In each part, you will listen to 1 conversation and 1 or 2 lectures. You will hear each conversation or lecture only **one** time.

After each conversation or lecture, you will answer some questions about it. The questions typically ask about the main idea and supporting details. Some questions ask about a speaker's purpose or attitude. Answer the questions based on what is stated or implied by the speakers.

You may take notes while you listen. You may use your notes to help you answer the questions. Your notes will not be scored.

If you need to change the volume while you listen, click on the **Volume** at the top of the screen.

In some questions, you will see this icon: This means that you will hear, but not see, part of the question.

Some of the questions have special directions. These directions appear in a gray box on the screen.

Most questions are worth 1 point. If a question is worth more than 1 point, it will have special directions that indicate how many points you can receive.

A clock at the top of the screen will show you how much time is remaining. The clock will not count down while you are listening. The clock will count down only while you are answering the questions.

CONTINUE

VOLUME

PART 1

00-02

Listening Directions

In this part, you will listen to 1 conversation and 1 lecture.

You must answer each question. After you answer, click on **Next**. Then click on **OK** to confirm your answer and go on to the next question. After you click on **OK**, you cannot return to previous questions.

You may now begin this part of the Listening Section. You will have **7 minutes** to answer the questions.

Click on **Continue** to go on.

01-01

1 Why does the student visit the professor?

Ⓐ To discuss the results of the midterm exam

Ⓑ To ask some questions about the last class

Ⓒ To get some help on a paper he is writing

Ⓓ To find out about applying to graduate school

2 Why does the professor give the student a compliment?

Ⓐ To praise him for doing his work ahead of time

Ⓑ To encourage him not to drop out of her class

Ⓒ To say that he is a good candidate for graduate school

Ⓓ To congratulate him on his final exam grade

3 What does the professor tell the student to do about his research?

Ⓐ Find a completely new subject

Ⓑ Make his topic more specific

Ⓒ Read some more scholarly books

Ⓓ Talk about it with some graduate students

4 What does the student imply about his research?

Ⓐ He has been conducting it for more than one month.

Ⓑ He believes that it is worthy of a high grade.

Ⓒ He needs to find more recent books on his topic.

Ⓓ He will decide on a new subject by the next class.

5 Listen again to part of the conversation. Then answer the question.

What can be inferred about the student when he says this: 🎧

Ⓐ His grades have not improved since his first year.

Ⓑ He received some poor grades his freshman year.

Ⓒ His grades go down whenever he has a part-time job.

Ⓓ He cannot understand why his grades are often low.

01-02

Environmental
Science

6 What aspect of tides does the professor mainly discuss?

Ⓐ When they most frequently occur in the oceans

Ⓑ The differences between spring and neap tides

Ⓒ How outside forces cause them to rise and fall

Ⓓ Why some tides are higher than others are

7 What comparison does the professor make between the sun and the moon?

Ⓐ The amount of gravitational force they possess

Ⓑ The effect that they have on the Earth's tides

Ⓒ Their relative sizes as they compare to the Earth

Ⓓ The distance from the Earth that both of them are

8 What is a spring tide?

Ⓐ A tide that takes place only during the spring

Ⓑ The lowest level that the tide reaches in a year

Ⓒ A tide that differs slightly from the normal sea level

Ⓓ The tide with the highest level in a month

9 What is the professor's attitude toward the student?

Ⓐ He is tolerant of her constant interruptions.

Ⓑ He is complimentary of her for one of her questions.

Ⓒ He becomes impatient because she asks several questions.

Ⓓ He is pleased that she has read the material.

10 Why does the professor discuss the Bay of Fundy?

Ⓐ To change the topic of the lecture to discuss tidal power

Ⓑ To have the students watch a video of the spring tides there

Ⓒ To show how tides are affected by the shape of the coastline

Ⓓ To answer one of the questions that the student asks him

11 What does the professor imply about tidal power?

Ⓐ It is a more efficient source of energy than fossil fuels.

Ⓑ He is in favor of using it for a couple of reasons.

Ⓒ It has the potential to be cheap and plentiful.

Ⓓ The cost of tidal power stations is currently too high.

CONTINUE

VOLUME

PART 2

00-02

Listening Directions

In this part, you will listen to 1 conversation and 1 lecture.

You must answer each question. After you answer, click on **Next**. Then click on **OK** to confirm your answer and go on to the next question. After you click on **OK**, you cannot return to previous questions.

You may now begin this part of the Listening Section. You will have **7 minutes** to answer the questions.

Click on **Continue** to go on.

01-03

1 Why does the student speak with the resident assistant?

Ⓐ To find out his plans for the Thanksgiving holiday

Ⓑ To get the train schedule for the weekend

Ⓒ To ask about transportation to the airport

Ⓓ To confirm the price of taking a taxi

2 What can be inferred about the student?

Ⓐ She takes a class with the resident assistant.

Ⓑ She wants to stay at school for the holiday.

Ⓒ She has a close relationship with her family.

Ⓓ She has met the resident assistant before.

3 Why is the student going to visit her family this vacation?

Ⓐ She will not be able to go home for Christmas.

Ⓑ One of her aunts is getting married.

Ⓒ She has not seen them in a long time.

Ⓓ Her next trip home will be in the summer.

4 Listen again to part of the conversation. Then answer the question.

What does the student mean when she says this: 🎧

Ⓐ She does not like to spend money.

Ⓑ She cannot afford to take a taxi.

Ⓒ She dislikes taking public transportation.

Ⓓ She is unsure of the price of a taxi.

5 Listen again to part of the conversation. Then answer the question.

What is the purpose of the resident assistant's response: 🎧

Ⓐ To change the topic of the conversation

Ⓑ To confirm that he is being serious

Ⓒ To ask the student for her opinion

Ⓓ To add some humor to the conversation

01-04

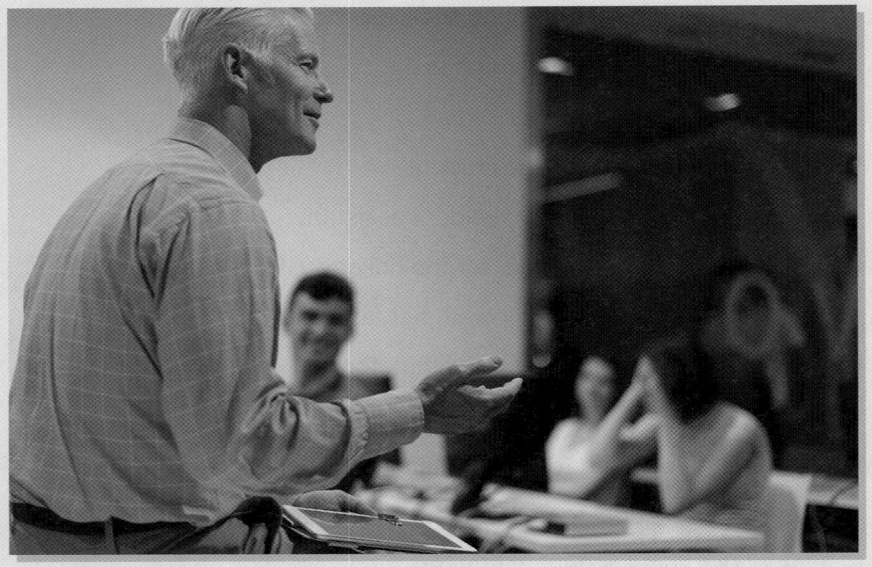

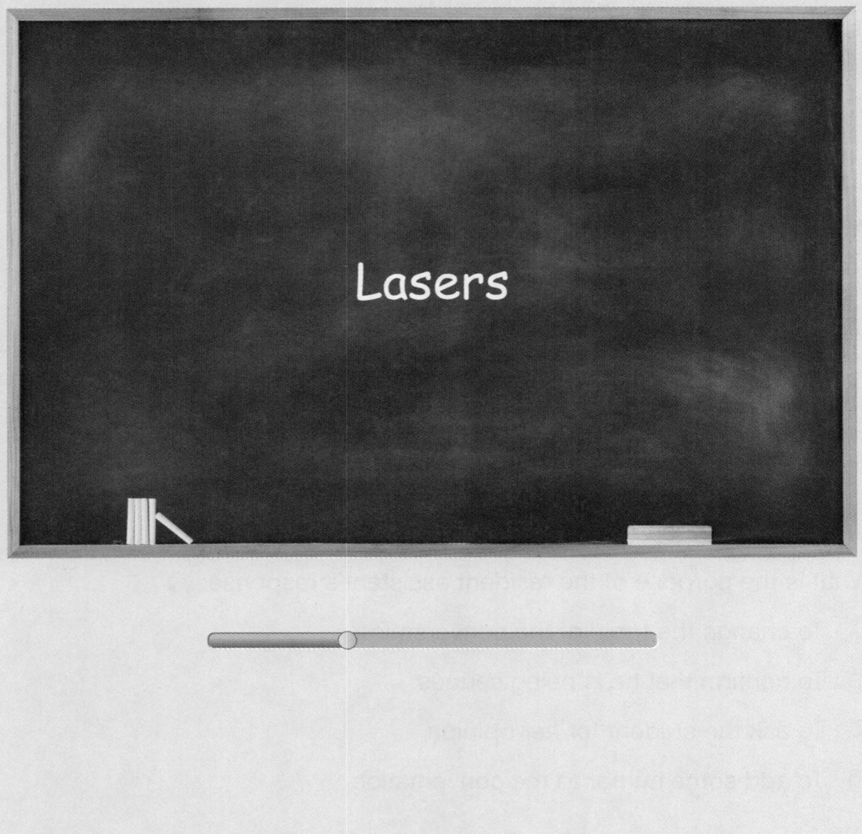

6 What aspect of lasers does the professor mainly discuss?

Ⓐ Who developed them

Ⓑ How they are produced

Ⓒ What they are used for

Ⓓ When they were first theorized

7 According to the professor, what is a gain medium?

Ⓐ A source of energy that enables a laser beam to be created

Ⓑ A low-energy state in which the photons are not yet excited

Ⓒ An optical cavity in a laser through which light will emerge

Ⓓ A substance used to increase the energy of the atoms in a laser

8 Why does the professor discuss the lasing threshold?

Ⓐ To note its relevance to the creation of a laser beam

Ⓑ To state that it can use crystal, gas, or some types of glass

Ⓒ To compare its importance with the gain medium

Ⓓ To explain what use scientists have for it

9 What will the professor probably do next?

Ⓐ Have the students conduct an experiment

Ⓑ Draw a diagram of a laser on the blackboard

Ⓒ Give a short demonstration for the students

Ⓓ Ask the students if they have any questions

10 Listen again to part of the lecture. Then answer the question.

Why does the professor say this: 🎧

Ⓐ To admit that he does not know the answer

Ⓑ To give the student permission to speak

Ⓒ To request that the students be polite

Ⓓ To make a remark about the student's comment

11 Listen again to part of the lecture. Then answer the question.

What does the student mean when she says this: 🎧

Ⓐ The professor needs to explain the information better.

Ⓑ She thinks that the professor made a mistake.

Ⓒ The material the class is learning is too difficult.

Ⓓ She does not understand what the professor said.

CONTINUE

VOLUME

PART 3

00-03

Listening Directions

In this part, you will listen to 1 conversation and 2 lectures.

You must answer each question. After you answer, click on **Next**. Then click on **OK** to confirm your answer and go on to the next question. After you click on **OK**, you cannot return to previous questions.

You may now begin this part of the Listening Section. You will have **10 minutes** to answer the questions.

Click on **Continue** to go on.

TOEFL® MAP **ACTUAL TEST**

VOLUME

LISTENING

00:10:00 HIDE TIME

01-05

1 What are the speakers mainly discussing?

(A) The definitions of some terms used in a class

(B) Some mistakes that the student made on a paper

(C) A class assignment the student must do

(D) Some material that the student recently read

2 According to the professor, what is an exotic species?

Click on 2 answers.

1 An organism that causes harm to its environment

2 An organism that is introduced to a new ecosystem

3 An organism that is originally from a tropical location

4 An organism that does not damage its environment

3 Why does the professor tell the student about the midterm paper?

(A) To remind him when the paper must be submitted

(B) To advise him to do his best on this assignment

(C) To assign him a topic that he should write about

(D) To go over some of the problems on his paper

4 What is the student's attitude toward the professor?

(A) He is pleased that she is so helpful to him.

(B) He feels that she should explain herself better.

(C) He believes she is not answering his questions.

(D) He is happy she has come up with an assignment for him.

5 What will the professor probably do next?

(A) Speak with a different student

(B) Teach a class

(C) Leave the campus

(D) Go to a staff meeting

TOEFL® MAP **ACTUAL TEST**

VOLUME

LISTENING

00:07:00 HIDE TIME

01-06

History

6 What is the main topic of the lecture?

Ⓐ Irish home rule in the 1900s

Ⓑ A battle during World War I

Ⓒ The Irish Easter Rebellion

Ⓓ British-Irish relations in the 1900s

7 According to the professor, how were the Germans involved in the Easter Rising?

Ⓐ They provided military advice for the Irish.

Ⓑ They attacked British forces to distract them from Ireland.

Ⓒ They funded the leaders of the Irish rebellion.

Ⓓ They attempted to send weapons to the Irish.

8 How is the lecture organized?

Ⓐ By describing events in chronological order

Ⓑ By engaging the students in a class discussion

Ⓒ By focusing on the key individuals in the revolt

Ⓓ By stressing the political implications of Irish home rule

9 What will the professor probably do next?

Ⓐ Continue lecturing on a similar topic

Ⓑ Begin a class discussion on what he just discussed

Ⓒ Provide his interpretation of the events he covered

Ⓓ Talk about revolutions in other countries

10 Listen again to part of the lecture. Then answer the question.

What does the professor mean when he says this:

Ⓐ He cannot remember most of the names of the people and the organizations.

Ⓑ He is not going to give the students any names of people or groups.

Ⓒ The students should look up the names of the leaders by themselves.

Ⓓ The names of the groups involved are of little historical significance.

11 Listen again to part of the lecture. Then answer the question.

What does the professor imply when he says this:

Ⓐ He respects the tactical abilities of the Irish.

Ⓑ No rebellion with bad military leaders has ever succeeded.

Ⓒ Ports and train stations are important to armies.

Ⓓ He has a lot of knowledge about fighting revolutions.

TOEFL® MAP **ACTUAL TEST**

VOLUME

LISTENING

00:04:00 HIDE TIME

01-07

Zoology

12 What is the lecture mainly about?

Ⓐ The biological connection between humans and other primates

Ⓑ The creation of both sign language and lexigrams

Ⓒ The experience researchers had with Washoe

Ⓓ Attempts to teach apes to communicate with humans

13 According to the professor, why did researchers first suggest teaching sign language to primates?

Click on 2 answers.

1 They thought that primates could use their hands to sign well.

2 They believed primates were unable to speak like humans.

3 They felt that primates were less intelligent than people.

4 They considered primates smart enough to learn complex motions.

14 How does the professor explain lexigrams to the students?

Ⓐ By showing the students a lexigram keyboard

Ⓑ By having the students look at some lexigrams in their books

Ⓒ By drawing some lexigrams on the blackboard

Ⓓ By asking a student to describe some lexigrams

15 Based on the information in the lecture, indicate whether the statements refer to Washoe or Kanzi.

Click in the correct box for each statement.

	Washoe	Kanzi
1 Uses lexigrams to speak with people		
2 Often signed faster than her trainers		
3 Learned to communicate by watching his mother be taught		
4 Knew around 350 words		

16 What can be inferred about the professor?

Ⓐ She has trained a primate to communicate with humans.

Ⓑ She believes it is possible to teach primates to communicate.

Ⓒ She thinks primates can learn to speak some English words.

Ⓓ She doubts some of the claims made by Washoe's trainers.

17 Listen again to part of the lecture. Then answer the question.

What can be inferred about the student when he says this:

Ⓐ He doubts that Kanzi is trying to speak.

Ⓑ He is interested in learning more about Kanzi.

Ⓒ He has seen Kanzi communicate in person.

Ⓓ He wants the professor to explain in more detail.

TOEFL® MAP

ACTUAL TEST

Listening 1

02

CONTINUE VOLUME

Listening Section Directions

00-01

This section measures your ability to understand conversations and lectures in English.

The Listening section is divided into separately timed parts. In each part, you will listen to 1 conversation and 1 or 2 lectures. You will hear each conversation or lecture only **one** time.

After each conversation or lecture, you will answer some questions about it. The questions typically ask about the main idea and supporting details. Some questions ask about a speaker's purpose or attitude. Answer the questions based on what is stated or implied by the speakers.

You may take notes while you listen. You may use your notes to help you answer the questions. Your notes will not be scored.

If you need to change the volume while you listen, click on the **Volume** at the top of the screen.

In some questions, you will see this icon: 🎧 This means that you will hear, but not see, part of the question.

Some of the questions have special directions. These directions appear in a gray box on the screen.

Most questions are worth 1 point. If a question is worth more than 1 point, it will have special directions that indicate how many points you can receive.

A clock at the top of the screen will show you how much time is remaining. The clock will not count down while you are listening. The clock will count down only while you are answering the questions.

CONTINUE

VOLUME

PART 1

00-02

Listening Directions

In this part, you will listen to 1 conversation and 1 lecture.

You must answer each question. After you answer, click on **Next**. Then click on **OK** to confirm your answer and go on to the next question. After you click on **OK**, you cannot return to previous questions.

You may now begin this part of the Listening Section. You will have **7 minutes** to answer the questions.

Click on **Continue** to go on.

02-01

1 What are the speakers mainly discussing?

- (A) A visit to a health clinic the student made
- (B) The student's proposal for a project
- (C) A paper that the student just submitted
- (D) An interview the student is going to conduct

2 Why does the student explain about Dr. Brown's Family Health Clinic?

- (A) To recommend that the professor go there
- (B) To talk about the treatment she received there
- (C) To discuss its connection with her project
- (D) To criticize the owner's marketing techniques

3 What does the professor imply about Dr. Brown's Family Health Clinic?

- (A) Its prices are the cheapest in the city.
- (B) It will likely go out of business sometime soon.
- (C) She will go there the next time she is sick.
- (D) The owner of it is a personal friend of hers.

4 What does the professor tell the student that she ought to do?

- (A) Come up with a new topic
- (B) Submit her proposal
- (C) Rewrite her entire paper
- (D) Interview Dr. Brown

5 Listen again to part of the conversation. Then answer the question.

What can be inferred about the student when she says this: 🎧

- (A) She believes that she made a mistake.
- (B) She is upset by the professor's response.
- (C) She is unfamiliar with how to use email.
- (D) She forgot the professor's address.

02-02

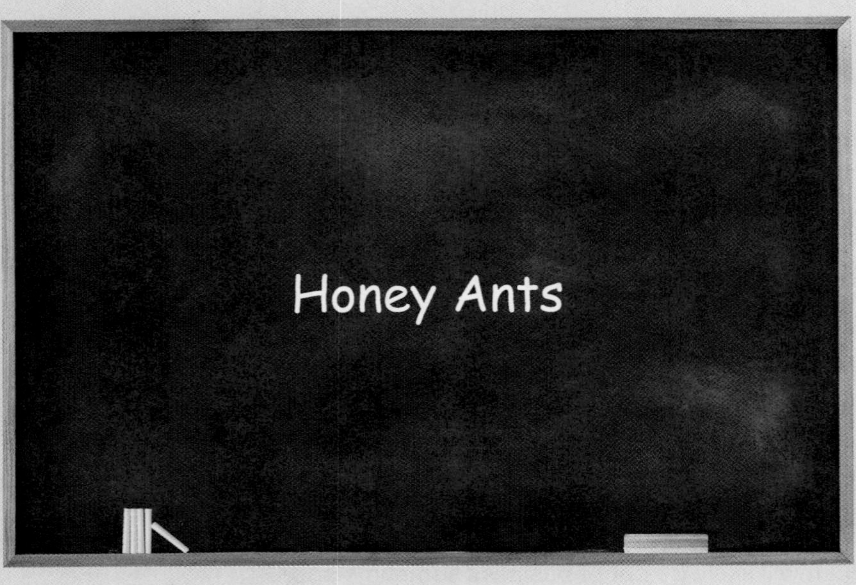

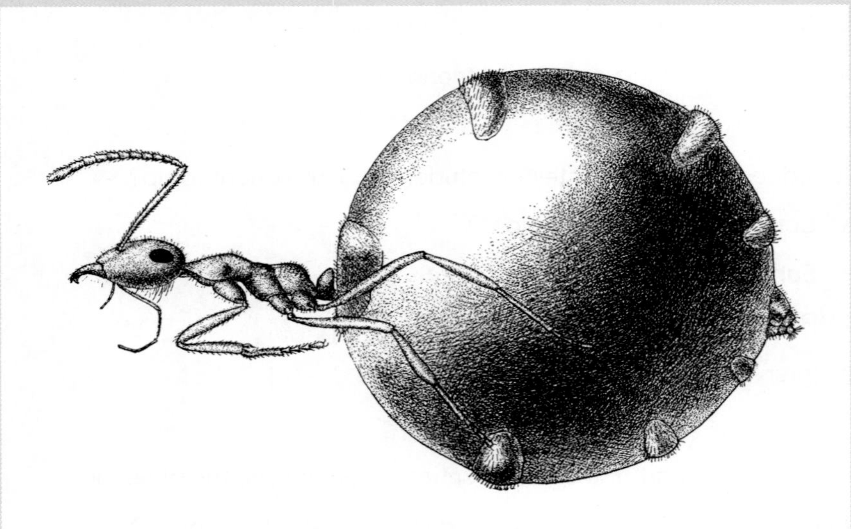

6 According to the professor, what do honey ants eat?

Click on 2 answers.

1 Honey

2 Aphids

3 Nectar

4 Insects

7 What can be inferred about storage honey ants?

(A) Fewer of them store water than store food.

(B) They do not leave the colony during their entire lives.

(C) Some of them lead hunting expeditions.

(D) There are more of them than forager ants in a colony.

8 What is a likely outcome of an attack by one honey ant colony against another?

(A) Most of the ants in the losing colony will be killed.

(B) The two colonies will combine into one larger colony.

(C) All of the ants in both colonies will fight until they die.

(D) Some ants in the losing colony will die of starvation.

9 Why does the professor mention the American Southwest?

Ⓐ To say that honey ants were first found there

Ⓑ To name one place where honey ants live

Ⓒ To focus on the harsh environment there

Ⓓ To talk about the research that she did there

10 What does the professor imply about the students in her class?

Ⓐ Not all of them are doing their homework.

Ⓑ They need to ask more questions in class.

Ⓒ Their grades ought to improve soon.

Ⓓ Some of them are falling asleep in class.

11 Listen again to part of the lecture. Then answer the question.

What does the professor imply when she says this: 🎧

Ⓐ She has eaten honey ants in the past.

Ⓑ She understands why animals like honey ants.

Ⓒ She wants the students to be more adventuresome.

Ⓓ She will prepare some honey ants in a later class.

CONTINUE VOLUME

PART 2

00-03

Listening Directions

In this part, you will listen to 1 conversation and 2 lectures.

You must answer each question. After you answer, click on **Next**. Then click on **OK** to confirm your answer and go on to the next question. After you click on **OK**, you cannot return to previous questions.

You may now begin this part of the Listening Section. You will have **10 minutes** to answer the questions.

Click on **Continue** to go on.

TOEFL® MAP **ACTUAL TEST**

VOLUME

LISTENING

00:10:00 HIDE TIME

02-03

1 What is the first problem that the student discusses?

Ⓐ There is water leaking into her dormitory room.

Ⓑ Both of her roommates make messes in their room.

Ⓒ Some insects in her room are stinging her.

Ⓓ She does not get along with her roommates.

2 What can be inferred about the housing office employee?

Ⓐ He has only been doing his job for a few weeks.

Ⓑ He is not sure how he can assist the student.

Ⓒ He attends classes at the school on a part-time basis.

Ⓓ He is eager to solve the student's problems.

3 According to the student, why are there ants in her dormitory room?

Ⓐ They came into her room because of the rain.

Ⓑ Her roommates leave uneaten food on the floor.

Ⓒ The students next door to her brought them in.

Ⓓ She is not sure what has attracted the ants.

4 What will the housing office employee probably do next?

Ⓐ Pay a visit to the student's dormitory room

Ⓑ Contact someone about the water in the student's room

Ⓒ Listen to the student describe her room's third problem

Ⓓ Have the student fill out some forms concerning her room

5 Listen again to part of the conversation. Then answer the question.

What does the housing office employee imply when he says this: 🎧

Ⓐ He did not enjoy the bad weather.

Ⓑ It is currently the rainy season.

Ⓒ A lot of rain fell during the storm.

Ⓓ It rarely rains in their location.

TOEFL® MAP **ACTUAL TEST**

VOLUME

LISTENING

00:07:00 HIDE TIME

02-04

6 What is the main topic of the lecture?

Ⓐ The European influence on American artists

Ⓑ The artists of the Hudson River School

Ⓒ Realism and Impressionism in American art

Ⓓ American art movements in the 1800s

7 What does the professor imply about the works by the Hudson River School artists?

Ⓐ They were comparable to those of J.M.W. Turner.

Ⓑ He believes that they look good.

Ⓒ They should have used more realism.

Ⓓ They were better than those made by the Impressionists.

8 Why does the professor mention Luminism?

Ⓐ To discuss its use in paintings of the American West

Ⓑ To state that it was utilized by Thomas Cole

Ⓒ To explain the effects of a painting technique

Ⓓ To criticize how it made some paintings look

9 According to the professor, how did painters that used Luminism differ from Impressionist painters?

Ⓐ The brushstrokes of Luminist painters could not be seen.

Ⓑ The Luminists were more inspired by European styles.

Ⓒ Luminist painters used brighter colors than the Impressionists.

Ⓓ Painters that utilized Luminism focused more on outdoor scenes.

10 Based on the information in the lecture, indicate whether the statements refer to the Hudson River School or the Impressionist Movement.

Click in the correct box for each statement.

	Hudson River School	Impressionist Movement
1 It gained influence in the United States in the 1870s.		
2 Its artists focused on one geographical area in the United States.		
3 One of its major artists was Theodore Robinson.		
4 The artists in it often utilized Luminism.		

11 What does the professor imply about Claude Monet?

Ⓐ He mostly painted landscapes.

Ⓑ He spent some time in the United States.

Ⓒ He was an Impressionist painter.

Ⓓ He was better than most American painters.

02-05

Meteorology

12 What is the main topic of the lecture?

Ⓐ The cells of air in the atmosphere

Ⓑ The effect that air has on the weather

Ⓒ Ferrel and Hadley cells

Ⓓ The Coriolis Effect

13 What causes the Coriolis Effect?

Ⓐ The rotation of the Earth

Ⓑ The changing of the seasons

Ⓒ The angle of the sun's rays

Ⓓ The moving of the ocean currents

14 Why does the professor tell the students to open their textbooks?

Ⓐ To read a passage

Ⓑ To examine a chart

Ⓒ To look at a diagram

Ⓓ To observe a picture

15 What can be inferred about Ferrel cells?

Ⓐ They are understood much less than Polar cells.

Ⓑ They are farther away from the equator than Hadley cells.

Ⓒ They cover less of the Earth's atmosphere than Polar cells.

Ⓓ They and Hadley cells were discovered by the same scientist.

16 Why does the professor explain the movement of air in Ferrel cells?

Ⓐ To show the students why the weather in Ferrel cells is fairly unchanging

Ⓑ To give a reason for the rapid temperature changes in Ferrel cells

Ⓒ To answer a question about them that a student asks

Ⓓ To contrast them with the movement of air in Polar and Hadley cells

17 What will the professor probably do next?

Ⓐ Collect the students' homework

Ⓑ Let the students go for the day

Ⓒ Explain a difficult concept again

Ⓓ Give a demonstration on air flow

TOEFL® MAP

ACTUAL TEST

Listening 1

03

CONTINUE

VOLUME

00-01

Listening Section Directions

This section measures your ability to understand conversations and lectures in English.

The Listening section is divided into separately timed parts. In each part, you will listen to 1 conversation and 1 or 2 lectures. You will hear each conversation or lecture only **one** time.

After each conversation or lecture, you will answer some questions about it. The questions typically ask about the main idea and supporting details. Some questions ask about a speaker's purpose or attitude. Answer the questions based on what is stated or implied by the speakers.

You may take notes while you listen. You may use your notes to help you answer the questions. Your notes will not be scored.

If you need to change the volume while you listen, click on the **Volume** at the top of the screen.

In some questions, you will see this icon: This means that you will hear, but not see, part of the question.

Some of the questions have special directions. These directions appear in a gray box on the screen.

Most questions are worth 1 point. If a question is worth more than 1 point, it will have special directions that indicate how many points you can receive.

A clock at the top of the screen will show you how much time is remaining. The clock will not count down while you are listening. The clock will count down only while you are answering the questions.

CONTINUE

VOLUME

PART 1

00-02

Listening Directions

In this part, you will listen to 1 conversation and 1 lecture.

You must answer each question. After you answer, click on **Next**. Then click on **OK** to confirm your answer and go on to the next question. After you click on **OK**, you cannot return to previous questions.

You may now begin this part of the Listening Section. You will have **7 minutes** to answer the questions.

Click on **Continue** to go on.

03-01

1 Why did the man ask to speak with the student?

Ⓐ To ask her for an employee's contact information

Ⓑ To find out when she has her next class

Ⓒ To discuss her work schedule with her

Ⓓ To convince her to work a longer shift

2 Why is the student unable to work on Friday?

Ⓐ She goes out of town then.

Ⓑ She has a class to attend.

Ⓒ She goes home every Friday.

Ⓓ She works at her second job then.

3 How does the woman propose to solve the man's problem?

Ⓐ She will withdraw from a class in order to work another shift.

Ⓑ She will ask some of her friends if they want a part-time job.

Ⓒ She and another student will rearrange the times that they work.

Ⓓ She will encourage another student to work more hours.

4 What will the student probably do next?

Ⓐ Telephone one of her coworkers

Ⓑ Continue working at her job

Ⓒ Attend her class on Russian history

Ⓓ Visit the student employment office

5 Listen again to part of the conversation. Then answer the question.

What can be inferred from the man's response to the student: 🎧

Ⓐ Calvin is one of the best workers he has.

Ⓑ Calvin and the student are coworkers.

Ⓒ The student is close friends with Calvin.

Ⓓ Calvin is considering quitting his job.

03-02

Literature

6 What is the main topic of the lecture?

(A) The scientific writings of Mary Shelley and Robert Louis Stevenson

(B) The possibility of people misusing science to do improper experiments

(C) The role of science in literature written in the nineteenth century

(D) The need for writers to use accurate descriptions of scientific experiments

7 What is the professor's attitude toward the 1800s?

(A) It was a relatively normal period of time.

(B) He considers it to have been a dangerous time.

(C) He offers no opinion on that time period.

(D) He is impressed by what happened then.

8 Why does the professor mention the movie versions of *Frankenstein*?

(A) To credit them for popularizing the novel by Mary Shelley

(B) To tell the students that they are different from the book

(C) To admit that they make use of too much pseudoscience

(D) To confess that he enjoyed them more than he did the book

9 Why does the professor explain galvanism?

Ⓐ To show the students why it was faulty science

Ⓑ To say why some people believed that they could create life

Ⓒ To describe an important part of the plot of *Frankenstein*

Ⓓ To blame it for having ruined Dr. Frankenstein's life

10 Based on the information in the lecture, indicate whether the statements refer to *Frankenstein* or *The Strange Case of Dr. Jekyll and Mr. Hyde*.

Click in the correct box for each statement.

	Frankenstein	*The Strange Case of Dr. Jekyll and Mr. Hyde*
1 One of the individuals in the story is rejected by the main character.		
2 The main character consumes a potion.		
3 The story ends with the possible suicide of the main character.		
4 Some of a main character's family members are murdered.		

11 What does the professor imply about Jules Verne?

Ⓐ His works were less popular than Mary Shelley's.

Ⓑ He thought that science could be a positive force.

Ⓒ He helped inspire the writings of Robert Louis Stevenson.

Ⓓ His books often contained stories using real science.

CONTINUE

VOLUME

PART 2

00-03

Listening Directions

In this part, you will listen to 1 conversation and 2 lectures.

You must answer each question. After you answer, click on **Next**. Then click on **OK** to confirm your answer and go on to the next question. After you click on **OK**, you cannot return to previous questions.

You may now begin this part of the Listening Section. You will have **10 minutes** to answer the questions.

Click on **Continue** to go on.

03-03

1 What are the speakers mainly discussing?

(A) A problem the student has with another professor

(B) The student's desire to improve his class grade

(C) An upcoming assignment the student must do

(D) The student's performance on a test that he took

2 Why does the student want to drop his astronomy class?

Click on 2 answers.

[1] His grade in it will keep him off the Dean's List.

[2] It starts too early in the morning for him to attend.

[3] The class is interfering with his other courses.

[4] He is not enjoying it as much as he had hoped to.

3 What can be inferred about the student?

(A) He is going to major in astronomy.

(B) He is not used to getting poor grades.

(C) He enjoys chatting with his advisor.

(D) He is going to graduate in one semester.

4 Listen again to part of the conversation. Then answer the question.

What does the student imply when he says this:

(A) He cannot do math problems without a calculator.

(B) He will register for a math class next semester.

(C) He took a math class the previous semester.

(D) He needs a tutor to help him in his math class.

5 Listen again to part of the conversation. Then answer the question.

What does the professor mean when he says this:

(A) He agrees with the student's decision to drop the class.

(B) He wants the student to study harder in the class.

(C) He believes the student should think more about his options.

(D) He feels that the student is making a hasty decision.

VOLUME

LISTENING

00:07:00 HIDE TIME

03-04

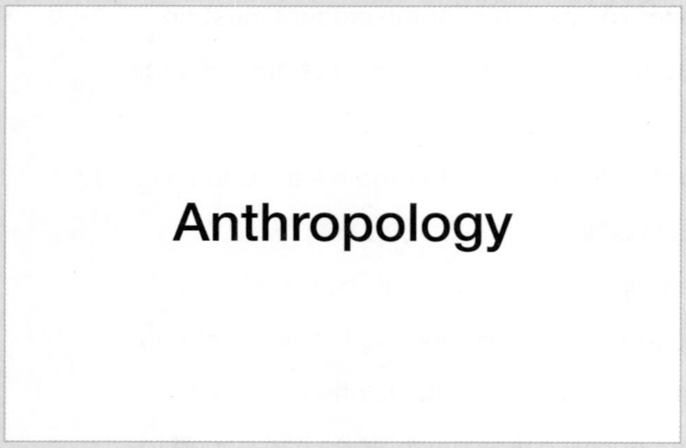

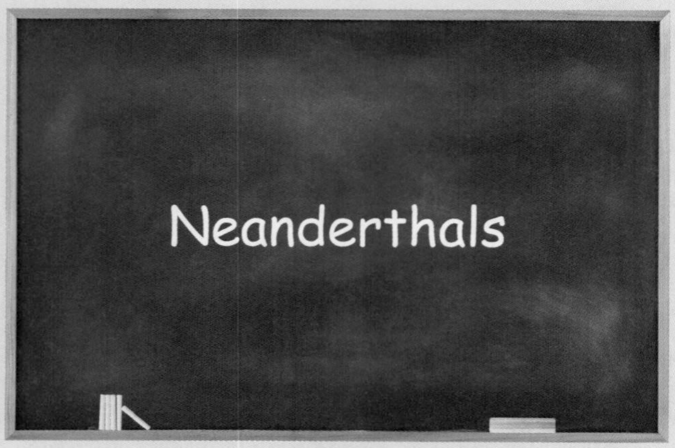

6 How does the professor organize the information about Neanderthal skulls that she presents to the class?

Ⓐ By showing slides of Neanderthal skulls

Ⓑ By providing a handout for the students to look at

Ⓒ By comparing them with human skulls

Ⓓ By describing the skulls in minute detail

7 According to the professor, why do anthropologists believe that Neanderthals looked after the elderly and sick?

Ⓐ They learned that by studying some cave art pictures left by the Neanderthals.

Ⓑ They arrived at that conclusion after examining the remains of some Neanderthals.

Ⓒ There is evidence in Neanderthals' DNA that many of them had long lifespans.

Ⓓ Proof that the Neanderthals made primitive types of medicine has been unearthed.

8 What does the professor imply about the presence of a hyoid bone in Neanderthals?

Ⓐ It enabled them to become very strong.

Ⓑ It prevented them from growing tall.

Ⓒ It permitted them to be able to speak.

Ⓓ It allowed them to move at fast speeds.

9 Why does the professor mention Cro-Magnon man?

(A) To cover one theory concerning the extinction of the Neanderthals

(B) To compare Cro-Magnon man's physical characteristics with those of Neanderthals

(C) To prove that Neanderthals were less evolved than Cro-Magnons were

(D) To describe the places where Cro-Magnon man primarily lived

10 Based on the information in the lecture, indicate whether the statements refer to Neanderthals or Cro-Magnons.

Click in the correct box for each statement.

	Neanderthals	Cro-Magnons
1 Were the ancestors of modern humans		
2 Possessed strong hands and arms		
3 Averaged 165cm in height for males		
4 Originally came from Africa		

11 Listen again to part of the lecture. Then answer the question.

Why does the professor say this:

(A) To make a joke with the student

(B) To apologize to the student

(C) To approve of the student's answer to her question

(D) To commend the student

03-05

Geology

12 What is the lecture mainly about?

Ⓐ Where in the world most islands are created

Ⓑ The world's most volcanic islands

Ⓒ The creation of long chains of islands

Ⓓ Some ways in which islands are formed

13 Why does the professor explain what happened at the end of the last ice age?

Ⓐ To note that the water level was once lower than it is today

Ⓑ To describe how glaciers created some islands

Ⓒ To say that melting ice increased the water level

Ⓓ To account for the creation of the Hawaiian Islands

14 According to the professor, how was Iceland formed?

Ⓐ By a sinking volcano

Ⓑ By receding glaciers

Ⓒ By volcanic eruptions

Ⓓ By moving tectonic plates

15 What can be inferred about coral atolls?

Ⓐ There are many of them in the Ring of Fire.

Ⓑ They are only located in the Pacific Ocean.

Ⓒ They can form in a rapid amount of time.

Ⓓ They sometimes sink beneath the ocean.

16 How is the lecture organized?

Ⓐ The professor compares the different types of islands in the Ring of Fire.

Ⓑ The professor covers the five major ways in which islands are formed.

Ⓒ The professor shows slides of islands and talks about their formation.

Ⓓ The professor focuses on the differences between islands and continents.

17 Based on the information in the lecture, indicate whether the statements refer to islands formed by glaciers or coral atolls.

Click in the correct box for each statement.

	Islands Formed by Glaciers	Coral Atolls
1 Have a lagoon in their centers		
2 Were created when the last ice age came to an end		
3 Are primarily in the Pacific Ocean		
4 May have once had a volcano		

CONTINUE VOLUME

PART 3

Listening Directions

00-02

In this part, you will listen to 1 conversation and 1 lecture.

You must answer each question. After you answer, click on **Next**. Then click on **OK** to confirm your answer and go on to the next question. After you click on **OK**, you cannot return to previous questions.

You may now begin this part of the Listening Section. You will have **7 minutes** to answer the questions.

Click on **Continue** to go on.

03-06

1 Why does the student visit the professor?

(A) To talk about a recent class that he attended

(B) To discuss the results of a paper he received

(C) To confirm which chapters in the book he must read

(D) To clarify a thesis that he does not understand

2 Why did the student get a poor grade?

(A) He failed to turn his assignment in on time.

(B) He did not provide enough examples in his paper.

(C) He wrote a report that was not long enough.

(D) He did not follow the professor's guidelines.

3 What can be inferred about the professor?

(A) She has another class to attend later in the day.

(B) She sometimes shows videos during her classes.

(C) She believes the student should have gotten a lower grade.

(D) She taught the student during a previous semester.

4 What does the student ask the professor to do?

(A) Let him write his paper again

(B) Regrade his assignment

(C) Give him a project for extra points

(D) Provide him with some study tips

5 Listen again to part of the conversation. Then answer the question.

What does the professor imply when she says this:

(A) She is willing to speak with the student now.

(B) She will be busy in around half an hour.

(C) She is planning to go home for the day.

(D) She has been attending meetings all day.

TOEFL® MAP **ACTUAL TEST**

VOLUME

LISTENING

00:04:00 HIDE TIME

03-07

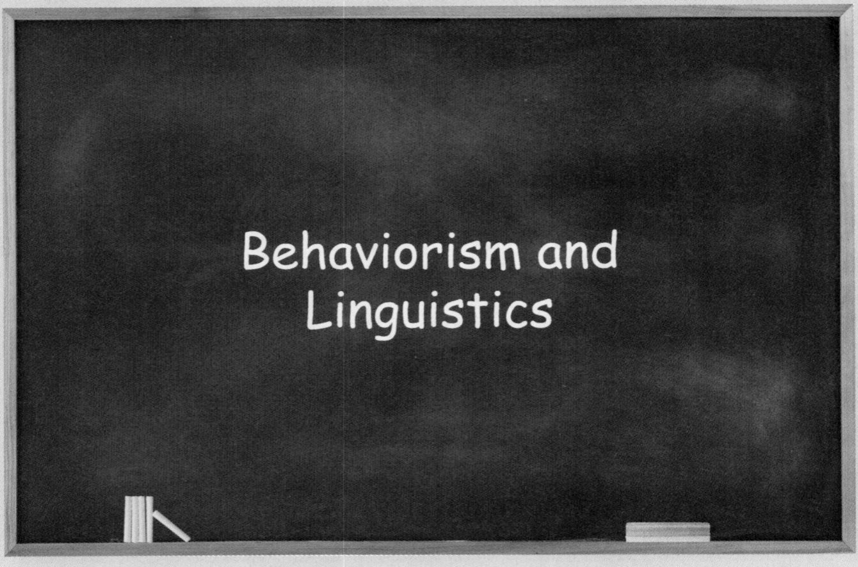

6 What is the lecture mainly about?

(A) The importance of environment in learning a language

(B) Opposing theories on language acquisition

(C) The lives of B.F. Skinner and Noam Chomsky

(D) The best manner for children to be taught a language

7 According to the professor, what is Noam Chomsky's area of specialization?

(A) Language stimulation

(B) The development of language

(C) Foreign languages

(D) Grammar structures

8 What can be inferred about the professor?

(A) He supports aspects of both Skinner's and Chomsky's theories.

(B) He believes that environment has little effect on language development.

(C) He is more familiar with Chomsky than he is with Skinner.

(D) He is able to speak more than three languages fluently.

9 How is the lecture organized?

Ⓐ The professor individually describes the opinions of two academics.

Ⓑ The professor provides details of his own research and defends his conclusions.

Ⓒ The professor focuses only on the defensible parts of each man's theory.

Ⓓ The professor points out how both theories have major flaws in them.

10 Based on the information in the lecture, indicate whether the statements refer to B.F. Skinner or Noam Chomsky.

Click in the correct box for each statement.

	B.F. Skinner	Noam Chomsky
1 Wrote a book that the other criticized		
2 Felt children were born with no ability to learn language		
3 Claimed a person could never learn a second language perfectly		
4 Believed in the reinforcement theory		

11 Listen again to part of the lecture. Then answer the question.

Why does the professor say this: 🎧

Ⓐ To repeat his main point

Ⓑ To explain a new theory

Ⓒ To make a clarification

Ⓓ To ask for student feedback

TOEFL® MAP

ACTUAL TEST

Listening 1

04

CONTINUE VOLUME

Listening Section Directions

00-01

This section measures your ability to understand conversations and lectures in English.

The Listening section is divided into separately timed parts. In each part, you will listen to 1 conversation and 1 or 2 lectures. You will hear each conversation or lecture only **one** time.

After each conversation or lecture, you will answer some questions about it. The questions typically ask about the main idea and supporting details. Some questions ask about a speaker's purpose or attitude. Answer the questions based on what is stated or implied by the speakers.

You may take notes while you listen. You may use your notes to help you answer the questions. Your notes will not be scored.

If you need to change the volume while you listen, click on the **Volume** at the top of the screen.

In some questions, you will see this icon: 🎧 This means that you will hear, but not see, part of the question.

Some of the questions have special directions. These directions appear in a gray box on the screen.

Most questions are worth 1 point. If a question is worth more than 1 point, it will have special directions that indicate how many points you can receive.

A clock at the top of the screen will show you how much time is remaining. The clock will not count down while you are listening. The clock will count down only while you are answering the questions.

CONTINUE VOLUME

PART 1

00-03

Listening Directions

In this part, you will listen to 1 conversation and 2 lectures.

You must answer each question. After you answer, click on **Next**. Then click on **OK** to confirm your answer and go on to the next question. After you click on **OK**, you cannot return to previous questions.

You may now begin this part of the Listening Section. You will have **10 minutes** to answer the questions.

Click on **Continue** to go on.

TOEFL® MAP **ACTUAL TEST**

VOLUME

LISTENING

00:10:00 HIDE TIME

04-01

1 What problem does the student have?

Ⓐ She has to pay some overdue book fines.

Ⓑ She lost some books that she had checked out.

Ⓒ She cannot find some books she needs.

Ⓓ She forgot to bring her student ID with her.

2 Why does the librarian explain the library's new program to the student?

Ⓐ To remind her always to return her books on time

Ⓑ To let her know an easy way to renew her books

Ⓒ To show her how to avoid paying some fees

Ⓓ To prove that the library is trying to improve its services

3 How much money does the student give to the librarian in total?

Ⓐ One dollar

Ⓑ Four dollars

Ⓒ Five dollars

Ⓓ Six dollars

4 What is the librarian's attitude toward the student?

Ⓐ He is condescending.

Ⓑ He is helpful.

Ⓒ He is amusing.

Ⓓ He is critical.

5 Listen again to part of the conversation. Then answer the question.

What is the purpose of the student's response: 🎧

Ⓐ To express her appreciation

Ⓑ To approve of the librarian's actions

Ⓒ To reject the librarian's offer

Ⓓ To give the librarian permission

04-02

6 What aspect of camels does the professor mainly discuss?

Ⓐ The places where they live

Ⓑ Their physical characteristics

Ⓒ Their usefulness to humans

Ⓓ Their traits as mammals

7 What comparison does the professor make between camels and some other mammals?

Ⓐ The amount of hair on their bodies

Ⓑ The number of toes on their feet

Ⓒ The physical sizes of their bodies

Ⓓ The distances that they can travel

8 How are the dromedary camel and the Bactrian camel different from one another?

Ⓐ The Bactrian camel is smaller than the dromedary camel.

Ⓑ The dromedary camel is easier to tame than the Bactrian camel.

Ⓒ There are fewer Bactrian camels than dromedary camels.

Ⓓ They each have a different number of humps on their backs.

9 Why does the professor mention the shape of camels' red blood cells?

Ⓐ To explain how well blood flows in camels' bodies

Ⓑ To note that this prevents camels from ever getting dehydrated

Ⓒ To stress that the blood cells look like circles

Ⓓ To state that the shape helps camels breathe more easily

10 In the lecture, the professor describes a number of facts about the camel's ability to survive in the desert. Indicate whether each of the following is a fact or not.

Click in the correct box for each statement.

	Fact	Not a Fact
1 Uses its nose to retain water		
2 Becomes inactive during cold desert nights		
3 Does not sweat at all		
4 Can drink lots of water at one time		

11 Listen again to part of the lecture. Then answer the question.

Why does the student say this: 🎧

Ⓐ To state a fact

Ⓑ To bring up a key point

Ⓒ To argue with the professor

Ⓓ To express his surprise

04-03

Psychology

12 What aspect of observation does the professor mainly discuss?

Ⓐ The most recent developments in observation methodology

Ⓑ The ideal way for scientists to observe their subjects

Ⓒ The varying manners in which people make use of it

Ⓓ The importance of watching animals in their natural habitats

13 Why does the professor explain how animals in captivity change their behavior?

Ⓐ To name one downside to the laboratory observation method

Ⓑ To show why scientists prefer not to observe captive animals

Ⓒ To decry the inhumanity of keeping wild animals in captivity

Ⓓ To express his doubt that observing these animals is useful

14 How does the professor organize the information about natural observation that he presents to the class?

Ⓐ By stressing that it is the best of the three main observation methods

Ⓑ By telling the students about his own experiences with it

Ⓒ By giving several real-life examples to illustrate it

Ⓓ By focusing more on its drawbacks than its benefits

15 What can be inferred about the professor?

Ⓐ He prefers to rely on laboratory observation for his research.

Ⓑ He has done participatory observation of primitive tribes.

Ⓒ He believes a perfect method of observation does not exist.

Ⓓ He is morally opposed to using laboratory observation on animals.

16 Based on the information in the lecture, indicate whether the statements refer to advantages or disadvantages of various observation methods.

Click in the correct box for each statement.

	Advantage	Disadvantage
1 Primitive people may begin to act differently.		
2 Scientists can work in a controlled environment.		
3 The subject cannot be observed at all times.		
4 Researchers do not get too close to the animals they are observing.		

17 Listen again to part of the lecture. Then answer the question.

What does the professor mean when he says this: 🎧

Ⓐ Primitive tribes make good subjects for participatory observation.

Ⓑ There are many advantages to participatory observation.

Ⓒ Participatory observation only works in certain situations.

Ⓓ Doing participatory observation can be dangerous at times.

CONTINUE

VOLUME

PART 2

00-02

Listening Directions

In this part, you will listen to 1 conversation and 1 lecture.

You must answer each question. After you answer, click on **Next**. Then click on **OK** to confirm your answer and go on to the next question. After you click on **OK**, you cannot return to previous questions.

You may now begin this part of the Listening Section. You will have **7 minutes** to answer the questions.

Click on **Continue** to go on.

04-04

1 Why does the student apologize to the professor?

Ⓐ She was unable to attend a recent class.

Ⓑ She failed to take notes during class.

Ⓒ She did poorly on a recent exam.

Ⓓ She interrupted the professor's lecture.

2 Why does the student ask the professor about the number of moons Saturn has?

Ⓐ To argue that she believes it only has a few moons orbiting it

Ⓑ To claim that the number is higher than she expected

Ⓒ To determine if it has the most moons of every other planet

Ⓓ To indicate her confusion about a number that she saw

3 According to the professor, what information is needed to confirm that a moon exists?

Click on 2 answers.

[1] Its orbit

[2] Its appearance

[3] Its composition

[4] Its lunar day

4 What can be inferred about Jupiter?

Ⓐ It is the largest planet in the solar system.

Ⓑ It has some unconfirmed moons orbiting it.

Ⓒ Some of its moons were once asteroids.

Ⓓ There are some rings around the planet.

5 Listen again to part of the conversation. Then answer the question.

Why does the professor say this: 🎧

Ⓐ To show her concern

Ⓑ To criticize the student

Ⓒ To warn the student

Ⓓ To express her surprise

04-05

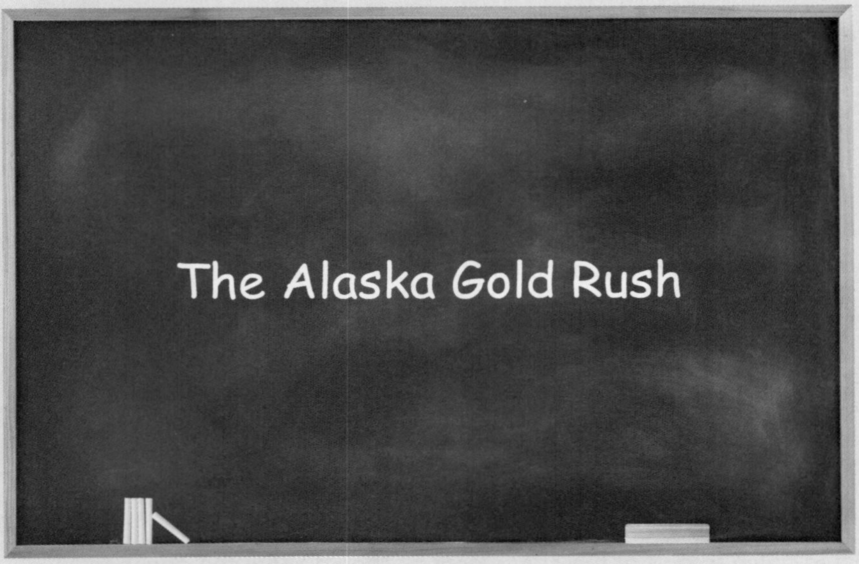

6 What is the professor's attitude toward the prospectors who first discovered gold in the Yukon?

- (A) They were tough men able to withstand the harsh northern climate.
- (B) They were lucky to have discovered such a large amount of gold.
- (C) They resorted to violence too many times when they were upset.
- (D) They acted thoughtlessly by telling people about their discovery.

7 According to the professor, why were so many Americans willing to go to Alaska to look for gold?

- (A) They were obsessed with the notion of becoming millionaires.
- (B) The United States was experiencing economic difficulties then.
- (C) The weather at the time of the discovery was not that harsh.
- (D) They felt that the natural obstacles were not too hard to overcome.

8 Why does the professor discuss the Northwest Mounted Police?

- (A) To talk about their role in dealing with incoming prospectors
- (B) To mention their relationship with the Royal Canadian Mounted Police
- (C) To criticize the actions that they took against the prospectors
- (D) To accuse them of trying to keep prospectors out of Canada

9 Why did the Canadian police confiscate the prospectors' guns?

Ⓐ To cut down on the illegal hunting some prospectors were doing

Ⓑ To stop the prospectors from attacking native Canadian tribesmen

Ⓒ To put an end to the robberies which were plaguing the Yukon

Ⓓ To prevent violence from erupting in the Yukon gold fields

10 What does the professor imply about the gold fields discovered near Juneau, Alaska?

Ⓐ They were extremely hard for most people to get to.

Ⓑ They required prospectors to travel by river for several days.

Ⓒ They were not as rich as the gold fields in the Yukon were.

Ⓓ They saw more violence than any other areas where gold was found.

11 Listen again to part of the lecture. Then answer the question.

What does the professor mean when he says this:

Ⓐ The prices people paid for goods in Alaska were somewhat fair.

Ⓑ Many people lacked enough money to buy the proper equipment.

Ⓒ The merchants were charging more money than was necessary.

Ⓓ It was easier to make money selling equipment than panning for gold.

TOEFL® MAP

ACTUAL TEST

Listening 1

05

CONTINUE

VOLUME

00-01

Listening Section Directions

This section measures your ability to understand conversations and lectures in English.

The Listening section is divided into separately timed parts. In each part, you will listen to 1 conversation and 1 or 2 lectures. You will hear each conversation or lecture only **one** time.

After each conversation or lecture, you will answer some questions about it. The questions typically ask about the main idea and supporting details. Some questions ask about a speaker's purpose or attitude. Answer the questions based on what is stated or implied by the speakers.

You may take notes while you listen. You may use your notes to help you answer the questions. Your notes will not be scored.

If you need to change the volume while you listen, click on the **Volume** at the top of the screen.

In some questions, you will see this icon: This means that you will hear, but not see, part of the question.

Some of the questions have special directions. These directions appear in a gray box on the screen.

Most questions are worth 1 point. If a question is worth more than 1 point, it will have special directions that indicate how many points you can receive.

A clock at the top of the screen will show you how much time is remaining. The clock will not count down while you are listening. The clock will count down only while you are answering the questions.

CONTINUE VOLUME

PART 1

00-03

Listening Directions

In this part, you will listen to 1 conversation and 2 lectures.

You must answer each question. After you answer, click on **Next**. Then click on **OK** to confirm your answer and go on to the next question. After you click on **OK**, you cannot return to previous questions.

You may now begin this part of the Listening Section. You will have **10 minutes** to answer the questions.

Click on **Continue** to go on.

05-01

1 What are the speakers mainly discussing?

Ⓐ A teaching assistant position that is available

Ⓑ A job that the professor wants the student to do

Ⓒ A class that the student would like to enroll in

Ⓓ A study group that the student often goes to

2 What does the professor tell the student about the study groups?

Click on 2 answers.

1 Her classes have had them for the past ten years.

2 She is going to select two students to lead them.

3 Their leaders will be just like teaching assistants.

4 The students that run them will receive money.

3 What does the professor imply about the student?

Ⓐ He is knowledgeable in physics.

Ⓑ He would make a good graduate student.

Ⓒ He needs to try harder in her class.

Ⓓ He is capable of lecturing in her classes.

4 What can be inferred about the student?

Ⓐ He is going to take five years to graduate from school.

Ⓑ He accepted the job because he needs to earn some money.

Ⓒ He did well in the classes he previously took with the professor.

Ⓓ He is uninterested in doing activities that he considers difficult.

5 Listen again to part of the conversation. Then answer the question.

What is the purpose of the professor's response: 🎧

Ⓐ To tell the student that he is correct

Ⓑ To compliment the student on his grades

Ⓒ To admit that he would be a good teacher

Ⓓ To imply that he is the best student in the class

05-02

Physiology

6 What is the main topic of the lecture?

Ⓐ How muscles provide energy for the body

Ⓑ The types of muscles and their roles

Ⓒ The differences between cardiac and striated muscles

Ⓓ Where in the body the muscles are found

7 Why does the professor explain what voluntary muscles are?

Ⓐ To provide another name for striated muscles

Ⓑ To compare their roles with those of smooth muscles

Ⓒ To point out where in the body they are located

Ⓓ To tell everyone which actions they are responsible for

8 Based on the information in the lecture, indicate whether the statements refer to striated or smooth muscles.

Click in the correct box for each statement.

	Striated Muscles	Smooth Muscles
1 Control involuntary actions in the body		
2 Are located in the esophagus and bladder		
3 Are composed of sarcomeres		
4 Are connected to the bones in the body		

9 Why does the professor tell the students about the muscles that control breathing?

Ⓐ To prove that they are smooth muscles

Ⓑ To mention their connection with the heart

Ⓒ To respond to a student's question

Ⓓ To state that breathing is an involuntary action

10 How does the professor organize the information about muscles that he presents to the class?

Ⓐ By engaging the students in a discussion in which they answer his questions

Ⓑ By showing the students a chart of the body and pointing out the muscles on it

Ⓒ By naming the types of muscles and discussing their characteristics and roles

Ⓓ By focusing on sections of the body and stating what muscles are found in them

11 Listen again to part of the lecture. Then answer the question.

What does the professor imply when he says this: 🎧

Ⓐ There is not much time left in the class.

Ⓑ Some of the words he said are hard to spell.

Ⓒ It is all right for the students to misspell the words.

Ⓓ He is afraid of making a spelling mistake.

05-03

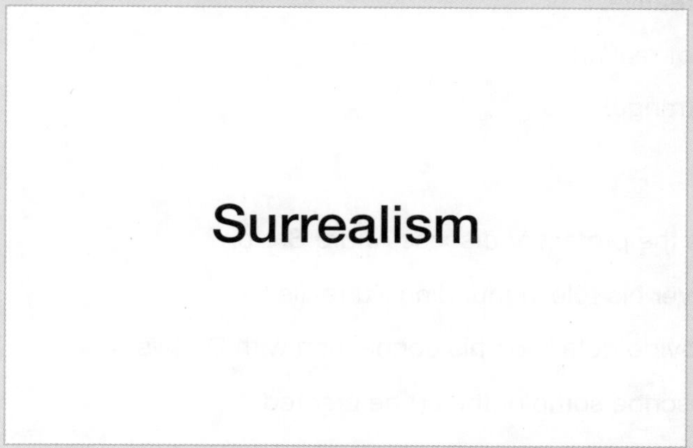

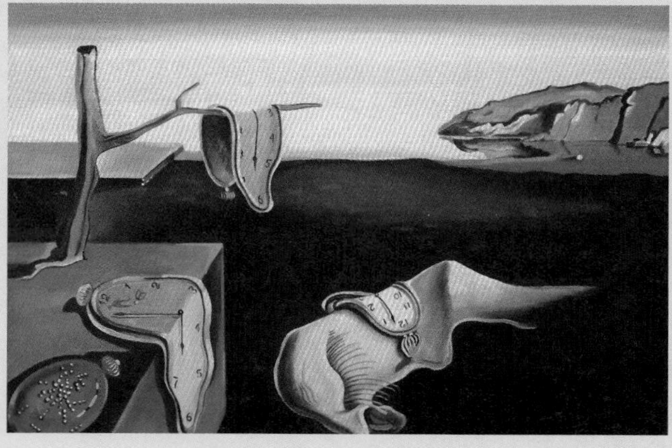

12 What aspect of Surrealism does the professor mainly discuss?

Ⓐ Its most famous artists

Ⓑ Its influence on later art movements

Ⓒ Its origins and early history

Ⓓ Its connection with Salvador Dali

13 What is the professor's opinion of Dadaist art?

Ⓐ It is brilliant.

Ⓑ It is creative.

Ⓒ It is not real art.

Ⓓ It is strange.

14 Why does the professor discuss Andre Breton?

Ⓐ To cover his role in founding Surrealism

Ⓑ To provide details on his connection with Dadaism

Ⓒ To describe some of the art he created

Ⓓ To talk about his friendship with Jacques Vache

15 According to the professor, what did Salvador Dali do?

Ⓐ He helped found the Surrealist Movement.

Ⓑ He introduced automatic drawing to Surrealism.

Ⓒ He produced Surrealist works of great imagination.

Ⓓ He was one of the first artists to join the Surrealists.

16 What can be inferred about Surrealism?

Ⓐ It produced art superior to that of other twentieth century movements.

Ⓑ Some of its artists have sold their works for millions of dollars.

Ⓒ Its influence on the art world is currently in dispute.

Ⓓ There are few art historians who study it nowadays.

17 Listen again to part of the lecture. Then answer the question.

What does the professor imply when she says this: 🎧

Ⓐ Andy is the only student not to have turned in his paper.

Ⓑ Andy has permission to answer her question.

Ⓒ It is Andy's turn to give his presentation.

Ⓓ Andy needs to raise his hand before speaking.

CONTINUE VOLUME

PART 2

00-02

Listening Directions

In this part, you will listen to 1 conversation and 1 lecture.

You must answer each question. After you answer, click on **Next**. Then click on **OK** to confirm your answer and go on to the next question. After you click on **OK**, you cannot return to previous questions.

You may now begin this part of the Listening Section. You will have **7 minutes** to answer the questions.

Click on **Continue** to go on.

05-04

1 Why does the student visit the student activities office?

Ⓐ To register as a member of one of the student clubs

Ⓑ To state her intention to run for president of a club

Ⓒ To sign up for a table during the student club day

Ⓓ To advertise her club in the student newspaper

2 Why is the upcoming event important to the student?

Ⓐ She hopes to increase the number of members in her club.

Ⓑ She wants to become the president of the drama club.

Ⓒ She is going to put on a performance during the event.

Ⓓ She believes she can raise some money for her club.

3 What can be inferred about the student?

Ⓐ She has been the president of her club for more than a year.

Ⓑ She knows little about the events that take place on campus.

Ⓒ She feels that she has too many responsibilities for her club.

Ⓓ She devotes more time to her club than she does to her studies.

4 What does the student have to do to get a table at the event?

Click on 2 answers.

1 Pay a fee

2 Register online

3 Complete a form

4 Show her student ID

5 Listen again to part of the conversation. Then answer the question.

Why does the woman say this: 🎧

Ⓐ To inspire the student

Ⓑ To answer the student's question

Ⓒ To attempt to be positive

Ⓓ To change the student's mood

05-05

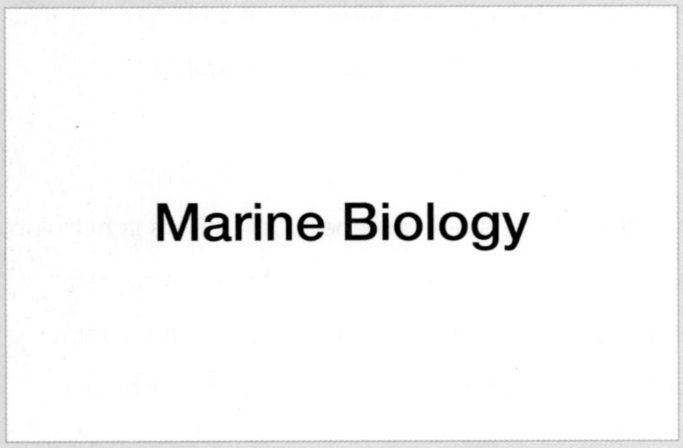

6 What is the main topic of the lecture?

Ⓐ The manner in which artificial reefs are created

Ⓑ Common organisms that live in artificial reefs

Ⓒ Some advantages of artificial reefs over natural reefs

Ⓓ Why artificial reefs are beneficial to humans

7 What is the professor's opinion of artificial reefs?

Ⓐ They have more positive effects than negative ones.

Ⓑ People should not be making so many of them.

Ⓒ The price of making them is worth the investment.

Ⓓ People need to learn to make them more efficiently.

8 According to the professor, what materials are good for building artificial reefs?

Click on 2 answers.

1 Automobiles

2 Subway cars

3 Ships' hulls

4 Tires

9 Why does the professor explain how a reef ball looks?

- Ⓐ Because he thinks the students should be aware of all aspects of artificial reefs
- Ⓑ Because he feels that a reef ball's size greatly affects the reef it creates
- Ⓒ Because he wants to show the students why reef balls are so effective
- Ⓓ Because he believes that the students are unfamiliar with its appearance

10 What can be inferred about artificial reefs?

- Ⓐ It takes many years for them to develop into complete ecosystems.
- Ⓑ Over time, they appear to look exactly like natural reefs do.
- Ⓒ The cost of producing them is decreasing, so more people are making them.
- Ⓓ The best artificial reefs are built in deep water far off the coast.

11 Listen again to part of the lecture. Then answer the question.

What is the purpose of the professor's response to the student:

- Ⓐ To encourage the student to think about what she just said
- Ⓑ To agree with part of what the student claimed
- Ⓒ To inform the student that her assumption is incorrect
- Ⓓ To provide evidence disputing the student's declaration

CONTINUE

VOLUME

PART 3

00-02

Listening Directions

In this part, you will listen to 1 conversation and 1 lecture.

You must answer each question. After you answer, click on **Next**. Then click on **OK** to confirm your answer and go on to the next question. After you click on **OK**, you cannot return to previous questions.

You may now begin this part of the Listening Section. You will have **7 minutes** to answer the questions.

Click on **Continue** to go on.

05-06

1 What are the speakers mainly discussing?

Ⓐ The student's satisfaction with her job

Ⓑ The student's current schedule

Ⓒ A job the man offers the student

Ⓓ A possible promotion for the student

2 What does the man instruct the student to do?

Ⓐ Check in some books that were returned

Ⓑ Put some books on the shelves

Ⓒ Submit her timesheet for the week

Ⓓ Assist a student at the circulation desk

3 Why does the student apologize to the man?

Ⓐ She arrived at her job a bit late.

Ⓑ She is unable to work this coming weekend.

Ⓒ She failed to respond to his message.

Ⓓ She could not find a replacement worker.

4 What can be inferred about the student?

Ⓐ She believes working during winter vacation will be easy.

Ⓑ Her family is encountering some financial difficulties.

Ⓒ Her grades have been falling during the past two semesters.

Ⓓ She intends to take a class during the upcoming break.

5 Listen again to part of the conversation. Then answer the question.

What does the man mean when he says this: 🎧

Ⓐ Several people have rejected his offer.

Ⓑ He considers the student an inferior worker.

Ⓒ Working during the break is difficult.

Ⓓ The library has hired many new employees.

05-07

6 Why does the professor discuss various emotions?

Ⓐ To get the students to remember some positive memories

Ⓑ To show how they are connected to memories

Ⓒ To make a point about retaining negative memories

Ⓓ To note their importance to people with Alzheimer's disease

7 What does the professor say about people's memories of everyday activities?

Ⓐ People forget them after one or two days because of their unimportance.

Ⓑ They are unclear because there are no strong emotions associated with them.

Ⓒ There are few people who are able to retain memories of these events.

Ⓓ Because they are short-term memories, people cannot remember them well.

8 Which of the following events is a person most likely to remember in great detail?

Ⓐ A class

Ⓑ A sporting event

Ⓒ A traffic accident

Ⓓ A presentation

9 According to the professor, why do women retain memories better than men?

Ⓐ Their emotions are more intense than men's emotions.

Ⓑ Their brains release more cortisol than men's brains do.

Ⓒ The hippocampus in women's brains tends to be large.

Ⓓ Men are less likely than women to have emotional experiences.

10 Why does the professor explain how the brain controls memories?

Ⓐ It is next on her list of topics to cover.

Ⓑ A student asks her a question about that.

Ⓒ She wants the students to study the brain in depth.

Ⓓ She believes the brain is crucial to memory.

11 What will the professor probably do next?

Ⓐ Show the students a film

Ⓑ Visit the class website

Ⓒ Examine the human brain

Ⓓ Return to talking about emotions

TOEFL® MAP

ACTUAL TEST

Listening 1

06

CONTINUE

VOLUME

Listening Section Directions

00-01

This section measures your ability to understand conversations and lectures in English.

The Listening section is divided into separately timed parts. In each part, you will listen to 1 conversation and 1 or 2 lectures. You will hear each conversation or lecture only **one** time.

After each conversation or lecture, you will answer some questions about it. The questions typically ask about the main idea and supporting details. Some questions ask about a speaker's purpose or attitude. Answer the questions based on what is stated or implied by the speakers.

You may take notes while you listen. You may use your notes to help you answer the questions. Your notes will not be scored.

If you need to change the volume while you listen, click on the **Volume** at the top of the screen.

In some questions, you will see this icon: This means that you will hear, but not see, part of the question.

Some of the questions have special directions. These directions appear in a gray box on the screen.

Most questions are worth 1 point. If a question is worth more than 1 point, it will have special directions that indicate how many points you can receive.

A clock at the top of the screen will show you how much time is remaining. The clock will not count down while you are listening. The clock will count down only while you are answering the questions.

CONTINUE

VOLUME

PART 1

00-02

Listening Directions

In this part, you will listen to 1 conversation and 1 lecture.

You must answer each question. After you answer, click on **Next**. Then click on **OK** to confirm your answer and go on to the next question. After you click on **OK**, you cannot return to previous questions.

You may now begin this part of the Listening Section. You will have **7 minutes** to answer the questions.

Click on **Continue** to go on.

06-01

1 Why does the student visit the financial aid office?

Ⓐ To apply for a scholarship

Ⓑ To pay the remainder of her tuition

Ⓒ To sign a form for a student loan

Ⓓ To inquire about getting more aid

2 How does the student pay for her tuition?

Click on 2 answers.

[1] Student loans

[2] An academic scholarship

[3] Work-study programs

[4] A school grant

3 What is the student's opinion of her grades?

Ⓐ She is embarrassed by them.

Ⓑ She feels they could be better.

Ⓒ She has no opinion of them.

Ⓓ She is proud of them.

4 Why does the man tell the student about special scholarships?

Ⓐ To get the student to describe her personal finances

Ⓑ To let the student know about a possible source of financial aid

Ⓒ To encourage the student to apply for one of them

Ⓓ To instruct the student on which forms she should fill out

5 What can be inferred about the student?

Ⓐ She will likely get to attend school next semester.

Ⓑ She is going to ask her parents for some more money.

Ⓒ She is disappointed with the man's treatment of her.

Ⓓ She believes that she needs to improve her grades.

06-02

Anthropology

6 What is the lecture mainly about?

Ⓐ The common ancestor of all primates

Ⓑ The similarities in DNA of various primates

Ⓒ The evolution of monkeys and apes

Ⓓ The manner in which primates differ from one another

7 What happens to the melting point of DNA when the DNA of two different species is combined?

Ⓐ It decreases.

Ⓑ It increases.

Ⓒ It remains the same.

Ⓓ It fluctuates randomly.

8 Why does the professor tell the students about the handout?

Ⓐ To advise them to look at it while he continues to lecture on the topic

Ⓑ To let them know that it has a few mistakes which need to be corrected

Ⓒ To inform them that they should study the pictures which are on it

Ⓓ To tell them that they do not have to take notes on some material

9 Put the following animals in the order in which they diverged from their common ancestor.

Click in the correct box for each statement.

Animal	Order
1 Gibbon	
2 Monkey	
3 Chimpanzee	
4 Human	

10 What does the professor imply about humans?

Ⓐ They have around the same level of intelligence that apes do.

Ⓑ There are several species of humans that have evolved.

Ⓒ Humans have virtually no similarities to monkeys.

Ⓓ They diverged from a common ancestor that lived in Africa.

11 Listen again to part of the lecture. Then answer the question.

What can be inferred about the professor when she says this:

Ⓐ She recognizes the difficulty of the material she is discussing.

Ⓑ She expects the students to recall everything she tells them.

Ⓒ She will have the students answer some questions in class soon.

Ⓓ She thinks that the topic she is covering is of great importance.

CONTINUE

VOLUME

PART 2

00-03

Listening Directions

In this part, you will listen to 1 conversation and 2 lectures.

You must answer each question. After you answer, click on **Next**. Then click on **OK** to confirm your answer and go on to the next question. After you click on **OK**, you cannot return to previous questions.

You may now begin this part of the Listening Section. You will have **10 minutes** to answer the questions.

Click on **Continue** to go on.

06-03

1 What are the speakers mainly discussing?

Ⓐ The required classes the student must take

Ⓑ Some classes the student is presently enrolled in

Ⓒ Which history class the student would enjoy more

Ⓓ The student's schedule for the next semester

2 What is the student's major?

Ⓐ Italian

Ⓑ Art History

Ⓒ Mathematics

Ⓓ History

3 What can be inferred about the student?

Ⓐ She is better at math than she is at chemistry.

Ⓑ She values the professor's opinion.

Ⓒ She is in her sophomore year.

Ⓓ She has no interest in the sciences.

4 Why does the professor tell the student about lab classes?

Ⓐ To warn her about their level of difficulty

Ⓑ To stress the amount of work required in them

Ⓒ To mention he knows a professor who will teach one

Ⓓ To recommend that the student enroll in one

5 Listen again to part of the conversation. Then answer the question.

What does the student imply when she says this: 🎧

Ⓐ She expects to receive a low grade in her math class.

Ⓑ She objects to math being a required course.

Ⓒ She will need tutoring to get a good grade in math.

Ⓓ She must take more than one math class to graduate.

VOLUME

LISTENING

00:07:00 HIDE TIME

06-04

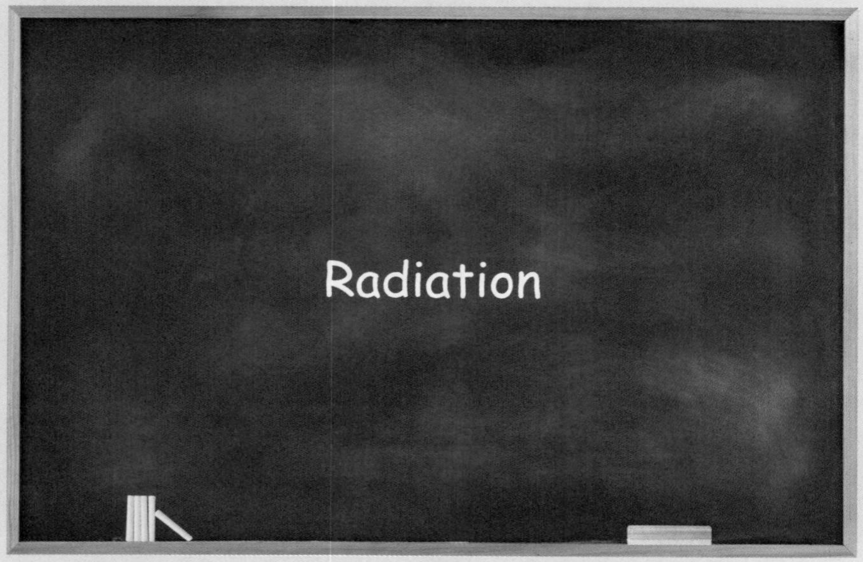

6 What is the main topic of the lecture?

(A) The damage that radiation can do to people

(B) The origins and various types of radiation

(C) Ways to prevent exposure to radiation

(D) The main sources of ionizing radiation

7 What does the professor imply about ultraviolet waves and microwaves?

(A) They are less dangerous than X-rays and gamma rays.

(B) Their wavelengths are longer than those of visible light.

(C) Even in large doses, they pose no danger to humans.

(D) They are produced by the sun and other stars.

8 What can be inferred about uranium?

(A) It is found in abundance in many places.

(B) It is difficult for people to detect.

(C) It is safe when consumed by humans.

(D) It is a radioactive element.

9 How is the lecture organized?

Ⓐ The professor shows the students important information from a website.

Ⓑ The professor lectures without accepting any input from the students.

Ⓒ The professor randomly moves from one topic to another while lecturing.

Ⓓ The professor asks questions and then proceeds to answer them himself.

10 What is a rad?

Ⓐ A dangerous form of ionizing radiation

Ⓑ A unit that measures exposure to radiation

Ⓒ A source of background radiation

Ⓓ A measurement of the wavelengths of radioactive substances

11 Listen again to part of the lecture. Then answer the question.

What does the professor imply when he says this:

Ⓐ The final exam for his class will take place sometime next week.

Ⓑ He is willing to help students who need assistance for the final exam.

Ⓒ The students will be tested on the information found on the class website.

Ⓓ It is important for the students to do well on the final exam.

06-05

12 What aspect of Dutch history does the professor mainly discuss?

(A) The wars the Dutch fought against Spain, France, and England

(B) The advances the Dutch made in trade, transportation, and science

(C) A period of success that the Dutch experienced in the 1600s

(D) The time in the 1500s when the Spanish attacked the Netherlands

13 What does the professor imply about the Netherlands?

(A) It was larger in the past than it is today.

(B) The majority of its people are Catholics.

(C) It plays a crucial role in modern European politics.

(D) It is still heavily influenced by France.

14 What event important to Dutch history took place in the sixteenth century?

Click on 2 answers.

[1] The Protestant Reformation

[2] The founding of the Dutch East India Company

[3] Spain's conquest of the Netherlands

[4] The independence of the Dutch from the Spanish

15 What is the professor's opinion of the Dutch system of pumps and levees?

Ⓐ It was highly advanced.

Ⓑ It was impressive.

Ⓒ It was inefficient.

Ⓓ It was too costly.

16 Why does the professor tell the students about the Dutch East India Company?

Ⓐ To note its role in the trade the Dutch engaged in with European countries

Ⓑ To emphasize the importance of trade in the Netherlands

Ⓒ To claim it was responsible for the founding of a stock market in Amsterdam

Ⓓ To state that it played a major role in Dutch colonies

17 Based on the information in the lecture, indicate whether the statements refer to the causes or effects of the Dutch Golden Age.

Click in the correct box for each statement.

	Cause	Effect
1 The Dutch spent much money on the arts.		
2 The Netherlands gained its independence from Spain.		
3 England and the Netherlands fought three wars in the 1600s.		
4 Dutch ships carried goods to many ports in Europe.		

TOEFL® MAP

ACTUAL TEST

Listening 1

07

CONTINUE

VOLUME

Listening Section Directions

00-01

This section measures your ability to understand conversations and lectures in English.

The Listening section is divided into separately timed parts. In each part, you will listen to 1 conversation and 1 or 2 lectures. You will hear each conversation or lecture only **one** time.

After each conversation or lecture, you will answer some questions about it. The questions typically ask about the main idea and supporting details. Some questions ask about a speaker's purpose or attitude. Answer the questions based on what is stated or implied by the speakers.

You may take notes while you listen. You may use your notes to help you answer the questions. Your notes will not be scored.

If you need to change the volume while you listen, click on the **Volume** at the top of the screen.

In some questions, you will see this icon: This means that you will hear, but not see, part of the question.

Some of the questions have special directions. These directions appear in a gray box on the screen.

Most questions are worth 1 point. If a question is worth more than 1 point, it will have special directions that indicate how many points you can receive.

A clock at the top of the screen will show you how much time is remaining. The clock will not count down while you are listening. The clock will count down only while you are answering the questions.

CONTINUE

VOLUME

PART 1

00-02

Listening Directions

In this part, you will listen to 1 conversation and 1 lecture.

You must answer each question. After you answer, click on **Next**. Then click on **OK** to confirm your answer and go on to the next question. After you click on **OK**, you cannot return to previous questions.

You may now begin this part of the Listening Section. You will have **7 minutes** to answer the questions.

Click on **Continue** to go on.

07-01

1 Why does the student visit the professor?

Ⓐ To request that he grade her paper again

Ⓑ To learn how to write a proper report

Ⓒ To have him go over an assignment with her

Ⓓ To prove that some of her facts are correct

2 Why does the student feel her grade should be higher?

Ⓐ She knows a lot about the topic of her paper.

Ⓑ The professor is known to be an easy grader.

Ⓒ She tried very hard while writing her paper.

Ⓓ She has perfect attendance in the class.

3 What is the professor's opinion of the student's paper?

Ⓐ It was poorly written.

Ⓑ It needed more facts.

Ⓒ It had many grammatical mistakes.

Ⓓ It covered the wrong topic.

4 Listen again to part of the conversation. Then answer the question.

Why does the professor say this:

Ⓐ To prove that he did not make a mistake

Ⓑ To criticize the student's choice of words

Ⓒ To hint that the student should leave his office

Ⓓ To show that he is upset with the student

5 Listen again to part of the conversation. Then answer the question.

What does the professor imply when he says this:

Ⓐ The student might be able to get a better grade.

Ⓑ He believes the student can get an A in his class.

Ⓒ The student needs to work hard to get a high grade.

Ⓓ Only a few students in his class get A's or B's.

07-02

6 What is the lecture mainly about?

Ⓐ What kinds of commodities people trade

Ⓑ The first commodities market in the United States

Ⓒ How the commodities market operates

Ⓓ The reasons why commodity prices fluctuate

7 Why does the professor discuss Chicago?

Ⓐ To explain why wheat farmers often had to visit it

Ⓑ To focus on the railroads that went through the city

Ⓒ To compare its markets with those found in other cities

Ⓓ To detail its role in the founding of the commodities market

8 What is a speculator?

Ⓐ A person only interested in profiting on the commodities market

Ⓑ A person primarily focused on selling various commodities

Ⓒ A person who acts as a go-between for farmers and dealers

Ⓓ A person that provides loans to people buying futures contracts

9 In the lecture, the professor describes a number of facts about the commodities market. Indicate whether each of the following is a fact about the commodities market.

Click in the correct box for each statement.

	Fact	Not a Fact
1 The first commodities market was established in Chicago, Illinois.		
2 More items are traded on it than on the stock market.		
3 It was founded to make buying and selling easier.		
4 The commodities that are sold on the market are all standardized.		

10 What comparison does the professor make between the commodities market and the stock market?

Ⓐ The prices that people pay for commodities and stocks

Ⓑ The conditions under which people buy and sell items

Ⓒ The amount of time people may hold onto commodities and stocks

Ⓓ The commissions buyers and sellers pay brokers

11 What is the professor's opinion of the commodities market?

Ⓐ It is too risky to invest his own money in it.

Ⓑ It is a good idea that could be more efficient.

Ⓒ He thinks more commodities should be sold on the market.

Ⓓ He finds the potential to make large profits appealing.

CONTINUE

VOLUME

PART 2

00-02

Listening Directions

In this part, you will listen to 1 conversation and 1 lecture.

You must answer each question. After you answer, click on **Next**. Then click on **OK** to confirm your answer and go on to the next question. After you click on **OK**, you cannot return to previous questions.

You may now begin this part of the Listening Section. You will have **7 minutes** to answer the questions.

Click on **Continue** to go on.

07-03

1 What are the speakers mainly discussing?

Ⓐ A conversation they had with Professor Douglas

Ⓑ A job the professor wants the student to do

Ⓒ A lab class that the student is going to teach

Ⓓ An opportunity for the student to take a lab class

2 What can be inferred about Professor Douglas?

Ⓐ He speaks with the student about personal matters.

Ⓑ He works in the same building as the professor.

Ⓒ He frequently has lunch with the professor.

Ⓓ He serves as the student's academic advisor.

3 Why does the professor have an opening in his laboratory?

Ⓐ He had to fire a lab assistant.

Ⓑ There are too many students in his class.

Ⓒ One of his student employees quit school.

Ⓓ The school gave him some additional funding.

4 Why does the professor explain what the student will do in the laboratory?

Ⓐ To describe the work that he needs done

Ⓑ To note why the student must work so many hours

Ⓒ To justify the money that he will pay the student

Ⓓ To prove that he trusts the student to lead a lab class

5 What can be inferred about the student?

Ⓐ He will only work on the weekend.

Ⓑ He cannot always attend lab classes.

Ⓒ He will accept the professor's offer.

Ⓓ He has no interest in cleaning the lab.

07-04

Literature

6 What is the lecture mainly about?

Ⓐ The impossibility of time travel

Ⓑ Time machines in various science-fiction books

Ⓒ Works of literature that use time travel

Ⓓ The works of H.G. Wells and Mark Twain

7 How does the Time Traveler in *The Time Machine* travel into the future?

Ⓐ By going into suspended animation

Ⓑ By using a chair that creates a time bubble

Ⓒ By inventing a room that can leap through time

Ⓓ By swallowing a pill that he made

8 Why does the professor explain the method of time travel in *A Connecticut Yankee in King Arthur's Court*?

Ⓐ To contrast Hank Morgan's experiences with the Time Traveler's

Ⓑ To focus on Mark Twain's interest in how his character went back in time

Ⓒ To encourage the students to read the book since none of them is familiar with it

Ⓓ To talk about a book that uses a means of time travel not reliant on machinery

9 What is the student's opinion of the book *Replay*?

Ⓐ He considers the book to be a masterpiece.

Ⓑ He claims that it is his favorite book.

Ⓒ He states that he enjoyed the book a lot.

Ⓓ He believes the book could have been better.

10 How is the lecture organized?

Ⓐ The professor asks the students for their input on time travel stories.

Ⓑ The professor focuses on her favorite stories that incorporate time travel.

Ⓒ The professor gives examples of different methods of time travel.

Ⓓ The professor goes over excerpts from stories that use time travel.

11 Listen again to part of the lecture. Then answer the question.

Why does the professor say this:

Ⓐ To talk about a scientific fact

Ⓑ To add some humor to her lecture

Ⓒ To contradict what Einstein believed

Ⓓ To let the students know her opinion

CONTINUE VOLUME

PART 3

Listening Directions

00-03

In this part, you will listen to 1 conversation and 2 lectures.

You must answer each question. After you answer, click on **Next**. Then click on **OK** to confirm your answer and go on to the next question. After you click on **OK**, you cannot return to previous questions.

You may now begin this part of the Listening Section. You will have **10 minutes** to answer the questions.

Click on **Continue** to go on.

VOLUME

LISTENING

00:10:00 HIDE TIME

07-05

1 What problem does the student have?

Ⓐ Some furniture in his dormitory room is missing.

Ⓑ He does not get along well with his roommate.

Ⓒ He cannot unlock his dormitory room door.

Ⓓ An appliance in his dormitory room is broken.

2 Why does the student tell the woman about his morning activities?

Ⓐ To explain why he cannot find his room key

Ⓑ To respond to a question that she asks him

Ⓒ To describe a normal day in his university life

Ⓓ To state why he arrived at the office so late

3 What can be inferred about the woman?

Ⓐ She has seen other people with the same problem as the student.

Ⓑ She will still be unable to solve the man's problem as soon as he pays a fee.

Ⓒ She is unwilling to help the student with his problem.

Ⓓ She has been employed at the university for a short period of time.

4 What does the woman tell the student to do?

Click on 2 answers.

1 Request that a new key be made

2 Make a payment at once

3 Visit another office on campus

4 Speak with the basketball coach

5 Listen again to part of the conversation. Then answer the question.

What does the student imply when he says this: 🎧

Ⓐ His grades are high enough to win him a scholarship.

Ⓑ He has to attend basketball practice soon.

Ⓒ He does not owe the university any money.

Ⓓ His roommate is a member of a sports team.

07-06

History of Science

6 What is the main topic of the lecture?

Ⓐ Ancient models of the universe

Ⓑ Planetary orbits of the sun

Ⓒ The composition of the solar system

Ⓓ Ptolemy's and Copernicus's lives

7 Why does the professor discuss the *Almagest*?

Ⓐ To show what the ancient Greeks thought about the universe

Ⓑ To point out the mistakes which were made in it

Ⓒ To describe Ptolemy's version of the universe

Ⓓ To compare the information in it with that learned by Galileo

8 According to the professor, why was Ptolemy's model of the universe believed for so long?

Ⓐ Telescopes were not used until centuries after his death.

Ⓑ Knowledge advanced at a slow pace in the past.

Ⓒ Ptolemy's work had the support of the Church.

Ⓓ Arab astronomers stated that his model was correct.

9 Based on the information in the lecture, indicate whether the statements refer to the model of the universe proposed by Ptolemy or Nicolas Copernicus.

Click in the correct box for each statement.

	Ptolemy	Nicolas Copernicus
1 Believed that Earth was stationary		
2 Described a sun-centered universe		
3 Was described in *On the Revolutions of Heavenly Spheres*		
4 Put the moon in a sphere closer to Earth than anything else		

10 What will the professor probably do next?

Ⓐ Continuing discussing Copernicus

Ⓑ Begin to talk about Galileo

Ⓒ Show models of two separate universes

Ⓓ Give the students a break

11 Listen again to part of the lecture. Then answer the question.

Why does the professor say this:

Ⓐ To ask the students a question about some terminology

Ⓑ To let the students know how to spell a term

Ⓒ To avoid having to give his opinion on a topic

Ⓓ To explain the derivation of an important word

07-07

Microbiology

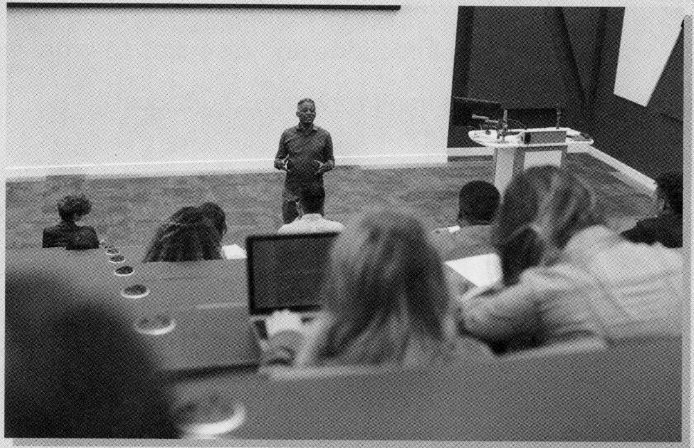

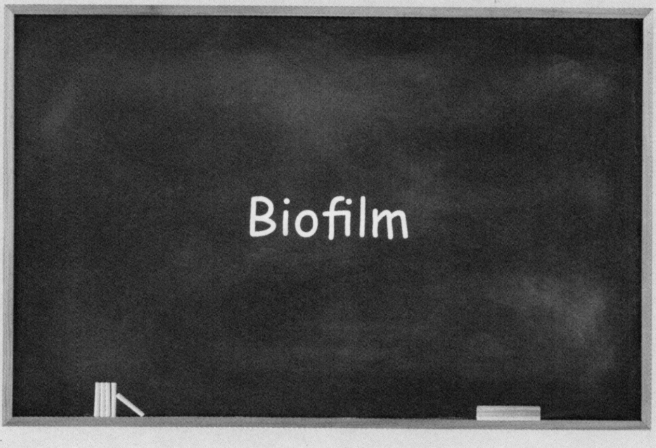

12 What does the professor imply about the class?

Ⓐ It is going to end in a few minutes.

Ⓑ He will give a short quiz after his lecture.

Ⓒ It is the last one before the final exam.

Ⓓ He thinks the students need to pay closer attention.

13 What does EPS do?

Ⓐ Helps biofilm increase in size by breaking down foreign material

Ⓑ Enables biofilm to communicate with others of its kind

Ⓒ Allows biofilm to spread infections and diseases to organisms

Ⓓ Permits biofilm to attach itself to various surfaces

14 What is the likely outcome of applying the same disinfectant to biofilm over a long period of time?

Ⓐ The biofilm will have all of its harmful material removed.

Ⓑ The biofilm will lose its ability to cling to a certain surface.

Ⓒ The biofilm will develop a resistance to the disinfectant.

Ⓓ The biofilm will no longer be able to transmit diseases.

15 According to the professor, what is a benefit of biofilm?

Ⓐ It can assist in the cleanup of spilled oil.

Ⓑ It can remove plaque from people's teeth.

Ⓒ It can eliminate barnacles from ships' hulls.

Ⓓ It can protect crops from harmful diseases.

16 Listen again to part of the lecture. Then answer the question.

What does the professor mean when he says this: 🎧

Ⓐ It is easy to destroy biofilm if people spot it in its early stages.

Ⓑ Biofilm is more common in manmade environments than in natural ones.

Ⓒ The biofilm that grows in manmade environments can be dangerous.

Ⓓ He has not told the students all of the places where biofilm may exist.

17 Listen again to part of the lecture. Then answer the question.

What is the purpose of the professor's response to the student: 🎧

Ⓐ To alleviate the student's concern

Ⓑ To offer a possibility the student had not considered

Ⓒ To confirm the student's statement

Ⓓ To suggest the student reread the material

TOEFL® MAP ACTUAL TEST

Listening 1

Answers, Scripts, and Explanations

Actual Test 01

p.13

Answers

PART 1

1 Ⓒ	2 Ⓐ	3 Ⓑ	4 Ⓓ	5 Ⓑ
6 Ⓒ	7 Ⓑ	8 Ⓓ	9 Ⓑ	10 Ⓒ
11 Ⓑ				

PART 2

1 Ⓒ	2 Ⓓ	3 Ⓒ	4 Ⓑ	5 Ⓑ
6 Ⓑ	7 Ⓓ	8 Ⓐ	9 Ⓒ	10 Ⓑ
11 Ⓓ				

PART 3

1 Ⓐ	2 [2], [4]	3 Ⓒ	4 Ⓐ	5 Ⓒ
6 Ⓒ	7 Ⓓ	8 Ⓐ	9 Ⓐ	10 Ⓑ
11 Ⓒ	12 Ⓓ	13 [2], [3]	14 Ⓒ	
15 Washoe: [2], [4] Kanzi: [1], [3]		16 Ⓑ	17 Ⓐ	

Scripts & Explanations

PART 1

Conversation 01-01

p.16

M Student: Professor Higgins, I know I scheduled our meeting for two o'clock, but, uh, is it all right if I come in a little early? Do you mind?

W Professor: Of course not, Allen. I don't mind if you drop in ten minutes early. Besides, I was just waiting for you to arrive, so you're helping me by being here now.

M: Sweet. Thanks.

W: All right . . . So you asked for this meeting after class yesterday. What exactly do you need to talk about? Are you having some problems following the material in class?

M: Oh, not at all. You know, I thought this class would be pretty difficult and that I might wind up having to drop it, but I find that I understand the material pretty well.

W: If I remember correctly, you got a 97 on your midterm exam, so I'd have to agree with your assessment. So it's not the material. Then, uh, what is it?

M: The paper.

W: The paper?

M: Yes, the big paper we need to turn in at the end of the semester. I've already decided on a topic, and I'm trying to do the research now.

W: Good for you. I love it when students show initiative.

M: [5]Uh, thanks. I just don't like waiting for the last minute to do papers. I tried that my freshman year two years ago, and . . . Ugh. **You wouldn't believe how badly that worked out.**

W: Actually, I probably would. I have several student advisees, and I see that happen each and every semester. Some of them, fortunately, see the light and shape up. It sounds like that's what you've done.

M: I'd like to think so. My grades have steadily improved since my first year. Anyway, uh, back to the paper.

W: Sure.

M: I decided to focus on the migration patterns of large mammals in Africa. You know, how they migrate depending on weather patterns . . . What troubles they encounter along the way . . . Where they breed and bear their young . . . That kind of stuff. But, uh . . .

W: Overwhelming, isn't it?

M: You can say that again.

W: First of all, Allen, it's great that you're being ambitious. But what you are proposing sounds more like a master's thesis than a ten-page paper. If you intend to go to graduate school, you could make that a course of study for a yearlong project. But you'd have to be really general for a paper on that topic in my class. And that's something I don't want.

M: Then what do you propose that I do?

W: Easy. Pare down your topic. First, focus on just one animal that migrates. I don't care which one it is. Just choose one. Next, look at only one aspect of its migrating habits. And then go into that in as much depth as you possibly can.

M: All right. That makes sense to me.

W: Do you know which animal you're going to choose? If you do, then I can suggest a few books that will definitely help you with your research.

M: I'm not positive yet, but I have a couple in mind. Let me think about it, and I will talk to you after class tomorrow. Then, if it's all right with you, I'll pick your brain for some research material.

1 **Gist-Purpose Question** | The student tells the professor he wants to talk about "the big paper we need to turn in at the end of the semester."

2 **Understanding Function Question** | The student says that he has already decided on a topic for his paper and is doing the research for it. The paper is due at the end

of the semester, and they have only recently taken the midterm exam. The professor then says, "Good for you. I love it when students show initiative." She compliments him because he is doing his work ahead of time.

3 **Detail Question** | The professor tells the student, "Pare down your topic. First, focus on just one animal that migrates. I don't care which one it is. Just choose one. Next, look at only one aspect of its migrating habits. And then go into that in as much depth as you possibly can." So she wants the student to focus on a more specific topic rather than a general one.

4 **Making Inferences Question** | The student tells the professor that he needs to think about his topic and that he will talk to her after tomorrow's class. So he implies that he will decide on a new subject by the next class.

5 **Understanding Attitude Question** | When the student says, "You wouldn't believe how badly that worked out," he implies that some of his grades during his freshman year were poor.

Lecture 01-02

p.18

M Professor: The world's ocean level rises and falls daily. This action is called the tide as you no doubt already know. Typically, the tide rises and falls twice a day, but it may happen only once a day in some places. Tides usually rise and fall over the course of many hours. When the water level begins rising or falling, this is called the turning of the tide. The time it takes for the tide to rise and fall varies from place to place, but, like I just said, most places experience four changes a day. Additionally, one low tide is lower than the other and is called the, uh, the lower low tide. Got that . . . ? Excellent.

So, uh, why do the tides occur . . . ? The tides occur because of gravity. The moon has a great effect on the Earth's tides. Think about it . . . The moon's gravity is trying to pull the Earth toward it, yet it is unsuccessful. However, the water on the Earth is not as resistant as the rest of the planet. Therefore, the water moves toward the moon. Of course, it doesn't go, uh, spiraling off into space because Earth has its own gravity, which is keeping the water on the planet. Nevertheless, the moon's gravitational pull on the water is noticeable in coastal regions where it manifests in the form of tides.

The sun also causes tides in much the same manner as the moon. But despite the sun's much greater size, the moon has a greater influence on the Earth's tides due to the fact that it's much closer to the planet. Just in case you're interested, the sun's gravitational influence on the Earth's tides is less than fifty percent of the moon's. However, since the two act in conjunction, they can have a significant effect on the tides. Here's an example . . . During a full moon or a new moon, the moon, the sun, and the Earth are all in conjunction. That is, uh, they're all lined up with each other. During these times, the gravitational forces of the moon and sun work together to produce the highest tides each month. These are called spring tides, and they happen twice a month.

W Student: I have a question. Does this mean that halfway between a new moon and a full moon that, uh, the tides are lower?

M: You figured that out rather quickly, Melissa. Yes, when the sun and the moon are at roughly ninety-degree angles to one another, which happens in both the first and third quarters of the moon's phases, the tides don't change much. These are called neap tides, and they also occur twice a month. Another question?

W: Yes, please. How big is the difference in terms of the height of the water between neap tides, spring tides, and normal tides?

M: Well . . . There's no simple answer to that question. I would estimate that the difference is roughly, oh, let's say, around twenty percent or so. But that's not an exact figure since the difference in water levels varies from place to place. The reason for this is that there are other forces which also affect the tides. For example . . . the Earth's rotation, the tilt of the Earth's axis, the condition of the seafloor, the currents, the depth of the coastal water, and the shape of the coastline. All of those factors play a role in how high and low the tides are. Oh, yeah, and remember that the distance of the moon from the Earth varies slightly as it orbits the planet. Depending on how close or how far from the Earth the moon is, the moon's effect on the tides can change.

Let's take a look at how the shape of the coastline can affect the tides. Up here on the screen is a scene from a port on the Bay of Fundy in Nova Scotia, Canada. As we watch this video, which has been accelerated to account for the passing of time, notice how extreme the tidal changes are. They're almost twenty meters in some places, making these tidal changes among the greatest in the world. See how much the tides are changing . . . Incredible, isn't it?

Now, look at this map of the Bay of Fundy. Notice that the bay is long and narrow and shaped like a funnel. That's why the tides are so high. The mass of water in the bay has nowhere to go when the gravitational forces pull on it. It can't spread out across the wide ocean, so it causes very high tides.

W: There must be a lot of tidal power stations there.

M: You'd think so, but, as far as I'm aware, there's only one small tidal power station in the Bay of Fundy. Some people are concerned it may negatively impact the environment, so no larger ones have been built yet. Hopefully, they'll start constructing more soon. Tidal power is cheap and clean. Anyway, I don't want to get distracted talking about that. Let's get back to discussing the tides.

6 **Gist-Content Question** | During the lecture, the professor mostly talks about how the sun and the moon can affect the tides and cause them to rise and fall.

7 **Connecting Content Question** | The professor tells the students, "The sun also causes tides in much the same manner as the moon. But despite the sun's much greater size, the moon has a greater influence on the Earth's tides due to the fact that it's much closer to the planet. Just in case you're interested, the sun's gravitational influence on the Earth's tides is less than fifty percent of the moon's."

8 **Detail Question** | The professor says, "During these times, the gravitational forces of the moon and sun work together to produce the highest tides each month. These are called spring tides, and they happen twice a month."

9 **Understanding Attitude Question** | After the student asks a question, the professor answers, "You figured that out rather quickly, Melissa." So he praises the student for her response. In addition, listen to his tone of voice. He has a praising tone of voice. So he is very complimentary of the student.

10 **Understanding Organization Question** | About the Bay of Fundy, the professor states, "Now, look at this map of the Bay of Fundy. Notice that the bay is long and narrow and shaped like a funnel. That's why the tides are so high. The mass of water in the bay has nowhere to go when the gravitational forces pull on it. It can't spread out across the wide ocean, so it causes very high tides."

11 **Making Inferences Question** | When the professor mentions tidal power stations, he claims, "Hopefully, they'll start constructing more soon. Tidal power is cheap and clean." So it can be inferred that he is in favor of tidal power for a couple of reasons.

PART 2

Conversation 01-03

p.22

W Student: Dave, I've got a couple of things that I need to talk to you about. Do you have a moment or two to spare?

M Resident Assistant: Sure, Susan. What can I help you with?

W: Well, uh, I'm planning to go home for the Thanksgiving holiday that's coming up in a couple of days. I didn't get the opportunity to go home during summer vacation since I was here taking classes, and my parents really want to see me even if it's just going to be for a few days. After all, my entire family, including all of my aunts and uncles, is getting together this year.

M: That's great. I'm glad to hear that.

W: Yeah, so, uh, I'm going to be heading to the airport on Wednesday morning to catch my flight. But the airport's kind of far away from the school you know.

M: You're totally right about that. Hey, I'd offer to drive you there in my car, but I'm going home on Tuesday night, so unless you want to spend the night in the airport, I don't think that I will be able to help you out.

W: Oh, you're going home as well? I had no idea that you were leaving.

M: It's been a while since I've seen my family, so I thought I'd go back home. But I live all the way across the country, so I have to take the redeye to get there.

W: Cool. Anyway, thanks for the offer, but I'm going to go to the airport on Wednesday in the morning. So, uh, that brings me to my question.

M: Which is?

W: Is there a bus that goes to the airport? [4]I mean, I usually just go there with a friend of mine, but nobody that I know is going to the airport at the same time as me. And I heard that a taxi to the airport can cost something like forty dollars. **That's way out of my price range.**

M: [15]Actually, there's a bus that leaves from campus and goes straight to the airport.

W: No way. Are you serious?

M: **I wouldn't pull your leg about that.** It's a new service. That's probably why you haven't heard about it. It leaves from the student services building. You can go there and get a schedule from a staffer.

W: Awesome. I didn't know that at all. Thanks a lot for the information.

M: No problem.

W: Oh, wait. So does that mean that the bus picks up students at the airport and takes them back to campus as well?

M: That's right. But what time are you going to get back?

W: A little after midnight on Sunday. Why do you ask?

M: Ah, the bus stops running at eleven at night. You're either going to have to take a taxi or the train to get back to school. In case you don't know, the train runs all night, but it's on a reduced schedule after ten PM.

W: Okay. Thanks for letting me know. I'll go to the student services building later and see if I have to make a reservation or anything for the bus. And I'll try to get a train schedule and figure out how I can get back here.

M: No problem. Oh, and if I don't see you before you leave, have a great holiday.

1 **Gist-Purpose Question** | After chatting with the resident assistant, the student then asks him, "Is there a bus that goes to the airport?" Right before then, she says, "So, uh, that brings me to my question." So she speaks with him to find out about transportation to the airport.

2 **Connecting Content Question** | The student and the resident assistant chat about their personal lives. They also know each other's first names, and they appear to be comfortable with one another. Thus it can be inferred that the student has met the resident assistant before.

3 **Detail Question** | The student comments, "I didn't get the opportunity to go home during summer vacation since I was here taking classes, and my parents really want to see me even if it's just going to be for a few days." So it has been a long time since she has seen her family.

4 **Understanding Attitude Question** | When a person says that something is out of his or her price range, it means that the person cannot afford that item. So the student cannot afford to take a taxi to the airport.

5 **Understanding Function Question** | When a person "pulls someone's leg," it means that the speaker is joking with that person. The resident assistant says that he would not pull the student's leg about the bus, so he is indicating to her that he is telling the truth and not joking.

Lecture 01-04

p.24

M Professor: Lasers are no longer fantasies found exclusively in science-fiction books and movies. Today, they are a reality and are used in a multitude of applications. For instance, we use lasers in CD and DVD players, in many types of surgery, and in the transmitting of electronic communications, to name but a few of their uses.

What is a laser? It's a type of light, but it is light that flows in one direction. Additionally, all the light particles in a laser are a single color, which means that they have the same wavelength. Just so you know, when something is a single color, it's said to be monochromatic. As for how a laser is made . . . Well, it's the result of the stimulated emission of photons. What happens is that a photon . . . uh, that's the basic unit of light . . . so a photon strikes an atom that's in an excited state. This causes the atom to release another photon, which is identical to the first one. Both photons travel in the same direction. They begin striking other atoms, which causes this release of more photons. Then, a chain reaction of sorts occurs as the laser beam is formed. [10]This is actually why we use the name laser. It's an acronym for light amplification by stimulated emission of radiation. That spells L-A-S-E-R. **Janice, you have your hand up?**

W Student: Yes, sir. Who discovered—or invented I guess I should say—the laser?

M: Good question. Hmm . . . The principles behind the laser were first proposed by Albert Einstein in a paper he wrote in 1917. After that, several scientists around the world worked on making a practical laser, but the first one wasn't built until the 1960s. This happened in the United States, but there wasn't just one person responsible. Instead, it was many people and one company, Bell Labs, that together played a significant role in making lasers a reality. The main problems they encountered in building a practical laser were first getting the atoms to become excited and then finding a way to focus the photons in a single direction. [11]You see, uh, when more atoms in a substance are in an excited state than in a low-energy state, you have what's called population inversion. To get these atoms excited to a state of population inversion, what's needed is an optical cavity with a gain medium as well as a source of power such as electricity. Understand . . . ?

W: **I'm sorry, sir, but that went completely over my head.**

M: All right . . . It appears that some of you are a bit confused. Let me define these terms for you then. First, the optical cavity. That's merely an enclosed space. Inside the optical cavity is something called a gain medium. That's a substance which allows the atoms to increase in energy so that they can reach the population inversion stage. Typical substances include crystals, gases, and special types of glass. The optical cavity also has two or more mirrors, which reflect light back and forth through the gain medium to the point that the atoms become excited and start releasing photons. One side of the optical cavity is more transparent than the other. This side is the direction that the focused beam of light—the laser itself—will emit from the optical cavity. This entire contraption requires a power source, which is most often electricity. The energy source is called the energy pump, and the process of applying energy is called pumping. Does that make sense for everyone now . . . ? Let's continue then.

Importantly, no laser will be produced if the energy pump is insufficient. Why's that? Well, the light passing through the gain medium won't produce enough of an excited state to enable a sufficient number of atoms to reach population inversion. Simply put, there won't be a laser beam unless enough energy gets pumped into the optical cavity. The point at which there's a sufficient amount of energy to create a laser beam is called the lasing threshold. The lasing threshold varies, by the way, depending upon the type of gain medium being used. And just so you know, everything I've described happens extremely fast . . . In the blink of an eye really.

There are many types of lasers, and they're built in different ways. Their intensity can be increased or lowered. Their intensity also depends on the distance they travel. For instance, over short distances, most laser beams are focused in a pencil-thin shape and are quite intense. Over longer distances, that same beam may diffuse and become wider, which makes it less intense. Additionally, lasers are either continuous or pulsed. A continuous beam operates at a steady rate while a pulsed laser has its beam interrupted at intervals.

Today, as I indicated a couple of minutes ago, lasers are used in a variety of applications. Since they can generate heat, they can be used as cutting tools in surgery and industry. But the most commonly used laser today is a laser diode. That's a small, simple laser used in electronic devices. Let me show you in brief how one of these works right now.

6 **Gist-Content Question** | The professor mostly focuses on the process of how lasers are produced.

7 **Detail Question** | The professor tells the class, "Inside the optical cavity is something called a gain medium. That's a substance which allows the atoms to increase in energy so that they can reach the population inversion stage. Typical substances include crystals, gases, and special types of glass."

8 **Understanding Organization Question** | About the lasing threshold, the professor says, "The point at which there's a sufficient amount of energy to create a laser beam is called the lasing threshold. The lasing threshold varies, by the way, depending upon the type of gain medium being used." So the professor discusses it to mention its relevance to the creation of a laser beam.

9 **Making Inferences Question** | At the end of the lecture, the professor states, "But the most commonly used laser today is a laser diode. That's a small, simple laser used in electronic devices. Let me show you in brief how one of these works right now." So he will probably give the students a short demonstration.

10 **Understanding Function Question** | When the professor asks the student, "You have your hand up?" he is acknowledging her and giving her permission to ask her question.

11 **Understanding Attitude Question** | When something "goes completely over one's head," it means that the person does not understand something. Thus the student means that she does not understand what the professor just told the class.

PART 3

Conversation 01-05

p.28

W Professor: Jeff, you said at the end of class this morning that you needed to speak with me. What's going on?

M Student: I guess I'm just a bit confused about something you lectured on in class today.

W: Yes? What is it?

M: It was the part of the class when you talked about exotic species and invasive species. If I remember correctly, you said that cows and chickens are exotic species. Um . . . How is that possible? I thought exotic species were, uh, plants or animals from the tropics or places like that.

W: Ah, I see your confusion. Yes, many people refer to exotic plants or animals as being from faraway lands such as tropic islands.

M: Right.

W: But that's not the scientific definition.

M: What is it then?

W: It's simple. An exotic species is simply an animal which has been introduced to an area that it's not native to, and . . .

M: Wait a minute. I thought that was an invasive species.

W: You need to let me finish, Jeff.

M: Er . . . sorry about that. Please go ahead.

W: An exotic species has been introduced to an ecosystem that's outside its native range. However—and this is very important—it's not harmful to that ecosystem. As for invasive species, well, they're plants, animals, or other organisms which have been introduced to a new place but are harmful in some manner. Invasive species may be harmful because they might have no natural predators, so they could reproduce very quickly. In the case of plants, such as kudzu, they could grow everywhere, which can cause native plants to die out.

M: Oh . . . So when you said that cows and chickens are exotic species, you simply meant that they now live in areas where they aren't originally from. Is that correct?

W: Precisely.

M: Okay, that makes sense to me. Can you tell me some other exotic species, please?

W: Sure. Cats and dogs are exotic species. So is the Venus flytrap, uh, if you want an example of a plant.

M: And what about some invasive species?

W: I just mentioned kudzu as one. The Burmese python, which is an enormous snake, is a terrible menace in the Florida Everglades. It's reproducing quickly and wiping out the native animals there. In fact, uh, I think that's what I'd like you to write your midterm paper on, Jeff. I want you to do a comparison on exotic and invasive species. Pick a couple of each, and then write about how they've affected the places where they were introduced. Be sure to propose what, if anything, we should do about them since they aren't native to their new environments.

M: Sounds great, Professor. Thanks so much for your explanation. I really appreciate your taking some time to clear things up for me.

W: It's my pleasure. If you have any more questions, feel free to email me. I'm not going to be on campus the rest of the week because I'm attending a conference in Dallas. In fact, I've got to head to the airport in just a few minutes.

M: Oh, I'm sorry to keep you waiting. I'll see you in class next week. Thanks again.

1 **Gist-Content Question** | During the conversation, the student and the professor mostly talk about the definitions of some terms that were used in a recent class.

2 **Detail Question** | The professor tells the student, "An exotic species has been introduced to an ecosystem that's outside its native range. However—and this is very important—it's not harmful to that ecosystem."

3 **Understanding Function Question** | The professor tells the student, "In fact, uh, I think that's what I'd like you to write your midterm paper on, Jeff. I want you to do a comparison on exotic and invasive species. Pick a couple of each, and then write about how they've affected the places where they were introduced. Be sure to propose what, if anything, we should do about them since they aren't native to their new environments."

4 **Understanding Attitude Question** | The student is pleased that the professor helps him by answering all of his questions.

5 **Making Inferences Question** | The professor states, "In fact, I've got to head to the airport in just a few minutes," so she will likely leave the campus next.

Lecture 01-06

p.30

M Professor: Today, Ireland is an independent nation, but at one time, the entire place belonged to the British Empire. The island was formally made a part of Great Britain in the Act of Union in 1801. Until then, Ireland had had its own parliament, but after the passing of the act, the Irish Parliament was closed down, and the Irish were given representation in the British Parliament. Over the next century or so, various attempts were made to grant Ireland something c-c-c-called home rule. This basically meant that the Irish Parliament would be revived, thereby giving the Irish some degree of autonomy. Unfortunately, all attempts at home rule failed. This, in turn, led to more radical forces in Ireland starting to push for an armed insurrection to throw the British out of the country.

The most significant event in the Irish struggle for freedom took place in 1916 at the height of World War I. This became known as the Easter Rebellion, or the Easter Rising. On Easter Monday, April 24, 1916, Irish nationalists seized several crucial points in Dublin, the capital city. For the next seven days, fighting took place in and around Dublin until the British succeeded in reestablishing control. The immediate results were that the rebellion was crushed, the leaders were captured and, in many cases, executed for treason, and Ireland's bid for independence seemed doomed. However, the Easter Rebellion sparked the building of an independence movement within Ireland that led directly to a wider war of independence, which saw the Irish nationalists achieve most of their goals by 1922.

[10] As for the 1916 Easter Rebellion . . . There were many factions involved. There were so many that listing them would cause you to drown in a sea of names and organizations. **So I won't distract you with them.** Suffice it to say, not all of these factions worked together, nor were all involved in the Easter Rebellion. Interestingly, many of these organizations sought help from the Germans. Remember that World War I pitted the Germans against the British, among others, so it seemed prudent for the Germans to get involved with the Irish in order to distract the British from the fighting on the European mainland. Thus the Germans supplied arms and a ship to transport them to Ireland. Unknown to them and the Irish nationalists, the British had broken the Germans' secret codes, so they knew the ship was heading to Ireland. On April 20, the Royal Navy intercepted the ship, yet its crew managed to sink it when they were forced into a harbor. Obviously, the weapons went to the bottom of the sea along with the ship.

This loss almost caused the Irish to abandon their plans, but they pressed on anyway. They merely delayed action from Easter Sunday, April 23, to the next day, Easter Monday, April 24. On that day, around 1,200 armed men took control of some key places in Dublin, including the post office, which became their headquarters. The Irish nationalists then declared the independence of the Irish Republic. Yet the Irish failed to take one key place: Dublin Castle. This was the center of British power in all of Ireland and was seen as a symbol of the hated British. Keeping the castle let the British maintain some measure of control in Dublin.

W Student: Didn't the British know the rebellion was going to take place? It seems that they must have since they knew about the German ship.

M: Well, they knew something was going on, but since it was Easter, they felt that nothing would happen then. The British did, however, have plans to arrest many of the people whom they believed were leading the movement, yet orders approving the arrests didn't arrive from London until after the rebellion had already begun. So, yes, the British were caught by surprise, and, in some clashes on the first day, many British soldiers were killed, uh, along with some nationalists and civilians who were caught in the crossfire.

[11] What happened next? Well, the British moved quickly to suppress the uprising. They were unintentionally helped by the Irish, who had failed to capture the port facilities and the main train stations. **Obviously, the leaders of the rebellion didn't possess much knowledge concerning military matters.** Anyway, this tactical error let the British move in reinforcements, including heavy artillery. The local commander declared martial law, and then the British slowly, but surely, began to regain control of Dublin. The next few days were a bloody affair. The British wore down the Irish mostly with artillery. There were some battles between infantry, during which the Irish inflicted a large number of casualties on advancing British troops. Still, by the next Sunday, the Irish were forced to surrender.

Many of the Irish leaders were killed. Those who survived were mostly captured, tried, and either executed or imprisoned. But the flame of rebellion had been lit. The Irish would be inspired to try both political and military means of gaining their independence. So let me tell you what they did next.

6 **Gist-Content Question** | The lecture is about the Irish Easter Rebellion and the events that happened during it.

7 **Detail Question** | The professor notes, "Thus the Germans supplied arms and a ship to transport them to Ireland." However, the ship sank, so the Irish never received the weapons.

8 **Understanding Organization Question** | The professor describes the events of the rebellion in chronological order.

9 **Making Inferences Question** | The professor states, "Many of the Irish leaders were killed. Those who survived were mostly captured, tried, and either executed or imprisoned. But the flame of rebellion had been lit. The Irish would be inspired to try both political and military means of gaining their independence. So let me tell you what they did next." So he is likely to continue lecturing on a similar topic.

10 **Understanding Attitude Question** | The professor indicates that there were many names and organizations involved in the Easter Rebellion. Then, he states that he will not distract the students with them. This means that he will not give the names of any of the people or groups to the students.

11 **Understanding Function Question** | The professor comments that the Irish did not capture the port

facilities and the main train stations. Then, he declares, "Obviously, the leaders of the rebellion didn't possess much knowledge concerning military matters." The professor thus implies that ports and train stations are important to armies.

Lecture 01-07

p.33

W Professor: The evidence appears irrefutable that humans and other primates shared a common ancestor millions of years ago. However, while we humans acquired the ability to use language, other primates did not. Well, uh, at least they didn't learn any sort of verbal communication that we can understand. However, here's an interesting question: Since primates—particularly gorillas and chimpanzees—share more than ninety-five percent of the DNA which humans have, could they not be taught to communicate as humans do? Could they, in fact, be taught to communicate with us? In recent decades, some researchers have put primates to the test, and they've reported that, in several cases, they've taught these primates how to communicate with humans. Nevertheless, the results are somewhat controversial.

I think I first need to explain how primates can talk with humans since they don't vocalize words like, uh, parrots do. Instead, researchers use two main methods to achieve communication. The first involves sign language. You know, what deaf and mute people use to communicate with others. Sign language was first proposed as a means of communication with primates for three reasons. First, many researchers thought primates weren't intelligent enough to use verbal language. Second, others believed that primates couldn't imitate sounds they heard in the way that human children do. Third, researchers thought that primates' vocal cords were physically incapable of making human-sounding vocalizations. As for the second method, it uses lexigram keyboards. Lexigrams, by the way, are symbols used to represent words. Let me write a couple on the board here . . . See this . . . And this one . . . Here's another . . . I think you can figure out what those mean. They're rather simple. Lexigrams are relatively new, with the first being made back in the early 1970s. Anyway, by using a lexigram keyboard—a keyboard with pictures of lexigrams—primates can communicate with humans.

Researchers have experienced success with both methods. Let me tell you about a couple of them. The first involves a female chimpanzee named Washoe. In the early 1970s, Washoe learned American Sign Language. Her caretakers raised her as if she were a human child, and they only used sign language with her. They didn't speak in front of Washoe since they thought that might confuse her and slow down her progress in learning sign language. After a few years of training, Washoe began using sign language. Eventually, she learned around 350 words. Interestingly, Washoe learned to use many of these signs in combinations that had not been taught to her. In doing so, she demonstrated the ability to put words into sentences in a spontaneous manner. After a while, Washoe became so proficient at signing that she was sometimes faster than her own trainers and often had to slow down so that they could understand her.

There's an ongoing experiment involving Kanzi, a male bonobo chimpanzee. Kanzi communicates by using a lexigram keyboard. Years ago, one researcher was trying to teach Kanzi's mother how to use a lexigram keyboard while Kanzi was merely observing. One day, Kanzi just, uh, just started using the keyboard to communicate. He learned ten words quickly, and, since then, he has picked up thousands of new words. He can make sentences, he follows instructions, and he even makes vocalizations. [17] Some recent studies involving Kanzi have proven that, when he makes a vocalization at the same time he presses a key on his keyboard for a word, the vocalization he's making represents that particular symbol.

M Student: **I'm sorry, but are you saying that Kanzi is actually speaking?**

W: Well, yes, he is in his own particular way. The team that handles Kanzi believes he might be trying to articulate English words; however, his vocal range is too high for them to understand what he's saying. If that hypothesis turns out to be true, that would be a, well, a remarkable breakthrough in primate-human communications.

There are lots of people—many of whom are experts on language—who claim that examples like Washoe and Kanzi are just that: They're examples. Uh, that is, they're exceptions to the general rule that primates lack the intelligence to communicate like humans do. This argument has some validity since of the many primates that researchers have tried teaching, only a few have successfully managed to communicate. And the two examples I gave you are the best of the bunch. Some skeptics even question these success stories. These doubters say that although the primates can make some words in sign language or with a keyboard, they're merely imitating actions they saw rather than making language. They state that the primates are simply trying to please their trainers instead of communicating their thoughts and feelings. Additionally, these skeptics note that, compared to the relative ease that human children learn language, primates lag far behind in the learning curve. That's certainly true. Yet it doesn't mean that primates can't communicate at all. In fact, I'm certain we'll see more success stories like Washoe and Kanzi in the future.

12 **Gist-Content Question** | The lecturer describes two separate attempts that people have made to teach apes to communicate with humans.

13 **Detail Question** | The professor states, "First, many researchers thought primates weren't intelligent enough to use verbal language," and, "Third, researchers thought that primates' vocal cords were physically incapable of making human-sounding vocalizations."

14 **Understanding Organization Question** | While talking about lexigrams, the professor says, "Lexigrams, by the way, are symbols used to represent words. Let me write a couple on the board here . . . See this . . . And this one . . . Here's another . . . I think you can figure out what those mean."

15 **Connecting Content Question** | According to the lecture, Washoe learned to sign very quickly and often had to slow down because she was so fast. She also knew around 350 words. As for Kanzi, he uses lexigrams to speak with people. He also learned to communicate with people by watching his mother be taught by researchers.

16 **Making Inferences Question** | At the end of the lecture, the professor declares, "Yet it doesn't mean that primates can't communicate at all. In fact, I'm certain we'll see more success stories like Washoe and Kanzi in the future." Thus she implies that it is possible to teach primates to communicate with humans.

17 **Understanding Function Question** | The student's tone of voice is important. He sounds very skeptical when he says, "I'm sorry, but are you saying that Kanzi is actually speaking?" He clearly doubts that Kanzi is trying to speak.

Actual Test 02

p.37

Answers

PART 1

1 (B)	2 (C)	3 (C)	4 (D)	5 (A)
6 [3], [4]	7 (A)	8 (D)	9 (B)	10 (A)
11 (A)				

PART 2

1 (A)	2 (D)	3 (D)	4 (B)	5 (C)
6 (D)	7 (B)	8 (C)	9 (A)	10 Hudson River School: [2], [4] Impressionist Movement: [1], [3]
11 (C)	12 (A)	13 (A)	14 (C)	15 (B)
16 (D)	17 (B)			

Scripts & Explanations

PART 1

Conversation 02-01

p.40

W1 Student: Professor Marconi, what did you think of my proposal for the class project?

W2 Professor: [5]Proposal? What proposal?

W1: The one that I submitted to you by email this morning. You didn't get it? **I must have sent it to the wrong address or something.**

W2: Ah, sorry, Kelly, but I haven't checked my email since last night. I've been up to my eyeballs with work, so I haven't gotten the opportunity to get on the Internet today. But since you're here, why don't you tell me what you propose to do? How does that sound?

W1: Perfect. Thanks.

W2: Okay. So, um, what do you want to do for your project?

W1: Are you familiar with that new medical clinic that's located near the campus?

W2: Which one?

W1: It's right across the street from Baker Hall. The name of the clinic is Dr. Brown's Family Health Clinic. There's a fairly big sign in front of the building. You can't miss it if you drive by it.

W2: Ah, sure. I know which clinic you're talking about. Hmm . . . I'm curious. What does that clinic have to do with your project?

W1: Well, I noticed that the clinic has been advertising on campus as well as in the local newspapers and elsewhere. So I thought I would take a look at exactly how effective Dr. Brown's marketing techniques are.

W2: What exactly are some of them?

W1: For one, patients don't require appointments when they feel ill. They can just walk right in and see a doctor within a few minutes. The clinic also doesn't accept health insurance but charges very small fees. According to Dr. Brown, he can still make money since he doesn't have to pay a bunch of people to do a lot of paperwork processing insurance claims.

W2: Hmm . . . That does sound interesting. Do you happen to know how popular his clinic is?

W1: Er, yes. I actually have firsthand experience with the clinic. And lots of people that I know have been there as well. Everyone I have spoken with has been highly satisfied.

W2: All right. I'll be sure to check it out myself in the future.

W1: So does this mean that my proposal is okay?

W2: Tentatively, yes. But I want to know what kind of approach you're going to take. I also hope that you will be able to schedule an interview with Dr. Brown so that you can find out from him how effective his marketing techniques are. And be sure to interview as many patients—both satisfied and unsatisfied ones—as you can.

W1: Don't worry, ma'am. I explain how I intend to do all of those things in my proposal. And I actually have an interview with Dr. Brown scheduled for this weekend.

W2: Outstanding. I look forward to seeing the results.

W1: Thanks.

W2: I'll check my email later today, and then I will get back to you tonight with a definite yes or no. But I imagine that the answer will be yes. I'll provide some feedback for you as well. You know, uh, suggestions on what kinds of questions you can ask and stuff like that.

W1: All right. That would be great. Anyway, um, I'll leave you to get back to your work in that case. It looks like you're pretty busy now.

W2: Sounds good. I'll talk to you later, Kelly.

1 **Gist-Content Question** | Most of the conversation is about a proposal for a project that the student must do.

2 **Gist-Content Question** | The student wants to do her project on the marketing techniques used by the health clinic, so that is why she talks to the professor about it.

3 **Making Inferences Question** | The professor tells the student that the health clinic's marketing techniques sound interesting. Then, she says, "I'll be sure to check it out myself in the future." So she implies that she will go there the next time that she is sick.

4 **Detail Question** | The professor tells the student, "I also hope that you will be able to schedule an interview with Dr. Brown so that you can find out from him how effective his marketing techniques are."

5 **Understanding Attitude Question** | When the student says that she must have sent the email to the wrong address, it can be inferred that the student believes that she made a mistake, so that is why the professor has not read her email.

Lecture 02-02 p.42

W Professor: Here is another species of ant up on the screen . . . Note its distended abdomen . . . how swollen it is. It's so big that it looks like it's the size of a grape or a cherry. What you're looking at is a honey ant—well, one species of honey ant at least. Honey ants have an unusual capability. They can store food in their bodies so that it can later be used by other members of their colonies.

Not all honey ants can do this though. Only certain females can. What happens is that some ants go out, gather food from various sources, and then carry the food back to the colony. Then, they pass this food on to certain females, who store the food in their bodies for a long period of time. These females hang from the interior roof of the colony. Hundreds—even thousands—of ants in one colony will store food for the benefit of others. As these ants gather more food, their abdomens swell until they are enormous. In fact, the bodies of the honey ants that store food typically become so swollen that those ants can neither leave the colony nor even move through the colony's tunnels for that matter. Over time, however, their abdomens shrink as the food they've stored internally is regurgitated and then consumed by the other ants in the colony.

Notice here . . . how some of these ants with swollen abdomens are amber in color . . . while others are more whitish. They all look as if they're ready to burst open, but, in fact, their abdomens are incredibly strong.

M Student: Professor Popper, what do these ants eat?

W: Honey ants eat a variety of foods. They enjoy sugary carbohydrates that come from the nectar of flowers. They also consume honeydew, which is produced by aphids. This sugary food accounts for the amber color in most of the swollen abdomens of the storage honey ants. Additionally, honey ants need to provide protein for the growing larvae, ah, the baby ants, in the colony. To obtain this protein, the food foragers often drag the bodies of dead insects back to the colony. The ants sometimes even form groups that attack other insects. Honey ants lack stingers like many ants, but they can spray a substance that's similar to caustic acid. This disables other insects and let the honey ants kill them. Later, the dead insects are offered to the storage honey ants. Finally, a few storage ants consume and store water, which accounts for the whitish color on some of their abdomens.

The abdomen of a storage honey ant is rather unusual. It contains many layers of a soft membrane that remains hidden under the hard outer plates, or segments, of the abdomen. When a honey ant starts to gorge on food, the plates move, and the soft membrane begins to expand. The abdomen is like a mammal's stomach in that it's flexible and has the ability to expand to a great size in order to store large quantity . . . er, quantities, of food. But the food is not digested, um, as it would be in the stomachs of mammals. Instead, it's stored for others to use.

Interestingly, these honey ants are frequently subject to attack. [11]The storage ants are considered a delicacy by some predators, such as, uh, badgers, and even humans are known to eat them. Seriously. **You should try them sometime. They're quite good.** You don't eat the entire ant . . . although other animals do. Instead, you eat the sugary nectar, which is squeezed out of the stomach. It tastes rather like, hmm . . . molasses I'd say. Okay, I'll stop since some of you are looking a little squeamish now. Ah, one more thing though . . . Honey ants often attack other honey ant colonies to try to capture their food storage ants. The victors drag the storage honey ants back to their own colonies as if the ants were spoils of war.

You're probably wondering what the motive behind the gathering and storing of food is, right? It's not too complicated. Many honey ant species live in dry climates such as the American Southwest. In desert-like conditions, food becomes scarce at times. So the food preserved by the storage honey ants enables the other colony members to survive. Without the benefit of the storage honey ants, it's likely that many species of honey ants would have gone extinct by now.

All right. I believe that we're at a sufficient stopping point for today. What I'd like for you all to do before our next class is read chapter ten in your textbooks. It's the chapter on arachnids, which is what we're going to turn our attention to for the next couple of lectures. Please be sure you read it as our class discussions haven't been as good as I've been expecting them to be. Are there any questions for me . . . ? Okay. I'll take your silence as a no. In that case, I'll see all of you this Friday. Enjoy the rest of the day, everyone.

6 **Detail Question** | The professor says, "They enjoy sugary carbohydrates that come from the nectar of flowers," and, "This disables other insects and lets the honey ants kill them. Later, the dead insects are offered to the storage honey ants."

7 **Making Inferences Question** | The professor states, "Finally, a few storage ants consume and store water, which accounts for the whitish color on some of their abdomens." Since she mentions this at the end of her description of the food that storage honey ants consume, it can be inferred that only a few of them store water while more store food.

8 **Connecting Content Question** | The professor says, "Honey ants often attack other honey ant colonies to try to capture their food storage ants. The victors drag the storage honey ants back to their own colonies as if the ants were spoils of war." Then, she states, "In desert-like conditions, food becomes scarce at times. So the food preserved by the storage honey ants enables the other colony members to survive. Without the benefit of the storage honey ants, it's likely that many species of honey ants would have gone extinct by now." Thus it can be assumed that without the storage honey ants, some ants in the losing colony will die of starvation.

9 **Understanding Organization Question** | The professor tells the students, "Many honey ant species live in dry climates such as the American Southwest."

10 **Understanding Attitude Question** | The professor says, "What I'd like for you all to do before our next class is read chapter ten in your textbooks. It's the chapter on arachnids, which is what we're going to turn our attention to for the next couple of lectures. Please be sure you read it as our class discussions haven't been as good as I've been expecting them to be." She implies that not all of the students are doing their homework.

11 **Understanding Function Question** | When the professor comments, "They're quite good," she is implying that she has eaten honey ants before.

PART 2

Conversation 02-03

p.46

M Housing Office Employee: Good morning. How may I be of assistance to you?

W Student: Good morning to you, sir. My name is Lisa Carter, and I'm a freshman here at the school. I live in Patterson Hall with two other roommates. But there are a couple of problems with our room. So, uh, I'm hoping that you can help me out and solve them.

M: I'll certainly do my best. In that case, why don't you tell me what's wrong with your dorm?

W: All right. The first problem is that there is a leak in the roof. We live on the seventh floor of the hall. That's the top floor. [5]And, uh, you remember how we got all that rain a couple of days ago?

M: Oh yeah. **That sure was some storm, wasn't it?**

W: You can say that again. Well, uh, there must still be a lot of water collected on the roof because parts of our ceiling are wet, and some water is even dripping onto the floor in a few places. We put some buckets in the room to catch the water, but . . . You know, that's going to cause mold and mildew to grow in our room, and we really don't want that.

M: Definitely not. Plus, the roof could collapse if there's still a lot of water up there.

W: Oh . . . I never even considered that.

M: All right. I'll make a call and have a work team head to your dorm right away so that they can check it out. This is something that absolutely can't wait. What room did you say that you're in again?

W: I'm in room 705 in Patterson Hall. And, uh, you might have those workers knock on some of the other students' rooms since I think I heard some other students complaining about water leaking into their rooms as well.

M: Hmm . . . That doesn't sound good at all. All right. Thank you very much for bringing that to my attention.

W: Sure. Now, as for the second problem . . .

M: Second problem?

W: Yeah, sorry. Anyway, um, the second problem is that there are ants in our room. And, no, before you ask, we don't leave uneaten food lying around on the floor.

M: Okay. That was the first question I was going to ask you.

W: I figured as much. But I make sure that we keep our room as clean as possible, so that's why I'm not sure exactly why we have ants. We've got them in one of our closets, and we can sometimes see them on the floor.

M: Hmm . . . That's not good either. I'll have a different person drop by to check out that problem. That should be sometime this afternoon . . . Uh, there's not a third problem, is there?

W: No, sir. That's it.

M: Well, that's a relief. All right. Expect to have some visitors within the hour. You're going back to your dorm room now, right? I hope so because someone needs to be there to let them in. They're not allowed into a room if no one is there.

W: Ah, that's fine. I don't have class today, so I'll go back to my room and stay there until the work teams take care of everything.

1 **Gist-Content Question** | At the beginning of the conversation, the student says, "Well, uh, there must still be a lot of water collected on the roof because parts of our ceiling are wet, and some water is even dripping onto the floor in a few places."

2 **Understanding Attitude Question** | The man seems helpful and is concerned about the student's problems. He also indicates that he will call the repairmen and have them visit the student's dormitory room quickly. So it can be inferred that he is eager to solve her problems.

3 **Detail Question** | About the ants, the student comments, "But I make sure that we keep our room as clean as possible, so that's why I'm not sure exactly why we have ants."

4 **Making Inferences Question** | In the middle of the conversation, the man says, "I'll make a call and have a work team head to your dorm right away so that they can check it out. This is something that absolutely can't wait." Since the problem cannot wait, as soon as the student leaves, he will probably call someone about the water problem.

5 **Understanding Function Question** | When the man says, "That sure was some storm, wasn't it?" he is indicating that a lot of rain fell during it.

Lecture 02-04

p.48

M Professor: We're going to continue examining American art by moving on to some movements in the nineteenth century. As I hope you remember from our last class, American artists during the colonial period in the eighteenth century concentrated mostly on portrait painting although some painted landscapes and other works. Many American artists during that time also traveled to Europe to learn the artistic techniques being taught there. These artists were, as you would expect, greatly influenced by European styles. This trend continued during the nineteenth century as various schools of European art, such as, uh, Impressionism, had a great impact on American artists. Still, American artists developed their own styles, and we can definitely state that, during the nineteenth century, American art began to develop a distinct style of its own.

The Hudson River School was one important art movement in the nineteenth century. As you can surmise from its name, the artists in it were associated with the Hudson River Valley, which is located in the eastern part of New York. Most of the paintings done by artists in this movement were landscapes depicting the natural scenery of the valley as well as the nearby Catskill and Adirondack mountains. And, I'd like to add, it is one of the most beautiful regions in the entire country. If you ever visit it, you'll see why it captivated so many artists during this period. That's actually exactly what happened to Thomas Cole, the widely acknowledged leader of the Hudson River School. In 1825, he took a boat trip up the length of the Hudson River. He promptly began painting landscapes of the area. Many of Cole's contemporaries took note of the landscapes he painted, and they, quite understandably I'd say, began traveling to the region in order to emulate his work.

Many of the Hudson River School artists were influenced by landscape artists such as J.M.W. Turner and John Constable of England, yet they also strove to make something new, something that was, well, uniquely American. Now, let me show you some works that the Hudson River School artists made. I'm just going to flash through them as I keep talking. First, note that their works were done in a panoramic style and showed the natural scenery of the valley and nearby mountains . . . Their paintings were romanticized versions of the landscape . . . and were often attempts to make a connection between nature and God. The artists frequently utilized light to make their paintings more dramatic . . . see here . . . and here. This is called Luminism. Luminism was primarily used during the latter half of the nineteenth century. Paintings that used Luminism had elements of water and sunlight that gave them a serene look. They typically depicted the landscape underneath a soft hazy sky and painted reflections on the water.

W Student: It sounds a lot like Impressionism.

M: In some ways, yes, but the Hudson River School actually predates the Impressionist Movement. In addition, the Hudson River School artists who used Luminism tried to hide their brushstrokes whereas the brushstrokes in the works of the Impressionists can be clearly seen.

Now, besides Thomas Cole, there were other famous artists in the Hudson River School. Frederic Church, who was one of Cole's students, was famous in his own right. Thomas Doughty, Sanford Gifford, and George Inness were some other notable artists. The Hudson River School remained influential in the U.S. until the 1870s. It was around that time that American artists once again began to be influenced by Europeans.

Most of this influence came from the Impressionists. Impressionism, which began in the 1860s and became more prominent in the 1870s, used light and heavy brushstrokes to give an impression, or, uh, an idealistic view of the natural world. The movement spread to the U.S. in two ways. First, in the 1880s, there were exhibits of Impressionist art in cities throughout the country. Second, some American artists traveled to Europe to study art and were influenced directly by Impressionist artists.

Theodore Robinson was the first major American Impressionist. He lived in France for eight years and studied under the painter Claude Monet. Upon his return to the U.S., Robinson worked as an art teacher to support himself, so he spread Impressionist ideas to his own students. Up here, notice some of Robinson's works . . . Nice, huh . . . ? You can clearly see the influence Monet had on him when you take a look at this work by Robinson here . . . and this one by Monet . . .

Another theme in nineteenth century American art concerned the works done of the American West and its people. Artists such as George Catlin and Frederic Remington painted dramatic landscapes of the great wide-open spaces in the American frontier in the West. They also painted images of Native Americans and the settlers who moved to the West to start new lives. Their works were of a more realistic nature than were those of the Hudson River School artists or the Impressionists. Let's look at some of their works right now.

6 **Gist-Content Question** | During the lecture, the professor talks about three different art movements in the United States during the 1800s.

7 **Understanding Attitude Question** | The professor says, "Many of Cole's contemporaries took note of the landscapes he painted, and they, quite understandably I'd say, began traveling to the region in order to emulate his work." So she implies that his paintings look good.

8 **Understanding Organization Question** | About Luminism, the professor comments, "This is called Luminism. Luminism was primarily used during the latter half of the nineteenth century. Paintings that used Luminism had elements of water and sunlight that gave them a serene look. They typically depicted the landscape underneath a soft hazy sky and painted reflections on the water." So she explains its effects.

9 **Detail Question** | The professor states, "In addition, the Hudson River School artists who used Luminism tried to hide their brushstrokes whereas the brushstrokes in the works of the Impressionists can be clearly seen."

10 **Connecting Content Question** | According to the lecture, the Hudson River school focused on the geographical area around the Hudson River Valley. Its artists also often used Luminism as a painting method. As for the Impressionist Movement, it became influential in the United States during the 1870s, and Theodore Robinson was one of its major artists.

11 **Making Inferences Question** | The professor lectures, "Upon his return to the U.S., Robinson worked as an art teacher to support himself, so he spread Impressionist ideas to his own students. Up here, notice some of Robinson's works . . . Nice, huh . . . ? You can clearly see the influence Monet had on him when you take a look at this work by Robinson here . . . and this one by Monet." Since Robinson, who was an Impressionist, was influenced by Monet and had a painting very similar to one by Monet, it can be inferred that Monet was an Impressionist painter.

Lecture 02-05

p.51

W1 Professor: All right. Those are the layers of the atmosphere. Now, let's explore how the atmosphere circulates. The atmosphere is not static. Instead, it's in constant motion. The fact that it circulates has a profound effect on atmospheric temperature as well as weather systems. In order to understand why the atmosphere circulates, we must first understand how it's heated by the sun. Sunlight strikes the Earth at different angles depending on the latitude. At the equator, sunlight is almost directly focused on the planet all year around. As a result, the equator gets more sunlight and more heat energy than other parts of the planet. As you move away from the equator and toward the poles, the angle of the Earth to the sun changes, so the planet's surface receives less sunlight and heat energy.

Because of this, the atmosphere near the equator is warmer than the atmosphere north and south of it. As we know from our studies, warm air rises and expands, which makes it less dense. On the other hand, cool air sinks and contracts, becoming denser as it does so. Warm air at the equator rises and moves north and south. As this air flows away from the equator, its temperature falls, so it eventually sinks and becomes cool. Then, the newly cooled air flows back toward the equator, where it will warm up again, rise, flow north or south, cool, sink, and then flow back toward the equator. It's, as you can see, circulating. This movement forms a convection cell of moving air. Christina, you have a question?

W2 Student: I do. Does the warm air from the equator flow as far as the North and South poles before it sinks?

W1: Not quite. This doesn't happen because another factor is involved: the Earth's rotation. Because the Earth rotates, it produces something that we call the Coriolis Effect. This is what causes water to spin quickly as it drains down a bathtub or toilet. What the Coriolis Effect does is cause large moving masses of air to shift sideways. It also breaks up the flow of warm air into three smaller types of convection cells in areas both north and south of the equator. Do you see the diagram on page seventy-three of your books . . . ? Now, keep in mind that the diagram is an idealized version of what we believe convection cells look like. The reality is a bit more chaotic and unpredictable for the most part. Still, the diagram should enable you to visualize what's happening.

So, uh, the convection cell closest to the equator is roughly between zero and thirty degrees latitude on both sides of the equator. These two convection cells—one in the north and one in the south—are called Hadley cells. Next to the Hadley cells are two more convection cells. They're called Ferrel cells. Both the Hadley and Ferrel cells are named for the scientists who first theorized their existence. Finally, above each of the poles are two more convection cells. They are aptly named Polar cells.

In each cell, the air circulates differently. Let me focus just on the Northern Hemisphere right now. In the Hadley cell, warm air rises at the equator and flows to around thirty degrees north. Then, it cools, sinks, and flows south again. The air in the Polar cell acts in the same manner. Oh, the Polar cell covers the area from roughly sixty to ninety degrees north latitude. Anyway, there, warm air rises, flows north, sinks, and then flows south again. Both the Polar and Hadley cells are considered to be complete convection cells.

The Ferrel cell, meanwhile, acts differently. It lies

between thirty and sixty degrees north latitude. There, warm air moves north along the surface. Then, it rises, becomes cool, and flows south. In the south, it sinks and repeats the process of moving north again. Why does the air in this cell behave in a reverse manner to the other two cells? One main factor is the jet stream. This moving current of air plays a role in moving warm air north. However, let me point out that the Ferrel cell is not a complete circular movement of air like the Polar and Hadley cells. At times, air does not flow as smoothly in the Ferrel cell as it does in the other two. The Ferrel cell also acts as a sort of buffer between the Polar and Hadley cells. It's kind of like a . . . hmm, like a ball bearing that is bouncing unstably between the other two stable convection cells. Another difference is that in both the Polar and Hadley cells, weather patterns can be predicted fairly accurately, but weather in the Ferrel cell tends to be unstable and unpredictable.

So what all this circulating air does in tandem with the Coriolis Effect is create the planet's wind and weather patterns. It also plays a role in how ocean currents move. Between the different cell systems are regions of mostly high and sometimes low pressure. These factors all combine to play a role in making our weather, which, since we don't have any more time, is something we'll explore in our next class.

12 **Gist-Content Question** | The professor mostly talks about cells of air in the atmosphere during the lecture.

13 **Detail Question** | The professor states, "This doesn't happen because another factor is involved: the Earth's rotation. Because the Earth rotates, it produces something that we call the Coriolis Effect."

14 **Understanding Function Question** | The professor asks, "Do you see the diagram on page seventy-three of your books?"

15 **Making Inferences Question** | The professor says, "So, uh, the convection cell closest to the equator is roughly between zero and thirty degrees latitude on both sides of the equator. These two convection cells—one in the north and one in the south—are called Hadley cells. Next to the Hadley cells are two more convection cells. They're called Ferrel cells." Since Hadley cells are next to the equator, then Ferrel cells must be farther away from the equator than Hadley cells.

16 **Gist-Purpose Question** | The professor says, "However, let me point out that the Ferrel cell is not a complete circular movement of air like the Polar and Hadley cells. At times, air does not flow as smoothly in the Ferrel cell as it does in the other two." So she contrasts the movement of air in the cells.

17 **Making Inferences Question** | At the end of the lecture, the professor says, "These factors all combine to play a role in making our weather, which, since we don't have any more time, is something we'll explore in our next class." Since she notes that they do not have any more time, she will probably let the students go for the day.

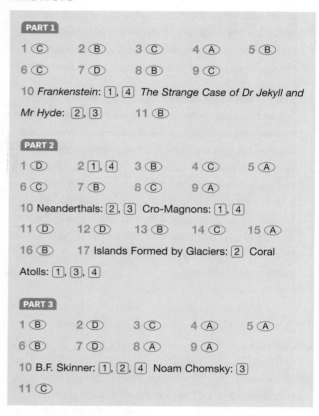

Actual Test 03

p.55

Answers

PART 1

1 Ⓒ 2 Ⓑ 3 Ⓒ 4 Ⓐ 5 Ⓑ
6 Ⓒ 7 Ⓓ 8 Ⓑ 9 Ⓒ
10 *Frankenstein*: [1], [4] *The Strange Case of Dr Jekyll and Mr Hyde*: [2], [3] 11 Ⓑ

PART 2

1 Ⓓ 2 [1], [4] 3 Ⓑ 4 Ⓒ 5 Ⓐ
6 Ⓒ 7 Ⓑ 8 Ⓒ 9 Ⓐ
10 Neanderthals: [2], [3] Cro-Magnons: [1], [4]
11 Ⓓ 12 Ⓓ 13 Ⓑ 14 Ⓒ 15 Ⓐ
16 Ⓑ 17 Islands Formed by Glaciers: [2] Coral Atolls: [1], [3], [4]

PART 3

1 Ⓑ 2 Ⓓ 3 Ⓒ 4 Ⓐ 5 Ⓐ
6 Ⓑ 7 Ⓓ 8 Ⓐ 9 Ⓐ
10 B.F. Skinner: [1], [2], [4] Noam Chomsky: [3]
11 Ⓒ

Scripts & Explanations

PART 1

Conversation 03-01

p.58

W Student: Mr. Wilkinson, you need to talk to me about something?

M Student Center Employee: Yes, Susan, I do. Uh, but first, uh, is your shift over yet? I don't want to interrupt you if you're busy working.

W: I'm all done for the day. I just finished up about five minutes ago. So after we're done chatting, I can go back to my dormitory for a couple of hours until my next class starts.

M: That's great to hear. Okay, this, uh, shouldn't take too long to discuss. I just want to let you know that there's another shift available for you to work this semester. I remember you told me you wanted to work twelve hours this semester. Right now, uh, I believe that you're only working nine. That's correct, isn't it?

W: Yes, sir, it is. So, um, there's another shift that's available? That sounds great. What is it?

M: Let me check my list here . . . It's at Friday from eleven to two. How does that sound? I know it's almost the weekend, but, uh, it's the best that I can do.

W: Friday . . . Oh, no, I can't do it.

M: Huh? How come?

W: I've got a Russian history class that finishes at eleven thirty. It's on the other side of campus, too, so I wouldn't be able to get here until noon. Um, is there any way that, uh, the person working before me could stay until noon? That way I could at least get two more hours of work. [5]What do you think of that?

M: Sorry, Susan, but that's totally impossible. **Calvin actually leaves a few minutes before eleven so that he can get to his class on time.** There's no way that he'd be able to stay any later. Oh well, I guess I'll have to find someone else.

W: Um . . .

M: Yes?

W: How about if I talk to a couple of other workers? I'm thinking of Peter and Rajiv. If I could convince one of them to take that shift and then switch one of their shifts with me, would that be okay with you?

M: To be honest, it doesn't matter to me at all which employee works which shift. All that I'm interested in is making sure that the shifts get filled.

W: All right. In that case, how about giving me half an hour to talk to both of them? I should be able to convince one of them to make a change . . . Uh, assuming that their schedules match of course.

M: Be my guest. You have their numbers?

W: I do. Peter and I live on the same floor in our dorm, and Rajiv and I are lab partners in physics. I actually know both of them pretty well.

M: Oh, I had no clue. Okay. It sounds like you should be able to solve my problem then. But, uh, if neither one of those two can handle that shift, then I'm going to have to post this job opening at the student employment office. So you need to be sure to get back to me as soon as possible. All right?

W: No problem, Mr. Wilkinson. I'll call you back on the office phone within thirty minutes.

M: Sounds great. Okay. I'll be waiting for your call.

W: Sure thing. Talk to you in a bit.

1 **Gist-Purpose Question** | The man tells the student, "I just want to let you know that there's another shift available for you to work this semester."

2 **Detail Question** | The available shift begins at eleven, but the student has a class that finishes at eleven thirty, so she cannot work on Friday.

3 **Detail Question** | The student says, "How about if I talk to a couple of other workers? I'm thinking of Peter and Rajiv. If I could convince one of them to take that shift and then switch one of their shifts with me, would that be okay with you?" So she will try to rearrange her schedule with that of another student employee.

4 **Making Inferences Question** | The man tells the student to hurry up and to call the students, and she indicates that she will get back to the man within thirty minutes. So she will probably call one of her coworkers next.

5 **Understanding Function Question** | Since they are talking about Calvin working one of his shifts, it can be inferred that the student and Calvin are coworkers.

Lecture 03-02

p.60

M Professor: The 1800s was a fascinating time, especially for the people who were living in it. There were all sorts of changes occurring in society. For instance, many colonies were gaining their independence, and there were revolutions in countries around the world, most notably in Europe. Not only were countries gaining their freedom, but so were people as slavery came to an end in the West. The Industrial Revolution was going on, so a number of practical and, uh, revolutionary, new inventions were being made. There were great discoveries in the realm of science as well.

That's what interests me today: science. In the 1800s, people began to take a more scientific look at the world. The secrets of science were starting to get unlocked. This fact simultaneously fascinated and frightened people. I think that you can see proof of this in the literature that was written during the 1800s. There was a genre that was produced then . . . we can call it science fiction, science horror, or even just plain horror I suppose . . . that focused on science to drive the plots of the stories. In many cases, the writers stressed the dangers of science and what bad—or even evil—things could result from science that was misused. In other instances, though, writers took a more positive view of science and looked at the great possibilities that existed when it was used properly. There were three major writers of this new genre. They were Mary Shelley, Robert Louis Stevenson, and Jules Verne.

Mary Shelley is best known for her novel *Frankenstein; or The Modern Prometheus.* Nowadays, we normally just shorten it to *Frankenstein*. Mary Shelley was from England and was the wife of the poet Percy Bysshe Shelley. Now, due to the numerous movies based on *Frankenstein*, there are several misconceptions about the novel. So let me cover it in brief. The plot focuses on the life of Dr. Victor Frankenstein and the monster that he created. And, no, the monster is not named Frankenstein in the novel. Thank Hollywood for that error.

Anyway, here's what happened. Dr. Frankenstein, who had studied at a university, was fascinated by the possibility of creating life from death. We'd call that pseudoscience today, but, in Mary Shelley's time, this notion was rather popular. The method thought to be able to create life was called galvanism. People back then believed that, um, by conducting electricity through the body of a dead person or other animal, the dead being would come back to life. The creature would be galvanized that is. Anyway, Dr. Frankenstein assembles a creature from spare parts and runs electricity through it. It comes alive but is misshapen and hideous to look at. Dr. Frankenstein is repulsed by the monster as is everyone else who sees it. The monster—an innocent at first—becomes a vengeful creature and seeks revenge on Dr. Frankenstein and those closest to him after being scorned and rejected. It essentially destroys Dr. Frankenstein's life and murders both his wife and some family members.

Shelley's work is a clear warning that science in the hands of the wrong person can have tragic consequences. Of course, galvanism isn't a real science, but that wasn't known back in Shelley's time. Now, Robert Louis Stevenson was another author who wrote about the dangers the misuse of science could pose in his work *The Strange Case of Dr. Jekyll and Mr. Hyde. Dr. Jekyll* is, as you can guess, a scientist. A good man, he becomes interested in exploring his darker, evil side. To do this, he concocts a potion that lets him transform into another person: Mr. Hyde. Hyde serves as Jekyll's alter ego in the story. Jekyll embodies that which is good while Hyde is the epitome of evil. To transform into Hyde, Jekyll must drink the potion. However, Hyde sometimes randomly attacks and even murders people as he walks the streets of London.

Eventually, Hyde begins to take over Jekyll and at times transforms even when Jekyll hasn't drunk any of the potion. In order to change back into himself, larger quantities of the potion need to be consumed by Jekyll. Needless to say, the story ends with the complete disappearance of Jekyll and the eventual death—possibly by his own hand—of Mr. Hyde. Much like Shelley in *Frankenstein*, Stevenson is warning people about the dangers that science poses. See, uh, Stevenson makes it clear that Dr. Jekyll doesn't totally understand the potion he has created. Unbeknownst to him, his first batch of the potion contained a chemical with an impurity that allowed him to transform back into himself. However, when Jekyll runs out of that particular chemical, he purchases more of it, and the new batch is in its pure form. When the pure chemical is added to the potion, Jekyll cannot easily transform back into his real self. In Stevenson's world, that's one of the consequences of messing with things that you don't completely understand.

While Shelley and Stevenson wrote warnings about the use of science, that's not quite the same for Jules Verne. He had an opinion of science that was the opposite of theirs and often wrote about how humanity could use it to its benefit.

6 **Gist-Content Question** | During the lecture, the professor talks about the role of science in the works of three writers in the nineteenth century.

7 **Understanding Attitude Question** | At the beginning of the lecture, the professor comments, "The 1800s was a fascinating time, especially for the people who were living in it. There were all sorts of changes occurring in society. For instance, many colonies were gaining their independence, and there were revolutions in countries around the world, most notably in Europe. Not only were countries gaining their freedom, but so were people as slavery came to an end in the West. The Industrial Revolution was going on, so a number of practical and, uh, revolutionary, new inventions were being made. There were great discoveries in the realm of science as well." He is clearly impressed by that period of time.

8 **Understanding Organization Question** | The professor states, "Now, due to the numerous movies based on *Frankenstein*, there are several misconceptions about the novel. So let me cover it in brief. The plot focuses on

the life of Dr. Victor Frankenstein and the monster that he created. And, no, the monster is not named Frankenstein in the novel. Thank Hollywood for that error." So he is letting the students know that the movie versions are different from the book.

9 **Gist-Purpose Question** | The professor states, "The method thought to be able to create life was called galvanism. People back then believed that, um, by conducting electricity through the body of a dead person or other animal, the dead being would come back to life. The creature would be galvanized that is." Then, he notes that Dr. Frankenstein used galvanism to make the monster come alive. This is therefore an important part of the plot of the book.

10 **Connecting Content Question** | According to the lecture, the monster is rejected by Dr. Frankenstein. In addition, the monster murders some of Dr. Frankenstein's family members as well as his wife. As for *The Strange Case of Dr. Jekyll and Mr. Hyde*, Dr. Jekyll must consume a potion to make the transformation into Mr. Hyde. Additionally, at the end of the store, Mr. Hyde dies, "possibly by his own hand," which means that he may have committed suicide.

11 **Making Inferences Question** | At the end of the lecture, the professor remarks, "While Shelley and Stevenson wrote warnings about the use of science, that's not quite the same for Jules Verne. He had an opinion of science that was the opposite of theirs and often wrote about how humanity could use it to its benefit." So the professor implies that Jules Verne believed that science could be a positive force.

PART 2

Conversation 03-03

p.64

M1 Professor: What's with that dejected look you've got on your face, Bruce? It seems like something bad happened. Is something not okay with you?

M2 Student: I'm not really doing very well, sir. I, uh, I kind of got some bad news today.

M1: Bad news? Goodness. Are your parents okay? I hope that nothing has happened to them.

M2: My parents? Oh, no. It's nothing like that. My parents are totally fine.

M1: All right. That's a relief. Well, why don't you take a seat over there and tell me about what's going on?

M2: Yes, sir.

M1: Here . . . Have a cup of coffee. I just made some on my coffee machine here. A cup of this should help you out a bit I imagine.

M2: Thank you for your kindness, sir. I really appreciate it.

M1: All right then . . .

M2: Ah, yeah. My problem. Here . . . Take a look at this test that I just got back a few minutes ago . . .

M1: A sixty-four? Er . . . Didn't you study for the test, Bruce? I don't think that I've ever seen you get a grade this low. And, uh, as your advisor, I get to see pretty much all of your grades. What happened?

M2: That's the problem, sir. I have no idea what happened.

M1: Explain. What exactly do you mean by that?

M2: Well, I thought that this astronomy class I had signed up for was going to be a lot of fun. You know, maybe we'd go to the school's observatory, look at some stars at night, and do other cool stuff like that . . . But this class is nothing like what I had imagined. It's just one boring lecture after another. [4]Not only that, but I am also totally lost in that class. There is a lot more math than I'm used to doing. **Uh, math, as you remember from last semester, isn't really my strong point.** And it's not like I didn't study for the test either. I studied for three straight days. And do you know the worst part?

M1: No. What's that?

M2: I still don't understand why I missed all of those questions. The professor went over the answers with us in class, but I just . . . I just didn't get it.

M1: What are you thinking of doing about this?

M2: Well . . . I think that the best idea for me is simply to drop the course. I mean, uh, I've already fulfilled my science requirements, so this is just an elective course. And if I stay in this class, there's no way that I'm going to make it onto the Dean's List this semester. That would kill my chances of getting into a good graduate school after I finish up here.

M1: [5]It sounds to me like your mind's already made up about dropping the class. **Well, you have my blessing.** But be sure to do that by tomorrow. That's the last day you can withdraw from a class without having it appear on your transcript.

M2: Oh, thanks for the reminder. In that case, I'm going to get a withdraw slip and visit Professor Danielson in his office right now. I know he's having office hours, so he'll definitely be there.

1 **Gist-Content Question** | The student and the professor mostly talk about the student's poor performance on the

astronomy test that he took.

2 **Detail Question** | The student says, "And if I stay in this class, there's no way that I'm going to make it onto the Dean's List this semester." He also says, "Well, I thought that this astronomy class I had signed up for was going to be a lot of fun. You know, maybe we'd go to the school's observatory, look at some stars at night, and do other cool stuff like that . . . But this class is nothing like what I had imagined. It's just one boring lecture after another."

3 **Making Inferences Question** | The professor tells the student, "Didn't you study for the test, Bruce? I don't think that I've ever seen you get a grade this low." The student is also clearly upset about his low grade, so it can be inferred that he is not used to getting poor grades at school.

4 **Understanding Function Question** | The student says, "Uh, math, as you remember from last semester, isn't really my strong point." So he implies that he took a math class last semester.

5 **Understanding Attitude Question** | When a person states, "You have my blessing," the person is giving permission to another to do something. So the professor is telling the student that he agrees with the student's decision to drop the class.

Lecture 03-04

p.66

W Professor: Neanderthals lived in Europe and parts of Asia and the Middle East between around 200,000 to 30,000 years ago. For years, we didn't know much about them. That changed when the first virtually complete set of Neanderthal remains was discovered in 1856 in a limestone quarry in the Neander Valley near Dusseldorf, Germany. That's where the name "Neanderthal" comes from. And if you're wondering, *thal* is the German word for "valley." Anyway, the remains of this hominoid were carefully preserved and then studied. The researchers examining it soon came to realize that it was a unique specimen that wasn't like modern humans.

M Student: How exactly do Neanderthals differ from modern humans, Dr. Watson?

W: In a number of ways. First, Neanderthals had stronger skeletons and larger bones than modern humans. On average, their hands and arms were much stronger than those of modern humans. They also had quite powerful legs. As for their height, male Neanderthals stood 165 centimeters tall on average while the females averaged about, um, about ten centimeters less in height than the males. Neanderthals' heads were also shaped differently from those of modern humans. [11] I believe that there is a picture of a Neanderthal skull in your books. I can't remember the page number off the top of my head though . . .

M: It's page 324, Dr. Watson.

W: **You're on the ball today, Tom.** Thanks . . . Ah, yes, does everyone see it now . . . ? Notice how it compares to the human skull next to it. As you can see, the Neanderthal skull is longer . . . the facial area around the nose protrudes more . . . and the jaw is larger as well. Note, however, that the forehead and chin do not protrude. Instead, the forehead is sloped back while the chin recedes. Finally, Neanderthals had large cranial cavities. That's the place in the skull where the brain is. So Neanderthals had brains that were slightly larger than those of modern humans. Does this mean that Neanderthals were more intelligent than modern humans . . . ? Hmm . . . That's hard to say. No one knows for sure.

That's enough about the physical aspects of Neanderthals. Let's proceed now to their behavior. First, like all early humans, Neanderthals were hunter-gatherers. They created simple stone tools, such as scraping tools, and they used spears for weapons. In their waning years, it's believed that they may have made tools from animal bones and antlers, but we don't have enough information to confirm the validity of that claim yet. Neanderthals did, however, know about fire and made use of it.

Anthropologists believe that Neanderthals lived in small social groups, much like our modern-day families. It's thought that they took care of the elderly and sick members of their groups. This evidence is based on the fact that some unearthed remains in caves appear to be those of Neanderthals who were rather old. Some of the bones bear evidence of healed injuries . . . uh, broken bones and stuff . . . as well as diseases. There's some evidence that Neanderthals buried their dead, but not everyone agrees as the evidence is rather, um, scanty. Another thing anthropologists are unsure of is whether or not Neanderthals could talk and, if they could, if they had language. Their brains were big enough to suggest intelligence, so the possibility exists that they produced both speech and language. In addition, in some Neanderthal remains, a hyoid bone has been found. That's the bone in our throats which is attached to the larynx and that we use mainly to make speech.

Now, Neanderthals are obviously extinct. What caused

them to die out is a question that has sparked a great deal of debate among experts. As you can guess, there are lots of unanswered questions about Neanderthals. Anyway, as to their extinction, one theory is that another hominid species, Cro-Magnon man, played a significant role. This hominid, from which modern man descended, originated in Africa and arrived in Europe around 40,000 years ago. For 10,000 years or so, Cro-Magnons and Neanderthals lived in close proximity to one another in Europe. But the Neanderthals then disappeared while the Cro-Magnons thrived. What happened? Did the Cro-Magnons outcompete the Neanderthals for resources? Did they purposely kill the Neanderthals? Again, we're not sure of the answers. What we do know is that by around 30,000 B.C., the Neanderthals were gone, and the Cro-Magnons were the dominant species in much of Europe.

M: Are Neanderthals related to modern humans?

W: Ah, that's yet another question whose answer we aren't positive about. It seems likely that Neanderthals and Cro-Magnons lived amongst one another for thousands of years. Did they comingle and produce offspring? Well, there are no physical characteristics in modern humans that suggest we're related to Neanderthals. However, thanks to modern DNA testing, we have the answer. Around one to four percent of the DNA of Europeans and Asians comes from Neanderthals. This suggests that, sometime after Cro-Magnons left Africa, some of them reproduced with Neanderthals. Interestingly, there is no Neanderthal DNA in Africans, which lends weight to the theory that this comingling happened only on the Eurasian landmass.

6 **Understanding Organization Question** | When the professor talks about Neanderthal skulls, she says, "Notice how it compares to the human skull next to it. As you can see, the Neanderthal skull is longer . . . the facial area around the nose protrudes more . . . and the jaw is larger as well. Note, however, that the forehead and chin do not protrude. Instead, the forehead is sloped back while the chin recedes." So she compares them with human skulls.

7 **Detail Question** | The professor says, "Anthropologists believe that Neanderthals lived in small social groups, much like our modern-day families. It's thought that they took care of the elderly and sick members of their groups. This evidence is based on the fact that some unearthed remains in caves appear to be those of Neanderthals who were rather old. Some of the bones bear evidence of healed injuries . . . uh, broken bones and stuff . . . as well as diseases."

8 **Making Inferences Question** | The professor notes, "In addition, in some Neanderthal remains, a hyoid bone has been found. That's the bone in our throats which is attached to the larynx and that we use mainly to make speech." So she implies that having the bone enabled Neanderthals to speak.

9 **Understanding Organization Question** | When the professor discusses Cro-Magnon man, she talks about how Cro-Magnon man may have been responsible for having caused the Neanderthals to become extinct.

10 **Connecting Content Question** | According to the lecture, Neanderthals' "hands and arms were much stronger than those of modern humans. They also had quite powerful legs" In addition, the professor remarks, "As for their height, male Neanderthals stood 165 centimeters tall on average while the females averaged about, um, about ten centimeters less in height than the males." As for Cro-Magnons, the professor states, "Anyway, as to their extinction, one theory is that another hominid species, Cro-Magnon man, played a significant role. This hominid, from which modern man descended, originated in Africa and arrived in Europe around 40,000 years ago."

11 **Understanding Function Question** | When a person tells another, "You're on the ball," that person is giving a compliment. So the professor is commending the student for knowing the correct page number.

Lecture 03-05

p.69

M Professor: There are literally hundreds of thousands of islands all over the world. But please don't think of all islands as being the same. That's a mistake some people make. In fact, there are several types of islands. By this, I'm referring to how the islands themselves were actually created. Right now, I want to briefly go over five major ways in which islands are created. Then, we're going to look at the creation of a few islands in more detail.

As you're aware, all throughout the Earth's existence, the face of the planet has changed dramatically. We already studied the theory of plate tectonics and discussed how the Earth's surface has moved over time. We talked about Pangaea as well as some of the other supercontinents that once existed. As the continents were busy moving around, all this movement occasionally resulted in some relatively small pieces of land getting separated from the larger pieces. Most geologists believe that the majority of our big islands . . . New Guinea, the British Isles, Newfoundland, and Baffin Island, to name just a few . . . uh, these islands were once probably parts of larger continents. They merely broke off.

W Student: Dr. Davidson, is Australia another example of this type of island?

M: Well, Mary, technically, Australia is a continent and not an island. I mean, okay, if you want to get fussy, we could call the Eurasian-African landmass an island, right? And the same could be said for the landmass that contains North and South America. After all, they're both land that's surrounded by water, aren't they? However, we don't do that, so that's why, uh, despite how it looks on a globe, we don't consider Australia to be an island. It's a continent. But that's a good question. Thanks for bringing that up.

The second way some islands formed happened at the end of the last ice age several thousand years ago. When the ice age ended, lots of water had been trapped as ice. The ice melted, which caused the ocean level to rise all around the world. One result of this was that islands were created from high points of land that were surrounded by lower ground which was suddenly covered in water. At the same time, large ice sheets, uh, glaciers, carved out the ground, making depressions that became both lakes and inland seas as soon as water filled them. However, the glaciers didn't carve the ground evenly, so the levels of the lakes and seas varied. In many places, high points of land in these lakes and seas suddenly became islands.

A third way in which islands were created was volcanic activity in the ocean. Volcanoes underneath the ocean's surface spewed molten magma, which cooled and formed solid rock underwater. Over time . . . er, millions of years that is . . . some volcanoes erupted again and again. Eventually, enough volcanic rock built up in places that the surface of the ocean was breached and islands were formed. In some cases, the volcanoes kept erupting, which, uh, which resulted in the creation of fairly large islands. Iceland was formed this way. So were major archipelagos such as Indonesia. There are volcanic islands and island chains scattered all around the world, but most, as you would presume, are found along the Earth's hot spots. Those are the places where volcanoes and earthquakes are the most common. The Pacific Ocean is home to many volcanic islands, particularly in the area known as the Ring of Fire.

Sometimes, these island chains created by volcanoes are the results of a hot spot that moves as the Earth's tectonic plates also move. It's believed that the Hawaiian Islands were created this way. You see, one weak spot in the Earth's crust on a tectonic plate allowed magma to bubble up from below. As the tectonic plate that this weak spot was on moved in an eastward direction over millions of years, every time there was considerable volcanic activity, new islands were formed. Take a look at a map of Hawaii sometime. You'll notice how it's a chain of islands that stretches from west to east.

The fifth way in which islands, most notably those in the Pacific Ocean, were created, um, is from coral. I'm referring to coral atolls. These are islands made from the remains of dead coral. Coral, by the way, are living organisms that attach themselves to shallow spots on the ocean floor. Over time, coral secrete a calcium substance that hardens. As the coral die, they get incorporated into this mass of solid material. This forms coral reefs. Gradually, coral reefs can grow so large that they break the ocean's surface and form islands. Most coral reefs are circular and surround— or almost completely surround— an inner body of water called a lagoon. It's thought that this lagoon once contained a volcanic island that sank into the ocean. Scientists base this belief on the fact that most coral reefs form close to islands. So here's what probably happened . . . A volcanic island rose from the ocean. Over time, a coral reef formed around it. Then, as time passed, forces in the Earth caused the volcano to sink beneath the water. But the coral reef remained and gradually became a coral atoll.

12 **Gist-Content Question** | The professor describes the five major ways in which islands are formed.

13 **Gist-Purpose Question** | The professor mentions the end of the last ice age to talk about the glaciers that melted during this time. It was these glaciers, the professor says, which caused many islands to form.

14 **Detail Question** | The professor tells the class, "In some cases, the volcanoes kept erupting, which, uh, which resulted in the creation of fairly large islands. Iceland was formed this way."

15 **Making Inferences Question** | The professor comments that coral atolls are believed to have formed around a volcanic island that sank into the ocean. Since the professor also notes that there are many volcanoes in the Ring of Fire, it can be inferred that many coral atolls are found in the Ring of Fire as well.

16 **Understanding Organization Question** | During the lecture, the professor individually covers the five major ways in which islands are made.

17 **Connecting Content Question** | According to the lecture, many islands were formed by glaciers when

the last ice age ended. As for coral atolls, they have a lagoon in their centers. In addition, most of them are in the Pacific Ocean, and they are believed to have once contained a volcano but that it sank beneath the ocean.

PART 3

Conversation 03-06

p.74

M Student: [5]Professor Crow, you're having office hours now, aren't you?

W Professor: **Well, they ended roughly half an hour ago, but I don't have any meetings or classes scheduled for the rest of the day.**

M: Great. Then you don't mind if I come in for a bit, right?

W: Not at all, Stuart. Shall I assume you're here to talk about the grade you just received on your paper?

M: Yes, ma'am. That's correct. I, uh, I was actually stunned when I received my paper back from you. I don't believe I've ever received a C- on a paper before. And, to be frank, I just don't understand why that happened.

W: It's actually pretty simple. You didn't follow the directions I gave the class regarding the paper.

M: Huh? I didn't follow the directions? But . . . but . . .

W: Tell me what they were, please.

M: Sure. You instructed us to write about how species can be either entirely eliminated or have their numbers greatly reduced. And that's what I did.

W: Hmm . . . Those were not the instructions I stated. I specifically stated—I even wrote the instructions on the board, and I know that many students took pictures of them with their smartphone cameras—I specifically stated that everyone was to write about several ways in which species could go extinct or become endangered. You didn't follow my instructions, and that's why you got a poor grade.

M: But . . . I wrote about how humans have caused so many species to go extinct and how we're making other species endangered. What's wrong with that?

W: Stuart, you don't actually think that humans are the only reasons certain species are endangered or extinct, do you?

M: Well, of course we are.

W: Okay, I'm going to assume you haven't done any of the assigned reading for the past couple of weeks. If you had, you would have learned about a large number of ways that something like this can happen. For instance, it's widely believed that the dinosaurs went extinct millions of years ago because of an asteroid striking the Earth. Likewise, numerous diseases have eliminated or reduced the numbers of both plants and animals a considerable amount. Supervolcano eruptions as well as tsunamis have reduced local populations of plants and animals all throughout history.

M: Oh . . . Yeah, I guess I see your point. I just, uh, I just wanted to focus on the problems humans are causing many plants and animals nowadays.

W: I understand that, but you didn't follow the directions. You're actually fortunate that you didn't receive a failing grade on the paper because you didn't write about what you were supposed to.

M: Ah, okay . . . Um, so I'm terribly sorry that I didn't follow the directions you gave. Would it be possible for me to do a rewrite or something? I mean, um, I don't want this one poor grade to prevent me from getting an A in the class.

W: I don't permit rewrites in my classes. Don't worry too much though. This paper only counts toward a small percentage of your final grade. So if you do well on the remaining two tests and one paper, I'm sure your final grade for the semester will be satisfactory.

1 **Gist-Purpose Question** | The student visits the professor to talk about a paper that she graded and returned to him.

2 **Detail Question** | The professor says, "You didn't follow my instructions, and that's why you got a poor grade."

3 **Making Inferences Question** | When the professor tells the student, "I understand that, but you didn't follow the directions. You're actually fortunate that you didn't receive a failing grade on the paper because you didn't write about what you were supposed to," it can be inferred that the professor believes the student should have gotten a lower grade.

4 **Detail Question** | The student asks the professor, "Would it be possible for me to do a rewrite or something?"

5 **Understanding Function Question** | In response to the student's question, the professor says, "Well, they ended roughly half an hour ago, but I don't have any meetings or classes scheduled for the rest of the day." She therefore implies that she is willing to speak with the student.

Lecture 03-07

p.76

M Professor: One issue that has troubled those studying education—particularly those in the field of language learning—is whether a child has an innate ability to learn a specific language or whether a child can be programmed to learn any language due to various influences on the child's environment. Two of the great minds that have touched on this subject are Americans B.F. Skinner and Noam Chomsky. Interestingly, they disagree widely on this aspect of learning. Their debate has shaped the fields of behaviorism and linguistics since the 1950s. Both men and their theories have supporters and detractors, and each of their theories has, well . . . each theory makes sense yet also has problems. Often, that's just the way it is in academia. Anyway, I'd like to give you a balanced account of both theories and leave it up to you to decide which theory is more appealing.

I'm going to start with Skinner's ideas on language learning. Skinner believed that children are born without any ability to perceive language. Their minds are clean slates in his view. Gradually, by interacting with their surrounding environment, they begin to learn language. This learning is aided by parental guidance and other outside stimuli. Skinner's views led to the development of what he called verbal behavior. In verbal behavior, verbal actions lead to responses from others. A central aspect of Skinner's theory is something he named the reinforcement theory. For example, let's say that a child learns the word, um . . . water. All right. So a little girl says, "Water," and her parents give her a glass of water. The child associates the word "water" with the actual thing, and, as time passes, this association is reinforced. As the girl ages, she acquires a larger vocabulary, becomes able to string words together to make sentences, and comes to understand grammatical structures as well. All of these things are conditioned into the child and are reinforced by her environment and the responses she gets from her parents whenever she speaks.

W Student: You're saying Skinner believed that a child born into any family could learn that family's language, right?

M: In Skinner's view, yes. And he's been proven correct time and time again. How is that? Well, think of all the international adoptions that take place nowadays. Say that a Russian baby is adopted by English-speaking American parents. The baby learns English, not Russian, and will never master the language of his birth parents even if he studies it for many years. Of course, there's a problem with Skinner's theory. Many people believe that it's only in our early years—our childhoods—that we can learn a language perfectly and that, as we age, our ability to learn a language diminishes even if we're totally immersed in the culture of the language we're trying to learn for many years. According to Skinner, the person should be able to learn the language by being in the environment and from other stimuli. But that doesn't always happen, does it?

What about Chomsky's theory? In 1957, Skinner published a book entitled *Verbal Behavior*, and Chomsky wrote a response to it. Chomsky, in case you don't know, is a linguist who specializes in grammar structures. He believes that all people are born with an innate ability to understand and learn the inherent grammatical structures of any language. [11]Imagine that you have a black box in your head when you're born. This black box contains a code that is just waiting to be programmed with a language. That's what Chomsky believes. **Uh, not in an actual black box of course. I'm referring to the idea.** See, uh, Chomsky feels that as a child grows and learns, the child discovers this innate ability and, over time, will fully develop the grammatical structures of his or her language.

Chomsky further notes that the rapid acquisition of language by a child is one thing that Skinner's theory does not account for. At certain stages, children learn languages by leaps and bounds . . . often, it seems, without having their language skills reinforced by any external factors. This makes Chomsky's theory of an innate ability to learn a language more plausible.

Chomsky further believes that after a person's initial language acquisition, that individual can never master a second language to its fullest extent because the human brain is hard-wired so that it only fully comprehends the structure of the first language that a person learns. Of course, there are many exceptions to this since there are a large number of people who have mastered two, three, or even more languages. This is a clear fault in Chomsky's reasoning I believe. Additionally, what about babies adopted into different cultures? Do their brains have the ability to learn their birth parents' language, their adopted parents' language, or both? By observing cases such as those of adoptees, it seems as though there is no, um, pre-assigned language. There's just an innate ability to learn. What language the child will learn depends upon that which the child hears in his or her first few years. Therefore, external stimulus from the child's environment seems essential to language acquisition, just as, uh, just as Skinner suggested.

6 **Gist-Content Question** | The professor describes the

opposing theories of language acquisition held by B.F. Skinner and Noam Chomsky.

7 **Detail Question** | The professor states, "Chomsky, in case you don't know, is a linguist who specializes in grammar structures."

8 **Understanding Attitude Question** | The professor says, "Both men and their theories have supporters and detractors, and each of their theories has, well . . . each theory makes sense yet also has problems." So it can be inferred that he supports aspects of both of their theories.

9 **Understanding Organization Question** | In his lecture, the professor first describes Skinner's ideas, and then he talks about Chomsky's ideas.

10 **Connecting Content Question** | According to the lecture, B.F. Skinner's book was criticized by Noam Chomsky. Also, B.F. Skinner believed "children are born without any ability to perceive language. Their minds are clean slates in his view." He also supported the reinforcement theory. As for Noam Chomsky, he believed that a person could never learn a second language perfectly.

11 **Understanding Function Question** | When the professor says that he is not talking about an actual black box, he is making a clarification to ensure that the students understand what he is talking about.

Actual Test 04

p.79

Answers

PART 1

1 (A) 2 (B) 3 (C) 4 (B) 5 (C)
6 (B) 7 (B) 8 (D) 9 (A)
10 Fact: [1], [4] Not a Fact: [2], [3] 11 (D) 12 (C)
13 (A) 14 (D) 15 (C) 16 Advantage: [2], [4]
Disadvantage: [1], [3] 17 (B)

PART 2

1 (A) 2 (D) 3 [1], [3] 4 (B) 5 (D)
6 (D) 7 (B) 8 (A) 9 (D) 10 (C)
11 (C)

Scripts & Explanations

PART 1

Conversation 04-01

p.82

W Student: Good evening. This is where I go to pay my library fines, isn't it?

M Librarian: That's correct. You have some fines? I'm really sorry to hear that.

W: Yeah, me too. I just hope that my overdue books aren't going to cost me that much.

M: So do I. Well, let's find out, shall we? Do you happen to have your student ID with you? I need to take a look at it so that I can scan your name on the computer.

W: Oh, yeah. Right . . . Here you are.

M: All right . . . Your name is Rebecca Mills, yes?

W: That's me. And I believe I turned in two books late a couple of days ago.

M: That is correct. The books were . . . *The Fatal Conceit* by F.A. Hayek . . . Uh, that one was eight days overdue, and . . . *The Knowledge Web* by James Burke . . . Excuse me. That one appears to be eight days overdue as well.

W: Yes, those are the two books that I returned. I can't believe I didn't renew them beforehand. I just didn't have time to visit the library since I've been so busy nowadays.

M: Actually, uh, you don't have to visit the library to renew your books. There are a couple of options available to you. Let's see . . . You can call us on the phone anytime we're open and renew your books that way. And we have a new program that lets you renew your books online as well. So you can do that from the comfort of your own dorm room. Of course, you can always drop by the circulation desk here if you want. That's what a large number of students and faculty prefer.

W: Yeah. I guess I'm just used to doing that. But thanks for the information. I didn't know that we're able to renew books over the Internet. I'll have to check that out.

M: Excellent. We're hoping that a lot of students start doing that.

W: So, uh, anyway . . . How much do I owe?

M: Ah, yes. You owe two dollars for each book. So that's a total of four dollars. Would you like to pay that now or have it put onto your bill that you pay at the end of the semester?

W: Well, it's tempting to let my parents take care of it, but I don't think they'd appreciate me making them pay for my overdue books. Here's five dollars.

M: Thank you very much. And here's your change.

W: Oh, uh, actually . . . Since I'm here, would you mind renewing the books that I have checked out right now? I think that I've got five of them.

M: [5]That won't be a problem at all. And . . . yes, you're right. You have five books. Do you need to know the titles?

W: **That's all right.** I know which books they are.

M: Oh, no . . . It looks like one of them is four days overdue. I can renew it, but you're going to have to pay a fine. If you want to take care of that now, I'm going to need that dollar back.

W: I can't believe it. I'm so forgetful. Here's the dollar. And I'm going to be sure to check out that Internet renewal system from now on.

1 **Gist-Content Question** | At the beginning of the conversation, the student asks, "This is where I go to pay my library fines, isn't it?"

2 **Gist-Purpose Question** | The librarian tells the student, "Actually, uh, you don't have to visit the library to renew your books. There are a couple of options available to you. Let's see . . . You can call us on the phone anytime that we're open and renew your books that way. And we have a new program that lets you renew your books online as well. So you can do that from the comfort of your own dorm room." So he is letting her know an easy way to renew her books.

3 **Detail Question** | The student first pays the librarian four dollars for her overdue books. Then, she gives him another dollar after she renews another overdue book. So she gives him a total of five dollars.

4 **Understanding Attitude Question** | The librarian is considerate and polite to the student. He is also helpful by telling her about the new program and by renewing her books for her.

5 **Understanding Function Question** | When the student says, "That's all right," she is rejecting his offer. She knows the titles of the books she has checked out, so she does not need him to tell her the titles.

Lecture 04-02

p.84

W1 Professor: Easily the best known of all desert animals is the camel. It's the most versatile animal that lives there. In the desert, the camel serves as a means of transportation, a beast of burden, a source of food, and even a commodity that can be traded for money or items.

Physiologically, camels are even-toed ungulates. This is the family of mammals that has an even number of toes on its feet. Ah, the number is typically two or four. In the case of camels, they possess two large toes on their feet. If you're curious, uh, some other animals that belong to this mammalian family include the pig, sheep, goat, giraffe, and cow. Camels are typically found in the desert regions of Africa and Arabia and parts of India, China, Mongolia, and Australia. [11]The vast majority of them are domesticated. The major exception is the large group of around, oh, a million camels or so, that lives wild in the Australian outback.

M Student: **Australia? How did they get there?**

W1: Ah, there's an interesting story behind that. In the nineteenth century, a small group of camels was taken to Australia to serve as beasts of burden. Eventually, the people got tired of raising them, so they simply let them go into the wild. Those camels have, uh, been breeding ever since, hence their big numbers. As for other large herds of camels, they exist in Somalia, Ethiopia, and the Sudan in Africa and also on the Arabian Peninsula.

Please be aware that not all camels are the same. That's a common misconception about them. In fact, there are two main groups of camels. They are the dromedary and the Bactrian camel. Telling them apart from one another is rather simple as the dromedary camel has a single hump while the Bactrian camel has two. In addition, the Bactrian camel is sometimes darker in color and tends to have longer hair than the dromedary camel. Take a look at this picture of both of them here . . . Now that you can see them side by side, it's easy to tell the difference between the two, isn't it? The Bactrian, as you can see, is the larger of the two. By the way, Bactrian camels are mostly found in Central Asia, and virtually all of them are domesticated. Now, the hump is the first thing that most people notice about camels. The hump . . .

W2 Student: I'm sorry to interrupt, Professor Collins, but I have a question.

W1: By all means, please go ahead.

W2: Thanks. Is the hump filled with water? Is that why the camel can travel so far in the desert?

W1: Ah, I was just about to cover that. The hump is not made of water but is actually made of fat. But you are right about one thing: The hump is what helps the camel survive the extreme heat and dryness of the desert. What happens to the fat in the hump is that it gets metabolized into water, so a camel can travel for a long period of time without replenishing its water supply.

Camels have some other features that enable them to thrive in the desert. Among mammals, they are the only ones with oval-shaped red blood cells. Those are what reptiles and fish have. Why is this important? Well, the oval shapes of the cells help the blood flow better than circular cells do when a camel's body gets dehydrated. Therefore, a camel may get dehydrated but can still survive longer than any other mammal because its blood will continue to flow smoothly to vital areas in its body.

Camels also sweat less than most other mammals, and it takes very high temperatures for them to start sweating. A camel won't start sweating until the temperature reaches more than forty degrees Celsius. Humans, on the other hand, sweat at much lower temperatures. Let's see. What other advantages do camels have . . . ? Ah, they can easily withstand the cold desert nights and the rapid changes in temperature between day and night in the desert. They can retain a lot of water because of their unique noses, which help trap water vapor as they breathe, so the water gets returned to their bodies. One other thing that helps them survive is their ability to imbibe massive amounts of water on the occasions when they do drink. They drink so much that consuming the same amount would kill another mammal. Finally, camels can eat almost anything—either plant or animal—although they prefer plants. And thanks to their incredibly hearty digestive systems, their bodies can process whatever they find to eat in the desert. In short, evolution has turned the camel into the perfect desert dweller.

And that's why camels are used as beasts of burden in the desert. They've been known to travel almost 200 kilometers a day while carrying a person or sixty kilometers a day while carrying loads of up to 200 kilograms. That, along with the camel's side-to-side motion when it walks, is how it received the moniker "the ship of the desert."

6 **Gist-Content Question** | The professor focuses on the physical characteristics of camels during her lecture.

7 **Connecting Content Question** | The professor states, "Physiologically, camels are even-toed ungulates. This is the family of mammals that has an even number of toes on its feet. Ah, the number is typically two or four. In the case of camels, they possess two large toes on their feet. If you're curious, uh, some other animals that belong to this mammalian family include the pig, sheep, goat, giraffe, and cow."

8 **Detail Question** | The professor notes, "Telling them apart from one another is rather simple as the dromedary camel has a single hump while the Bactrian camel has two."

9 **Understanding Organization Question** | The professor remarks, "Among mammals, they are the only ones with oval-shaped red blood cells. Those are what reptiles and fish have. Why is this important? Well, the oval shapes of the cells help the blood flow better than circular cells do when a camel's body gets dehydrated."

10 **Detail Question** | According to the lecture, "They can retain a lot of water because of their unique noses, which help trap water vapor as they breathe, so the water gets returned to their bodies." In addition, the professor comments, "One other thing that helps them survive is their ability to imbibe massive amounts of water on the occasions when they do drink. They drink so much that consuming the same amount would kill another mammal." On the other hand, the professor does not say that they become inactive at night. And camels sweat, but it takes very high temperatures for them to start sweating.

11 **Understanding Function Question** | The student's tone of voice is important. He sounds surprised when he asks about camels being in Australia. He clearly did not expect to hear that camels live there.

Lecture 04-03 p.87

M1 Professor: In different fields of science, most notably sciences like biology and zoology, which involve the study of living creatures, the use of observation has enabled researchers to understand the subjects they are studying much better. This may seem an obvious truism. However, the types of observation that researchers do can have an influence on the data that they collect and the conclusions that they reach. There are three main types of observation. They are natural . . . participatory . . . and laboratory . . . Let me go over the advantages and disadvantages of each method in brief.

The natural method of observation is probably the most common. Please be aware that it's also called field observation and field research. In this type of observation, the researcher does nothing but observe the subject in its natural surroundings. This is an extremely common method when observing wildlife. I guess you could say that it's the safest method as well since researchers can stand off at a distance and record what they see without having to get too close to their subjects. Aside from safety, there are several other advantages. Mostly, um, it permits an observer to watch the subject as it interacts with its natural environment. The subjects, hopefully unaware of the observers, act as they normally do. This is of particular importance when it comes to understanding a subject's behavior.

Yet natural observations also have a-a-a-a number of problems. For one, getting close to a subject in the wild isn't, um, isn't always easy. Even today, when modern technology provides researchers with all kinds of cameras and sound-detection equipment as well as satellite tracking devices on tagged animals, it's impossible to observe a subject one hundred percent of the time. Animals may hide, move to a new territory, or get killed. For instance, I remember reading about a field researcher in Africa who studied how one troop of chimpanzees would often attack other troops. They never actually killed the other chimps as the beaten chimps would merely move on to another place. But, uh, once, the researcher couldn't find a chimp in the losing troop. He concluded that the chimp had died—possibly from its injuries—but he couldn't be certain of that. Yes, in the front row? You have your hand up?

M2 Student: Yes, sir. I'm curious, uh . . . Why don't we just study these animals in a zoo or laboratory? That would be a lot easier than studying them in the wild.

M1: That's a true statement. It would be easier . . . But this method, which we call laboratory observation, has problems of its own. First, the benefits . . . By examining a subject closely in a controlled environment, researchers can conduct many test that would be, uh, simply impossible to do if they were engaged in field research. In a lab, they can conduct experiments in a safe environment, with a greater measure of control, and with access to facilities and equipment that aren't available in the field. Now, the problems . . . Animals confined in cages are taken out of their natural habitats and often don't behave in the same way when they're in captivity. They develop different habits when they aren't in the wild. They eat different food, they have different life spans, and they even mate and reproduce differently than they do in the wild. Simply put, laboratory observation doesn't capture animals in their authentic environments.

Now, the third main type of observation is participatory observation. Here, a researcher takes an active role in interacting with the subjects that he or she is studying. This is a common type of observation for anthropologists studying primitive tribes of people. As I'm sure you can imagine, it has both good and bad points. First, the researcher must gain the trust of the people, enter their lives, stay with them for an extended period of time, learn their language, and finally observe their lives. This all entails a lot of risk and a steep learning curve. That's particularly true if the people are very primitive, live in a remote setting, or have an obscure language. [17]Imagine, for instance, doing participatory observation of, say, a tribe living deep in the Amazon Rainforest. That wouldn't be the easiest of assignments. **However, the benefits are myriad.** The researcher can get a firsthand working knowledge of the people's society, culture, and ideals. The researcher can likewise learn about the tribe's history and may, if he or she is fortunate enough, be permitted to participate in some of their rituals.

On the downside, some observers may become too involved with the people they are observing. This may cause their judgment to become cloudy, and they become too biased to be impartial observers. Additionally, researchers tend to see primitive people from their own cultural prism. By that, I mean that they might judge these people according to the standards of their own cultures. Finally, the mere presence of an outsider may cause primitive people to change their behavior. They may act differently than normal, and they may hide aspects of their culture they don't want outsiders to know about.

12 **Gist-Content Question** | The professor gives some examples of how people use the different types of observation when he discusses it.

13 **Gist-Purpose Question** | The professor tells the class, "Now, the problems . . . Animals confined in cages are taken out of their natural habitats and often don't behave in the same way when they're in captivity. They develop different habits when they aren't in the wild. They eat different food, they have different life spans, and they even mate and reproduce differently than they do in the wild. Simply put, laboratory observation doesn't capture animals in their authentic environments."

14 **Understanding Organization Question** | The majority of the professor's talk about natural observation focuses on its drawbacks.

15 **Making Inferences Question** | The professor mentions that each type of observation has advantages and disadvantages. Thus it can be inferred that the professor does not believe a perfect method of observation exists.

16 **Connecting Content Question** | According to the lecture, it is an advantage that scientists can work in a controlled environment while observing organisms. It is also an advantage when researchers can avoid getting too close to the animals that they are observing. As for

disadvantages, some primitive people may act differently when they are being observed, and it is impossible to observe the subject at all times.

17 **Understanding Attitude Question** | When the professor says, "The benefits are myriad," he means that there are many advantages to participatory observation.

PART 2

Conversation 04-04

p.92

W1 Student: Good morning, Professor Fried. Thank you very much for permitting me to miss yesterday's class. I'm very sorry, and I promise it won't happen again.

W2 Professor: It's all right, Stephanie. But please inform your boss at your internship about your class schedule so that he doesn't cause you to miss any more classes. Yesterday's lecture was a very important one, and the information we covered is going to be on the final exam that's coming soon.

W1: Don't worry, ma'am. The only reason I had to arrive early was that the company CEO came for an inspection, and he wanted to meet all of the interns. It definitely won't happen again.

W2: I'm pleased to hear that.

W1: [5]But, um, I wonder if you have a moment to answer a question I have. It, uh, it pertains to yesterday's lecture.

W2: Oh? Did you already get notes from another student? **That was fast.**

W1: Ah, yes, I did. Eric Anderson let me borrow his notes. We live on the same floor in Harper Hall, so it was no problem for me to get them.

W2: That's great. So . . . what's your question?

W1: It concerns the number of moons that each of the gas giants in our solar system has. In Eric's notes, he wrote that Saturn only has fifty-three moons, but I remember reading that it has a much higher number than that. I think the article I read stated that Saturn has more than eighty moons. In addition, the number that he wrote for the moons of Jupiter was somewhat lower than what I have seen before. So, uh, did he write the numbers down wrong or something?

W2: Not at all. He wrote down exactly what I said in class.

W1: Er . . . So Saturn really only has fifty-three moons? I could have sworn that the number was higher.

W2: It has fifty-three confirmed moons.

W1: Confirmed? What do you mean by that?

W2: I mean that the confirmed moons of Saturn all have names. Their orbits are known. And they are definitely moons, not, uh, not asteroids, for instance. These are moons such as Titan, Enceladus, and Phoebe.

W1: So does that mean that there are more moons orbiting Saturn but that they're unconfirmed?

W2: That's correct. Basically, we need more information about these moons before we can state for sure that they're moons.

W1: Would that be information like their orbits, sizes, and composition?

W2: Yes, that's right. So as of now, Saturn has twenty-nine moons which are unconfirmed, giving it a potential total of eighty-two moons.

W1: Aha! So I was right about it having more than eighty moons.

W2: Yes, you were. Once we obtain more information from telescopes and space probes, we'll likely be able to confirm that many of these objects really are moons. Then, they'll get names and be entered as confirmed moons of Saturn. It's the same thing for the other gas giants. You know, Jupiter, Uranus, and Neptune. We need to learn more about some of the bodies orbiting them before they can be considered actual moons. Does that clear everything up now?

W1: It does. I really appreciate the in-depth explanation. Thank you.

1 **Detail Question** | The student missed the previous class because of her internship, so she apologizes to the professor.

2 **Understanding Attitude Question** | The student is clearly confused when she says, "In Eric's notes, he wrote that Saturn only has fifty-three moons, but I remember reading that it has a much higher number than that. I think the article I read stated that Saturn has more than eighty moons. In addition, the number that he wrote for the moons of Jupiter was somewhat lower than what I have seen before. So, uh, did he write the numbers down wrong or something?"

3 **Detail Question** | When the student asks, "Would that be information like their orbits, sizes, and composition?" the professor confirms that the student is correct.

4 **Making Inferences Question** | When the professor says, "It's the same thing for the other gas giants. You know, Jupiter, Uranus, and Neptune. We need to learn more about some of the bodies orbiting them before they can be considered actual moons," it can be inferred

that Jupiter has some unconfirmed moons orbiting it.

5 **Understanding Function Question** | The professor expresses her surprise that the student already got the notes for the class that she missed by stating, "That was fast."

Lecture 04-05

p.94

M Professor: Gold . . . There. I knew that would get everyone's attention. Virtually everyone loves gold. So when the news that gold had been found in the Yukon, which is near Alaska, reached the outside world in the late nineteenth century, there was a rush by people to reach the gold fields in order to get rich. This event is often called the Alaska Gold Rush and sometimes the Klondike Gold Rush. However, to put it into perspective, there were actually two separate gold rushes: The first was in the Yukon in Canada while the second smaller one happened in various parts of Alaska.

In 1896, several prospectors, ah, miners, that is, were panning for gold in a creek in the Klondike region of the Yukon Territory in Canada nearby the border with Alaska. They discovered a large deposit of gold there in August 1896, and they were soon bragging about it. That was a foolish move on their part since many local miners hurried to the area and, by winter, had struck it rich as well. However, because it was winter, the land was frozen, and no one could get out until the weather improved. In July 1897, a boat docked in Seattle, Washington. It was carrying several dozen miners and a few tons of gold. That, in case you are unaware, is simply a phenomenal amount of gold. It was also the first news of the Yukon gold strike to reach the U.S. mainland. Within days, thousands of people in Seattle had abandoned their jobs and were booking passage to Skagway, Alaska, which was the entry point to the Yukon gold fields.

W Student: Is that why it's sometimes called the Alaska Gold Rush, Professor Gorey?

M: Yes, in part because most of the prospectors arrived in Alaska and had to travel overland and then upriver to reach the gold fields. But gold was also discovered in Alaska, so calling it the Alaska Gold Rush is not a misnomer.

Anyway, within a few years, more than, oh, 100,000 people from all over the world—but mostly from the U.S. and Canada—had gone to Alaska to get to the Yukon gold fields. If you're wondering why that number is so high, be aware that there was an economic depression in the U.S. at that time. As a result, many people felt that they had nothing to lose by heading north and risking their lives to make a fortune.

[11] However, there were numerous obstacles for them to overcome. First, the prospectors needed supplies, and the merchants there charged exorbitant prices for everything. **There was some serious price gouging going on by merchants in Alaska.** Second, the prospectors had to traverse mountain passes in the Yukon. As there were no roads, they either traveled on foot, on dog sleds, or by boat up various rivers. And they could only travel for a few months each year due to the frigid climate.

Another problem was that at the Alaska-Canada border, the police were stopping everyone. The Northwest Mounted Police . . . uh, they were the predecessors of the RCMP, the Royal Canadian Mounted Police . . . the NMP were the ones who were doing the stopping. They were checking prospectors for two things. First, they wanted to make sure that no known criminals were attempting to enter the region. Second, they took away all of the guns that the prospectors were carrying. They did this since they were hoping to limit any potential violence when some prospectors found gold while others didn't. They were somewhat successful although there were scattered bits of fighting. Ah, there was a third reason as well. The police were ensuring that everyone had enough supplies, especially food. They wouldn't let anyone in if they deemed that person had an insufficient amount of supplies. They did this because in the first year of the gold rush, many people had faced starvation since they hadn't brought enough food with them.

Despite these human and natural obstacles, quite a large number of people . . . hmm, tens of thousands that is . . . reached the gold fields. Like during the California Gold Rush of 1849, the Alaska Gold Rush produced its share of success stories, yet these were often overshadowed by the more numerous failures. Some people just stayed in Skagway and got rich by supplying the prospectors with the food and equipment that they needed. Others moved on to the Alaska gold fields. After all, gold had been discovered near Juneau, Alaska, in 1880. This find, obviously, didn't immediately attract as many people as did the 1896 Yukon discovery, but some people headed there instead of going to the more perilous Yukon. In 1898, gold was also discovered far north of Nome, Alaska. This prompted a second wave of prospectors to head to the region. But Nome is in an extremely remote place, so fewer people went there. Anyway, after a few years, most of the easily accessible gold in the Yukon was taken, and the gold rush died out. Most of the prospectors went back home either bankrupt or wealthy, but some stayed in the

Yukon and Alaska and made their homes in those places.

6 **Understanding Attitude Question** | The professor remarks, "They discovered a large deposit of gold there in August 1896, and they were soon bragging about it. That was a foolish move on their part since many local miners hurried to the area and, by winter, had struck it rich as well."

7 **Detail Question** | The professor says, "If you're wondering why that number is so high, be aware that there was an economic depression in the U.S. at that time. As a result, many people felt that they had nothing to lose by heading north and risking their lives to make a fortune."

8 **Understanding Organization Question** | The professor tells the students, "Another problem was that at the Alaska-Canada border, the police were stopping everyone. The Northwest Mounted Police . . . uh, they were the predecessors of the RCMP, the Royal Canadian Mounted Police . . . the NMP were the ones who were doing the stopping. They were checking prospectors for two things." So he is letting them know how the NMP dealt with the incoming prospectors.

9 **Detail Question** | The professor states, "Second, they took away all of the guns that the prospectors were carrying. They did this since they were hoping to limit any potential violence when some prospectors found gold while others didn't. They were somewhat successful although there were scattered bits of fighting."

10 **Making Inferences Question** | The professor says, "Others moved on to the Alaska gold fields. After all, gold had been discovered near Juneau, Alaska, in 1880. This find, obviously, didn't immediately attract as many people as did the 1896 Yukon discovery, but some people headed there instead of going to the more perilous Yukon." Since the Juneau gold fields did not attract as many people as the Yukon ones, the professor implies that the Juneau fields were not as rich as those in the Yukon.

11 **Understanding Attitude Question** | When people engage in "price gouging," they are charging more money than is necessary.

Actual Test 05

p.97

Answers

PART 1

1 Ⓑ 2 [2], [4] 3 Ⓐ 4 Ⓒ 5 Ⓐ
6 Ⓑ 7 Ⓐ 8 Striated Muscles: [3], [4] Smooth Muscles: [1], [2] 9 Ⓒ 10 Ⓒ 11 Ⓑ
12 Ⓒ 13 Ⓓ 14 Ⓐ 15 Ⓒ 16 Ⓒ
17 Ⓑ

PART 2

1 Ⓒ 2 Ⓐ 3 Ⓑ 4 [1], [3] 5 Ⓒ
6 Ⓐ 7 Ⓐ 8 [2], [3] 9 Ⓓ 10 Ⓐ
11 Ⓒ

PART 3

1 Ⓒ 2 Ⓑ 3 Ⓒ 4 Ⓐ 5 Ⓐ
6 Ⓑ 7 Ⓑ 8 Ⓒ 9 Ⓐ 10 Ⓑ
11 Ⓒ

Scripts & Explanations

PART 1

Conversation 05-01

p.100

W Professor: Okay, that should take care of that little problem . . . And now that we've gotten that out of the way, I need to speak with you about the, uh, real reason why I called you into my office today, Matt.

M Student: Sure, Professor Jacobson.

W: You've been a student of mine in three classes already, haven't you? I believe that's right.

M: Yes, ma'am. That's correct. I took one class with you my freshman year and two classes with you my junior year. I suppose that the class we just started this week is the fourth that I'm going to take with you. Why do you ask?

W: Well, I've got a proposition for you.

M: Oh? What is it?

W: Let me tell you a little about this class first. As you are aware, this is an upper-level physics class. The class has an initial enrollment of sixty students. However, I've been teaching this class off and on for the past ten years. In my experience, by the time that this semester is finished, more than half of the students that originally signed up for the class will have dropped it. For instance, the last time I taught this class, I ended up with twenty-seven students out of the original group of sixty.

M: That many dropped the class? Uh-oh. Um, is this class going to be that hard?

W: Not for you, I believe, but it is going to be a lot of work for the majority of the students who are taking it. And this semester, I intend to do something about it. This is where I think you can be of great help to me.

M: Uh, how so?

W: Well, unfortunately, we don't have a teaching assistant for this class. But I did manage to get the department to provide some funds for me for this class. What I propose to do is to have a couple of students lead study groups each week. You know, the study groups could meet, oh, let's say, once a week for an hour and a half each time. [5]That way, the students who are behind can get some extra tutoring in the class.

M: And you want me to lead one of the study groups?

W: **That's what I like about you, Matt. You catch on fast.**

M: Thanks, ma'am.

W: So what do you think of my offer? I can pay you and the other student I hire for your time. It wouldn't be much. You'd get about fifteen dollars an hour. But I really hope that you accept my offer. I would love to retain as many students as possible this semester.

M: Okay. It sounds like a challenge. I'll do it.

W: Great. I'm thinking of having the study groups at night, so why don't you let me know a couple of days and times during the week—not the weekend though—that would be good for you? I can make all of the arrangements and then tell the students about the new study groups in next Monday's class.

M: No problem. Let me think about when I'd like to do it. I can send you an email with my preferred times later this evening.

1 **Gist-Content Question** | The professor talks to the student about doing a job that she wants him to have.

2 **Detail Question** | The professor states, "What I propose to do is to have a couple of students lead study groups each week." She also says, "I can pay you and the other student I hire for your time. It wouldn't be much. You'd get about fifteen dollars an hour."

3 **Understanding Attitude Question** | Since the professor wants the student to lead a study group for a difficult physics class, she implies that he is knowledgeable in physics. She also says that she believes the class will not be difficult for him.

4 **Making Inferences Question** | The professor wants the student to lead a study group for a difficult class. She also tells the student that while the class is difficult, she does not believe that he will have a hard time in the class. Finally, the student has taken three classes with the professor previously, so she is familiar with his work. So it can be inferred that the student did well in the classes that he took with the professor in the past.

5 **Understanding Function Question** | When the professor tells the student, "You catch on fast," she is acknowledging that he is correct in saying that she wants him to lead a study group.

Lecture 05-02

p.102

M Professor: The skeleton is the frame of the human body, and the muscular system is its power. We use our muscles for many reasons. Let me see . . . Thanks to our muscles, we can move, eat, digest food, make the heart beat, and breathe, to name just a few actions. There are two main types of muscles in the body. There are those that move voluntarily and those which move involuntarily. Some of the body's muscles are striated while others are smooth. There is also a third type of muscle—the cardiac muscle—which is found in the heart.

The majority of the muscles in the body are striated. They're attached to the bones in the skeleton so are therefore often referred to as skeletal muscles. We can move them voluntarily as well, so some people call them voluntary muscles. For instance, if I ask you all to raise your arms and you do so, then you're making a voluntary movement that you decided to do with your brain. In other words, you made a conscious choice to move.

These muscles are mostly composed of bundles of muscle fibers that are made up of thousands of smaller parts called sarcomeres. [11]These sarcomeres . . . uh, that's S-A-R-C-O-M-E-R-E in its singular form . . . So, uh, these sarcomeres are themselves made up of more bundles of much smaller parts called myofibrils. Myofibrils are made up of two proteins called actin and myosin. **Uh, I'm not going to spell all of these words.** You can look up their spellings in the book. Okay?

So, uh, to continue . . . these proteins, ah, actin and myosin, play key roles in a person's ability to contract his or her muscles. In the skeletal muscle system, the muscles are long and have a striated appearance. They look as if, hmm . . . as if lines were carved into them. Check out the diagram of the human body on page ninety-four in your textbooks . . . Notice the long bundles of muscle fibers and their striations. Note also that the largest muscles in the body, such as those in the thighs, are skeletal muscles.

It should be obvious to you that skeletal muscles differ from one another not only in size but also in function and in how they work. Some are designed for endurance, so they can resist fatigue, yet other muscles tire more easily. This ability depends upon the number of mitochondria in the muscle fibers. As you should recall . . . at least I hope you recall . . . from my last lecture, mitochondria are like factories in each cell that take oxygen and nutrients to make ATP, the main source of energy for the body. Different muscles also have different blood flow properties and oxidation. For example, the types of muscles that are designed for endurance have more capillaries for blood flow and oxidation and more mitochondria for producing energy than other muscles.

Next up are the smooth muscles. These are the muscles that control involuntary functions. These are actions like digestion, the passing of waste from the body, blood flow, and, um, the opening and closing of the iris in the eye. They are all controlled by the involuntary movements of the body's smooth muscles. So, naturally, these muscles are found in the eyes, the esophagus, which passes food to the stomach, the stomach, the intestines and bowels, and also the bladder. Additionally, smooth muscles are located in blood vessels as they help pump blood all throughout the body. Like striated muscles, actin and myosin are the two main active proteins that make up smooth muscles and help them function. Smooth muscles, as their name suggests, appear smooth looking without any striations. And remember that smooth muscles are out of people's control most of the time.

W Student: But what about breathing, Professor Newton? Do smooth muscles control breathing? I mean, we can control our breathing, but it's normally something that we don't think about.

M: That's a good question, Kimberly. Most of the time, we're unaware that we're breathing. Yet we can hold our breath or breathe faster than normal when we want to. The muscles that control breathing are skeletal muscles in the diaphragm and ribcage. Therefore, they're part of the skeletal muscle group. Perhaps because we constantly do it, breathing has come to seem practically like an involuntary movement of the muscles. But it's not.

Finally, we come to the cardiac muscles, which control the beating of the heart. Cardiac muscles are like skeletal muscles in that they're striated. Yet cardiac muscles are not long like skeletal muscles are. Instead, they're shorter and more compact. They're also different from skeletal muscles because they're more involuntary. Because of these two facts—their striated and involuntary natures—we put cardiac muscles in a category all by themselves. Now, cardiac muscles, which are perhaps the most important muscles in the entire body, are highly resistant to fatigue. They also have a superior ability to take in oxygen and to produce energy with their mitochondria.

6 **Gist-Content Question** | The professor describes the various types of muscles in the body and explains what their functions are as well.

7 **Gist-Purpose Question** | The professor states, "The majority of the muscles in the body are striated. They're attached to the bones in the skeleton so are therefore often referred to as skeletal muscles. We can move them voluntarily as well, so some people call them voluntary muscles." So he is giving another name for striated muscles.

8 **Connecting Content Question** | According to the lecture, striated muscles are made of sarcomeres and are connected to the bones. As for smooth muscles, they control the body's involuntary actions, and some of them are found in the esophagus and bladder.

9 **Understanding Function Question** | A student asks a question about the muscles that control breathing, so the professor tells the class about them.

10 **Understanding Organization Question** | The professor first names the different types of muscles, and then he provides their characteristics and talks about their roles in the body.

11 **Making Inferences Question** | The professor spells one word, and then he says some other words that are somewhat unusual. When he says, "Uh, I'm not going to spell all of these words," he is acknowledging that some of the words are difficult to spell. However, he wants the students to look them up in their textbooks to learn how to spell them.

Lecture 05-03

p.105

W Professor: Have you all handed in your reports . . . ?

Okay, good. I'm looking forward to reading them. I'll do my best to return them by Thursday of next week. All right. Now that we're done with that, why don't we get started with class . . . ? [17] We're going to take a look at Surrealism in today's class. When I mention Surrealism, what's the first thing that comes to mind? Anyone . . . ? **Andy, I believe your hand was the first to go up.**

M Student: Thank you, Professor Dodd. When I hear the word Surrealism, I think of melting clocks and Salvador Dali.

W: Those were actually the two responses I was hoping to hear. That particular image and the artist, class, are precisely what most people think of when they consider Surrealism. And that's only natural, especially in the case of Salvador Dali, who was the most famous Surrealist. But I want to start by examining the roots of Surrealism before I hit on the history of the movement.

It's generally agreed that the roots of Surrealism lie in Dadaism, which started in 1916 and lasted for approximately a decade. Dada was a protest movement. Its members were protesting the violent of, uh, violence of World War I. Dadaism started in Switzerland when some intellectuals got together to discuss the war and their feelings about it. They wanted to show their disgust and anger with the war's brutality by doing something that would outrage society. The writings, paintings, and sculptures the Dadaists produced reflected a world gone mad and were very much against the traditions of the art world. Personally, I find Dadaist art to be rather bizarre. It's a feeling many others share, too. Anyway, these artists never intended for Dadaism to become an actual art movement, but that's what happened. After the war ended, Dadaism slowly died out. It was around 1925 that it had completely disappeared. Well, I suppose it's more precise to say that Dadaism sort of, uh, morphed into Surrealism. One reason was that those who had been attracted to Dadaism were also attracted to Surrealism.

The person most responsible for the founding of Surrealism was the Frenchman Andre Breton. He was a psychiatrist who helped French soldiers recover from the trauma they had suffered on the battlefield. During the war, Breton met a young soldier named Jacques Vache, who was also a writer. Vache's writings about his war experiences were done in a, hmm . . . a nontraditional way I guess I should say. Breton was inspired by Vache's work, and he began associating with some Dadaists in Paris around 1919. With them, Breton started experimenting with what he called automatic writing. This was a method of writing in which he wrote as he thought, um, without any constraints imposed by morality or reason. Basically, it was a way of writing in which he freed his mind of any restrictions. Some Dadaists also engaged in automatic drawing, in which they let their pencils flow freely across the paper without any plan or structure. Some even engaged in dream analysis as a way of-of-of expressing their freedom of thought. Essentially, Breton and his fellow Dadaists were trying to unlock the unconscious mind.

In its early years, Surrealism was focused more on automatic writing than on any other type of art. But Surrealism embraced all aspects of art, including filmmaking and, of course, painting. As time passed, more visual artists joined the movement. The Surrealists' experiments with automatic drawing in the mid-1920s started causing the movement's members to stress the more visual aspects of art. So, um, many of the visual artists that had been Dadaists began moving in Surrealist circles, particularly in Paris. Paris became such an important city for the Surrealists that, in 1925, the first exposition of Surrealist art was held there.

Yet Surrealism wasn't confined to France. Its center remained in Paris, but its influence spread throughout Europe. Anyway, in the 1930s, the movement entered its most formative years. Much of this was due to the work of Salvador Dali, a Spaniard who had joined the movement in 1929. In the early 1930s, he produced some of the best-known pieces of Surrealist art. His images of melting clocks and wildly imaginative dreamscapes are what most people have come to associate Surrealism with.

Surrealism continued as a movement for decades. It wasn't until Breton himself died in 1966 that many considered the movement to be over. Of course, some art historians argue that Surrealism ended long before that event. Others, naturally, contend that the spirit of Surrealism continued in a number of movements, including Pop Art and Postmodernism. I agree with them. It's also clear that the generation of American writers from the 1950s and 1960s, who were called the Beat Generation, were influenced by Surrealism, particularly automatic writing. Well, I think that's enough of an introduction to the movement. Let's look at some examples of Surrealist art now, and, as we do so, I will fill you in on more aspects of the movement.

12 Gist-Content Question | In the lecture, the professor focuses on the origins and early history of Surrealism.

13 Understanding Attitude Question | The professor comments, "Personally, I find Dadaist art to be rather bizarre." So she thinks that it is strange.

14 Understanding Organization Question | The professor says, "The person most responsible for the founding of

Surrealism was the Frenchman Andre Breton." Then, she describes how he founded the Surrealist Movement.

15 **Detail Question** | While talking about Salvador Dali, the professor mentions, "In the early 1930s, he produced some of the best-known pieces of Surrealist art. His images of melting clocks and wildly imaginative dreamscapes are what most people have come to associate Surrealism with."

16 **Making Inferences Question** | The professor states, "It wasn't until Breton himself died in 1966 that many considered the movement to be over. Of course, some art historians argue that Surrealism ended long before that event. Others, naturally, contend that the spirit of Surrealism continued in a number of movements, including Pop Art and Postmodernism." As people disagree on the effects of Surrealism, its influence can be said to be in dispute.

17 **Understanding Function Question** | The professor asks a question. Then, she tells Andy that she saw his hand go up first. So she is implying that he has permission to answer her question since he was the first to respond.

PART 2

Conversation 05-04

p.110

W1 Student: Hi. Do you happen to be Ms. Laura Redding?

W2 Student Activities Office Employee: Yes, that's me. Is there something I can do for you today?

W1: I think so. You're the person in charge of the upcoming student club day, aren't you? One of my friends that works here told me you're the woman I need to speak with.

W2: Ah, yes. You've come to the right person if you're interested in learning about the student club day. I'm in charge of the entire event. What exactly about the program do you need to know?

W1: Well, uh, I need to know how to get a table for the event. I'm the president of the student drama club, and we're trying to recruit some more members. Our membership has been declining in the past couple of years, but I think we might be able to attract some more people if we can, uh, advertise and stuff at the event.

W2: You need a table? Aren't you applying a little late? I mean, the event is supposed to start in two days.

W1: Er . . . Yeah, I guess I'm late. Sorry about that. I actually wasn't aware there was going to be a student club day until last night.

W2: You weren't aware? But we've been advertising for it in the student newspaper every day for the past two weeks. How could you not have seen it?

W1: To be totally honest, I rarely read the student newspaper. I simply don't have the time this semester. Plus, uh, I've never really been impressed with the quality of the writing in it. So I tend to ignore it.

W2: I understand what you're saying, but, as a club president, you need to be aware of these sorts of activities. It's part of your leadership obligations.

W1: Yes, I can see that now. Thank you for the reminder.

W2: Anyway . . . I tell you what. You seem like you care about your club. That's not always the case for some club presidents. So I'm going to give you a slot. I was saving one last spot in case we got a last-minute applicant, and it seems like you fit the bill.

W1: Seriously? That's great news. Thank you so much.

W2: [5]Now, the only drawback is that it's not in the most public part of the student center. So you won't get a great number of students walking by your table. **But I suppose it's better than nothing.**

W1: You can say that again. So, uh, what do I need to do to get the table?

W2: Fill out this form here . . . And you need to pay a fee of thirty dollars.

W1: Thirty dollars?

W2: Yes. Oh, don't worry. It doesn't have to come out of your pocket.

W1: That's a relief.

W2: Well, I mean that you need to pay the money now, but you can apply to this office to have the money reimbursed. Yeah, I know that seems a little bureaucratic, but that's the way things get done around here.

W1: All right. If you say so. Here's the thirty dollars. Let me fill out this form. And if you can let me know how I can get my money back, that would be great, too.

W2: Of course. I've got the form for that right here. It will take a week or two for your request to be approved though. So you won't get a refund until then.

1 **Gist-Purpose Question** | The student tells the woman, "Well, uh, I need to know how to get a table for the event."

2 **Detail Question** | The student mentions, "I'm the president of the student drama club, and we're trying to recruit some more members. Our membership has

been declining in the past couple of years, but I think we might be able to attract some more people if we can, uh, advertise and stuff at the event."

3 **Understanding Attitude Question** | The student says, "To be totally honest, I rarely read the student newspaper. I simply don't have the time this semester. Plus, uh, I've never really been impressed with the quality of the writing in it. So I tend to ignore it." She also admits that she did not know about the club day event even though it has been advertised for two weeks. So it can be inferred that the student knows little about the events that take place on campus.

4 **Detail Question** | The woman tells the student, "Fill out this form here . . . And you need to pay a fee of thirty dollars."

5 **Understanding Function Question** | When a person says that something "is better than nothing," the person is not happy about what is happening but is trying to be positive. So the student is not happy about the location of her table, but she is pleased to have one, so she is being positive about the result.

Lecture 05-05

p.112

M Professor: As you can see, natural reefs are home to many forms of aquatic life. These reefs are frequently teeming with life since they contain plenty of food and offer places of sanctuary from the oceans' fiercest predators. Yet the number of natural reefs in the world is limited, and some are even being destroyed for reasons both natural and human. Because of that, people have begun building artificial reefs. These are structures that are placed in the ocean and which transform into reefs over time. There are hundreds along the east coast of the United States as well as the coast of the Gulf of Mexico. They serve a number of purposes.

First, the construction of artificial reefs provides places for old ships and other manmade structures to be disposed of. Many artificial reefs, you see, are comprised of ships, subway cars, oil rigs, and even structures called reef balls that are made specifically to be turned into artificial reefs. [1]Yes? You have something to add to the conversation?

W Student: Professor Rand, how can people do that? I mean, aren't they harming the environment by sinking those objects in the ocean?

M: **You might think that, but the environmental damage that the ocean suffers is practically zero.** Let me tell you why . . . The building of artificial reefs is carefully controlled and monitored to ensure that the environment is protected. Take ships for example. Every ship that is designated to be turned into an artificial reef must be cleansed of all harmful elements first. The oil and other liquids in it are pumped out, all metals—except for the ship's hull and structure of course—are removed, and anything else that could possibly cause even the slightest amount of damage to the environment is removed prior to the ship being sunk. However, I admit there have been a few bad episodes concerning artificial reefs. Back in the 1970s in Florida, someone had the not-so-bright idea to use millions of old rubber tires to build an artificial reef. That wasn't a good idea at all. Coral and other marine life forms didn't grow on the tires, so few life forms were attracted. Later, the bundles of tires broke apart, so tires started washing up on Florida's beaches. That was something of a minor disaster.

Fortunately, we've learned what does and doesn't work well as material for artificial reefs. As a result, you won't ever see a repeat of the tire incident again. Let me tell you about the various materials now. Ships' hulls are commonly used and for good reason. They can last underwater for decades before breaking apart. Subway cars and oil rigs can also last for years, and artificial reef balls work quite well, too. Oh, uh, I doubt that any of you have ever seen a reef ball, so let me describe what one looks like. A reef ball resembles a beehive. It's rounded, has numerous holes, and is made of concrete. Reef balls come in many sizes, but most are, oh, around two meters wide and high. When used to make an artificial reef, they're placed in clusters on the ocean floor. These reef balls and other structures provide strong anchoring points for coral and other life forms that attach themselves to things. When these creatures are attracted to a reef, they, in turn, cause many other animals, particularly fish, to move to the reef.

But I'm getting a bit ahead of myself. I need to backtrack now. First, a question: Why do life forms live around artificial reefs in the first place? We're not exactly sure, but what seems to happen is that the artificial reefs block the flow of ocean currents. When a current of water hits the reef, the water moves up and carries plankton and other tiny life forms with it. This creates an uplifting column of nutrient-rich water. This column thus attracts many fish. First, small ones such as sardines and minnows come. Gradually, larger fish, including tuna and some sharks, are attracted. After that come marine life forms that enjoy hiding in places. Some of these are groupers, snappers, eels, and various shellfish such as crabs, shrimp, and lobsters. Then, over a period of many months and even years, coral and other life forms attach themselves to the artificial reefs. Soon, the reefs are encrusted with these life forms, and it becomes difficult to tell which parts of the reef belong to its original structure.

As I'm sure you can imagine, with all of this life surrounding artificial reefs, they make great diving spots for recreational divers. That's yet another advantage of artificial reefs. If you dive—or take up diving in the future—be sure to dive on an artificial reef. I've done that several times, and it's an impressive sight. Of course, you'll have to avoid the numerous sport fishermen who also visit the reefs. They typically find it much easier to catch fish around the reefs than anywhere else.

6 **Gist-Content Question** | The professor focuses on how people create artificial reefs.

7 **Understanding Attitude Question** | The professor admits that artificial reefs sometimes have problems, but he notes that they have many advantages, too.

8 **Detail Question** | The professor says, "Ships' hulls are commonly used and for good reason. They can last underwater for decades before breaking apart. Subway cars and oil rigs can also last for years, and artificial reef balls work quite well, too."

9 **Gist-Purpose Question** | The professor remarks, "Oh, uh, I doubt that any of you have ever seen a reef ball, so let me describe what one looks like. A reef ball resembles a beehive. It's rounded, has numerous holes, and is made of concrete."

10 **Making Inferences Question** | The professor comments, "Then, over a period of many months and even years, coral and other life forms attach themselves to the artificial reefs. Soon, the reefs are encrusted with these life forms, and it becomes difficult to tell which parts of the reef belong to its original structure." So it can be inferred that it takes years before artificial reefs can become complete ecosystems.

11 **Understanding Function Question** | When the professor responds to the student, he is letting her know that artificial reefs actually do not harm the environment. So he is telling her that her assumption is incorrect.

PART 3

Conversation 05-06

p.116

W Student: Good morning, Mr. Anderson. I'm here for my shift.

M Librarian: Good morning, Sheila. I don't think we're going to be very busy today because it's a holiday. Since we won't have too many patrons coming to check out books this morning, I'd like you to help Robert by shelving some of those returned books over there.

W: No problem. But, uh, who's going to work at the circulation desk while I'm away?

M: I'll handle anyone that comes here. I don't mind sitting at the desk for a while. Why don't you shelve books for the next half hour or so, and then you can come back here to the desk for the remainder of your shift?

W: Sure thing.

M: Oh, hold on. Before you go, I need to talk to you about something.

W: Yes?

M: Did you receive the email I sent you a couple of days ago?

W: Email?

M: I guess that means no. Anyway, uh, I emailed you to inquire about your interest in working here during winter vacation. As you know, the library doesn't close during the holidays, so we still need people to run the circulation desk.

W: Ah, yeah, actually, I did get that email. I'm really sorry I didn't respond to it. I was so busy writing a paper for my anthropology class that I didn't have time to reply.

M: What do you think? I seem to recall you stating that you aren't planning on going home for the holidays this winter.

W: Yes, that's correct. Now that winter vacation is only a couple of weeks long, it's not really worth the price of a plane ticket to go home for such a short amount of time. So, uh, yeah, I'm definitely interested in working. After all, I might as well make some money if I'm going to be here. It's better than doing nothing.

M: [5] All right. That's great news. **I've already asked almost everyone who works here about working during the break.** I'm very pleased that you can do it. How many hours do you want to work?

W: How many are available?

M: Well, if you want, you can work eight hours a day. The school permits students to work up to forty hours a week. And the library will have reduced hours during the holiday. We'll only be open from nine to six, so you can work all day long, uh, with a one-hour lunch break.

W: Oh . . . Can I get back to you on that?

M: Not interested in working the entire day?

W: No, it's not that. It actually, um, sounds a bit appealing. You just kind of caught me off guard. I was thinking I'd work maybe twenty hours a week instead of forty. But, hmm . . . Now that I think about it, working all day doesn't sound too bad. How busy does it get here during the holidays?

M: Not busy at all. We mostly have professors and graduate students here during that time. But it's quiet for the most part. You'd be able to study or read while you're on the job if we're not busy.

W: You know . . . That sounds pretty good. I've been meaning to catch up with my reading, and now I can get paid to do it. You've convinced me. Count me in for the entire shift.

M: Excellent. Thanks so much, Sheila.

1 **Gist-Content Question** | The speakers spend most of the conversation talking about a job during vacation that the man offers the student.

2 **Detail Question** | The man tells the student, "Why don't you shelve books for the next half hour or so?"

3 **Detail Question** | The student says, "Ah, yeah, actually, I did get that email. I'm really sorry I didn't respond to it. I was so busy writing a paper for my anthropology class that I didn't have time to reply."

4 **Making Inferences Question** | About working during vacation, the student says, "I've been meaning to catch up with my reading, and now I can get paid to do it." So it can be inferred that the student believes working during winter vacation will be easy since she thinks she will be able to read a lot on the job.

5 **Understanding Attitude Question** | In saying, "I've already asked almost everyone who works here about working during the break," the man means that several people have rejected his offer since he still has not found someone to do the work.

Lecture 05-07

p.118

W1 Professor: I want everyone to think of some positive memories. You know, uh, something that happened in the past that made you happy . . . Okay. Now, think about something bad that happened to you, uh, a negative memory . . . Got one . . . ? Great. Raise your hand if you remembered more details from the positive memory . . . And raise your hand if you remembered more about the negative memory . . . Ah, just as I had expected, uh, the majority of you recall more details from your negative experiences. Okay, I've got one more question . . . How many of you can remember what you were doing last night at, say, seven thirty . . . ? Not so many, huh? Well, in all likelihood, nothing special happened at that time, so you can't remember what you were doing or what happened.

The point I'm trying to make is that emotion and memory are linked to one another. The two memories I asked you to think about—the positive and negative ones—took place when you were in heightened states of emotions. You were either very happy or sad. Perhaps you were even ecstatic or terrified at the time. More importantly, you have fairly clear memories of these events. But how about rather mundane everyday actions, like eating dinner, watching TV, or studying? There's no heightened emotion associated with any of those memories, so the details are a bit fuzzy. Even those of you who remembered what you were doing last night at seven thirty . . . I bet that if I ask you the same question next week, you will have completely forgotten what you were doing then. The reason for this is that the brain doesn't store neutral memories the same way in which it stores emotional ones.

One major difference between positive and negative memories concerns how people perceive them. Most people who have a positive emotional experience remember it in broad detail yet tend to forget certain minor aspects. Conversely, with negative memories, people often remember the minor details while forgetting some of the broader issues. There's a reason this happens. Some studies suggest that it's the result of the more powerful emotions which are associated with negative memories. Think about some of the basic negative emotions . . . Sadness, depression, shame, and embarrassment are four. You may recall a family member's funeral in detail since it was a sad event in your life. And the time that you spilled a drink on your clothes right before you gave a class presentation might be a vivid memory since you were so embarrassed then. Even more powerful negative emotions, such as fear and terror, can enable a person to retain strong memories. If you've ever been in a car accident, a house fire, or a fistfight or have been robbed or perhaps chased by an angry dog, you probably remember the incident in great detail because of the heightened state of fear or terror that was involved.

There are some other factors besides emotion that are related to memory retention and retrieval. In general, women are better at retaining and retrieving memories than men. Some studies indicate that the reason for this is that women have more emotionally heightened states than men when emotional events occur. Therefore, they remember better and can also retrieve their memories more easily. Additionally, younger people tend to have less control over their emotions than older people, so they retain negative memories better than older people. Conversely, older people tend to remember more positive events than negative ones. Why that happens is unknown. Oh, a person's mood is related to memory retrieval, too. People remember positive memories more often when they're in good moods but recall negative memories when they're in bad moods.

W2 Student: Professor Bean, how does the brain store memories?

W1: Good question. Hmm . . . I wasn't going to cover that yet, but I guess I can do it now. You know, um, a great deal of research has been done on this subject. Much of it has been conducted in group studies where the subjects were connected to devices that did brain scans on them. The almost-universal conclusion experts have reached is that two parts of the brain control memories. They are the amygdala and the hippocampus. Both are small parts of the brain. When a person is in an emotion state, the body releases stress hormones. One hormone, called cortisol, interacts with the amygdala, which, in turn, acts on the hippocampus to help with memory retention. The term that psychologists use for this is memory consolidation. Sadly, these regions of the brain are the places that Alzheimer's disease usually damages, which may be why sufferers begin to lose their memories as the disease progresses.

Now, since you asked me that question, Erika, I need to show all of you a schematic of the brain. Take a look at the screen up here. I want to point out where in the brain the different centers of memory retention are located. Look carefully, please, everyone.

6 **Understanding Organization Question** | The professor says, "The point I'm trying to make is that emotion and memory are linked to one another."

7 **Detail Question** | The professor tells the students, "But how about rather mundane everyday actions, like eating dinner, watching TV, or studying? There's no heightened emotion associated with any of those memories, so the details are a bit fuzzy. Even those of you who remembered what you were doing last night at seven thirty . . . I bet that if I ask you the same question next week, you will have completely forgotten what you were doing then. The reason for this is that the brain doesn't store neutral memories the same way in which it stores emotional ones."

8 **Connecting Content Question** | The professor claims, "If you've ever been in a car accident, a house fire, or a fistfight or have been robbed or perhaps chased by an angry dog, you have probably remembered the incident in great detail because of the heightened state of fear or terror that was involved."

9 **Detail Question** | The professor mentions, "Some studies indicate that the reason for this is that women have more emotionally heightened states than men when emotional events occur. Therefore, they remember better and can also retrieve their memories more easily."

10 **Gist-Purpose Question** | A student asks the professor how the brain controls memories. She says that she was not going to cover that yet but she will now because the student asked her about it.

11 **Making Inferences Question** | At the end of the lecture, the professor says, "Now, since you asked me that question, Erika, I need to show all of you a schematic of the brain. Take a look at the screen up here. I want to point out where in the brain the different centers of memory retention are located. Look carefully, please, everyone." So she will probably examine the human brain next.

Actual Test 06

p.121

Answers

PART 1

1 Ⓓ	2 [1], [4]	3 Ⓓ	4 Ⓑ	5 Ⓐ
6 Ⓑ	7 Ⓐ	8 Ⓓ	9 [2], [1], [4], [3]	
10 Ⓓ	11 Ⓐ			

PART 2

1 Ⓓ	2 Ⓑ	3 Ⓑ	4 Ⓐ	5 Ⓓ
6 Ⓑ	7 Ⓐ	8 Ⓓ	9 Ⓓ	10 Ⓑ
11 Ⓒ	12 Ⓒ	13 Ⓐ	14 [1], [3]	15 Ⓑ
16 Ⓑ	17 Cause: [2], [4] Effect: [1], [3]			

Scripts & Explanations

PART 1

Conversation 06-01

p.124

M Financial Aid Office Employee: Greetings. You wouldn't happen to be Susan Sanders, would you?

W Student: Um, no. Sorry. My name is Emily Jenkins. I have an appointment at three twenty.

M: Ah, I see. Well, it's already three fifteen, and Susan's appointment was for three o'clock. It doesn't look like she's going to be showing up today, so why don't we get started with our meeting a little early?

W: That works for me.

M: Okay . . . What brings you to the financial aid office today?

W: Next semester's tuition. It's increasing by something like ten percent, and that's too much for my parents and me to handle.

M: I see. Do you receive any financial aid right now?

W: Yes, I do.

M: Could you be a little more specific?

W: Ah, yes. Sure. I receive a grant from the school for five thousand dollars. I also have two separate loans that total . . . um, I believe that it's thirty-five hundred dollars. As for the rest of my tuition and room and board, my parents and I pay several thousand dollars each.

M: Okay . . . I've got your information up here on my computer now. You've been getting financial aid ever since you started here, right?

W: That is correct. Without the extra help, I would have to transfer to a school that's a lot cheaper than this one. Either that or I would have to drop out and get a job, uh, I guess.

M: Let's hope that doesn't happen.

W: If the school can see fit to increase my financial aid by, uh, around a thousand dollars or so, I will definitely be able to remain here. Do you believe that is possible?

M: How are your grades?

W: I received a 3.92 GPA last semester. I had four A's and one A-. It was my best semester yet. I made the Dean's List for the fourth semester in a row, and I should be able to graduate with honors since my GPA is high enough.

M: Outstanding. What, may I ask, is your GPA right now?

W: It's . . . 3.51. I'm hoping to get it up to 3.60 before I finish. I'm not sure if that's going to be possible, but I'm going to try my hardest.

M: All right . . . Since your grades are pretty high, it looks like you might qualify for a special scholarship.

W: A special scholarship?

M: Yes. You see, a lot of people—usually alumni—endow scholarships here. They're typically worth, oh, several hundred dollars a year. Some might be worth a thousand or more. You can't apply for them individually. But the school looks over deserving—and needy—students each semester and hands them out. I'm going to recommend you for a couple of different scholarships. They're academic in nature but are only awarded to students who need the aid.

W: Wow. That's awesome. Do I have to do anything?

M: Just coming here was good enough. That started the process. Now, I'm not promising anything. Please understand that. There's even a chance that you won't get any kind of award. But I'd have to say that the odds are better than average that you'll receive a scholarship for at least a few hundred dollars. You'll be notified if you get anything by the end of next week.

W: That sounds great. Thank you so much for your time.

1 **Gist-Purpose Question** | The student indicates that she needs some more financial aid to continue attending the school.

2 **Detail Question** | The student states, "I receive a grant from the school for five thousand dollars. I also have two separate loans that total . . . um, I believe that it's thirty-five hundred dollars. As for the rest of my tuition and room and board, my parents and I pay several thousand dollars each."

3 **Understanding Attitude Question** | When the student talks about her grades, her tone of voice is very important. She has a high GPA, so she sounds proud while talking about it.

4 **Understanding Function Question** | The man tells the student about the special scholarships to let her know that they are a possible way that she can get some more financial aid in the coming semester.

5 **Making Inferences Question** | The man says, "But I'd have to say that the odds are better than average that you'll receive a scholarship for at least a few hundred dollars." So it can be inferred that the student will most likely be able to attend school the next semester since she will probably get some financial aid.

Lecture 06-02 p.126

W Professor: It's generally accepted that humans and other primates descended from a common ancestor. Of all primates, the ones that most closely physically resemble humans are apes. And by apes, um, I mean the branch of primates that includes the gorilla, orangutan, chimpanzee, and the siamang gibbon. There are, by the way, two types of chimps—the common chimp and the pygmy chimp—and two types of gibbons. They are, uh, the common gibbon and the siamang gibbon. When comparing humans with all of these apes, we are most closely related to the pygmy chimp and the gorilla. In fact, we're only separated from these two apes by a few percentage points of DNA. Interestingly enough, it's due to both the similarities in our DNA and our physical appearances that we know we shared a common ancestor many years ago. But the question is how long ago that happened. Hmm . . . Here are some clues to that mystery. Gorillas diverged from our common ancestor around ten million years ago, we diverged about seven million years ago, and pygmy chimps and common chimps diverged about three million years ago.

The reason we know these facts is through analysis of DNA. It turns out that the DNA of every species has a specific melting point. And if you mix the DNA of two different species, the melting point gets reduced to a level that's below the melting point of the DNA of the individual species. Here's something you need to remember: The melting point decreases by one degree Celsius for every one percent difference there is in the species' DNA structures. For example, human DNA and gorilla DNA mixed together melt at a temperature 2.3 degrees lower than human DNA by itself. [11] This means that humans and gorillas differ only in 2.3 percent of our DNA. As you can see, we share 97.7 percent of our DNA with gorillas. **Is everyone with me so far . . . ?** All right. That's good. A lot of classes have trouble understanding that point. Let's move on then.

Now, here's something else that's useful about the melting points of DNA. We can utilize it as a clock. However, we need to examine the fossil record of apes and monkeys in order to get solid support for this method. Sometime around thirty million years ago, the common ancestor of what would eventually become monkeys, apes, and humans lived. By studying the fossil record, we've learned roughly when monkeys and orangutans both diverged. For monkeys, it was around thirty million years ago. Monkeys, by the way, have a 7.3 percent difference in DNA with humans. Orangutans diverged around fifteen million years ago and have a 3.6 percent difference in DNA with humans. This suggests that, when there is a near doubling of the difference in DNA, there is also a near doubling of the difference in time from when each species diverged. Okay. I know this is complicated stuff, but I've got a handout to give you in a bit that has all of this information laid out nice and neatly. So please don't get too stressed. And don't worry about writing this information down. It's listed on the handout.

What this common ancestor actually was is something we don't know yet. However, it most certainly possessed traits that were both similar and different to those of modern-day humans. But keep this in mind . . . The species that diverged from the original ancestor had new species similarly diverge from them. Again, remember that monkeys first developed around thirty million years ago. During that period of time, several new species of monkeys have evolved as well. Here's another example. The gibbon diverged about twenty million years ago, and, later, around eight million years ago, it further subdivided into the common gibbon and simiang gibbon. Then, as I mentioned, the divergence of orangutans happened fifteen million years ago, gorillas ten million years ago, humans seven million years ago, and pygmy chimps and common chimps three million years ago.

So gorillas developed as a distinct species before humans while humans emerged prior to chimps. Gorillas, humans, and chimps all evolved within seven million years of one another. It should therefore be obvious that humans' closest relatives in the animal kingdom are gorillas and chimps. But these differences in our DNA are crucial. After all, thanks to our DNA, humans have created modern civilization while gorillas and chimps continue to live in the wild. We use complex tools, communicate in languages, and exclusively walk upright. Other primates don't.

Let me make a quick point about our common ancestor. Nobody knows exactly what it was. Several hominids, which are the ancestors of modern man, have been unearthed and added to the fossil record. Some—or one—of them may be the link between men, monkeys, and apes. But we don't know for sure. Perhaps later in the future someone will dig up a new species in Africa that will let us know who or what our common ancestor was. But until that happens, what we're doing is mostly guesswork.

6 **Gist-Content Question** | The professor's lecture is mostly about the DNA of various primates and how similar it is to one another.

7 **Detail Question** | The professor says, "And if you mix the DNA of two different species, the melting point gets reduced to a level that's below the melting point of the DNA of the individual species."

8 **Understanding Function Question** | The professor tells the students, "And don't worry about writing this information down. It's listed on the handout." So the students do not need to take any notes on that material.

9 **Connecting Content Question** | The professor states, "Then, as I mentioned, the divergence of orangutans happened fifteen million years ago, gorillas ten million years ago, humans seven million years ago, and pygmy chimps and common chimps three million years ago."

10 **Making Inferences Question** | The professor mentions, "Perhaps later in the future someone will dig up a new species in Africa that will let us know who or what our common ancestor was." So the professor implies that humans had their origin somewhere in Africa.

11 **Understanding Attitude Question** | When the professor asks, "Is everyone with me so far?" she is acknowledging that the material she is discussing is difficult, so she is checking to make sure that the students understand it.

PART 2

Conversation 06-03

p.130

M Professor: Ah, Martha, I am so sorry to have kept you waiting. I know we had an appointment for two o'clock, but the faculty meeting went a little bit too long. You have no idea how much some of those professors love to talk. Anyway, have you been waiting here long?

W Student: Just a few minutes, sir. It's all right. I did some reading while I was waiting outside your office.

M: Good, good. Well, please come in and have a seat. Let me take off my jacket . . . All right. Now, what do we need to chat about today?

W: My schedule for next semester, sir. I've been working on it, but I am simply stuck on a couple of classes. Would you mind helping me decide which classes to take?

M: Not at all. As your advisor, that's part of what I'm supposed to do.

W: Great. Now, I've decided to register for the following three classes . . . I'm going to take Art History 104. It's an introductory class in modern art. [5]I'm also going to take Mathematics 102. It's just an algebra class. **I want to get my first math requirement out of the way, so I'm going to enroll in that class.** And the third class is Italian 101.

M: Italian?

W: I've always wanted to learn it, and, uh, since I'm majoring in Art History, it seems like it would be a good language to know. After all, a lot of great art was produced by Italians, so . . .

M: Good point. That's logical. Okay. These three classes look like they're pretty good. What are the other two that you are trying to make up your mind on?

W: Okay. I'd really like to take a class in the History Department. I'm trying to choose between one on modern America and one on medieval Europe. Which do you think that I should select?

M: Why are you taking history? Because you want to major in it, uh, or simply because you're interested in it?

W: Both actually. I might do a double major, so it seems to me that I should take at least one history class before my freshman year is over.

M: That's a prudent decision. In that case, which are you more interested in?

W: The medieval history class. Definitely.

M: Then go with that one. I know the professor who is going to teach it, and she's excellent. You'll enjoy her class a lot. Now, what about the second class?

W: I'm thinking about taking either an introductory chemistry class or a philosophy class. The philosophy class looks fun, but, uh, if I take the chemistry class, I can get rid of a science requirement.

M: You are aware that most chemistry classes have labs, aren't you? Those aren't easy, especially for students in the liberal arts.

W: Ah, I checked on that. The class I'm thinking of registering for . . . It's called Chemistry 110 . . . Uh, it doesn't have a lab.

M: Really? In that case, why don't you take it and polish off a science requirement? That way, you'll have time in later semesters to take more electives.

W: That sounds like a good plan. Thank you so much for your help, sir.

1 **Gist-Content Question** | When the professor asks the student what she wants to talk about, she says, "My schedule for next semester, sir. I've been working on it, but I am simply stuck on a couple of classes. Would you mind helping me decide which classes to take?"

2 **Detail Question** | The student mentions, "I've always wanted to learn it, and, uh, since I'm majoring in Art History, it seems like it would be a good language to

know."

3 **Making Inferences Question** | Since the student is asking the professor about which classes she should take, it is clear that she values the professor's opinion.

4 **Understanding Attitude Question** | The professor warns the student, "You are aware that most chemistry classes have labs, aren't you? Those aren't easy, especially for students in the liberal arts."

5 **Understanding Function Question** | When the student says that she wants to get her "first math requirement out of the way," she implies that she has to take more than one class in order to graduate.

Lecture 06-04

p.132

M Professor: It's time to turn our attention to radiation. To begin, what is it . . . ? Simply put, radiation is a form of energy that exists all around us. There are two main types of radiation: ionizing and non-ionizing radiation.

Ionizing radiation derives its name from the fact that it can ionize an atom. When an atom is ionized, it has a positive electric charge. This happens when an electron in an atom receives enough energy to enable it to escape from its bond. The resulting loss of that electron leaves the atom with a positive charge. As you ought to remember from basic chemistry, a neutral atom has an equal number of negatively charged electrons and positively charged protons. But take away an electron, and you have a, uh, greater number of protons, which gives the atom its positive charge. That's what happens with ionizing radiation. There are several types of ionizing radiation, including alpha particles, beta particles, neutrons, neutrinos, muons, gamma rays, and X-rays. [11] Each has different characteristics and can potentially harm life forms in various ways. There's a table on the class website that highlights the differences between these particles. **I strongly suggest that you check it out as your final exam grade may depend on it.** Got it . . . ?

The second type is non-ionizing radiation. What's this? Well, it consists mostly of things that have longer wavelengths on the electromagnetic spectrum. As we learned early in the semester, the electromagnetic spectrum consists of waves of energy. The parts with longer wavelengths, including visible light and radio waves, are mostly harmless. As wavelengths decrease in length, uh, starting with ultraviolet waves and microwaves, the danger to living organisms increases. Finally, at the end of the spectrum are X-rays and gamma rays, which have very short wavelengths. They pose significant danger to living organisms.

Um, it's obvious that various types of radiation are all around us. But what are their sources . . . ? There are both natural and manmade sources of radiation. There's one type that's around us at all times but, um, in low doses. We call it background radiation. Interestingly, much of it comes from space. This is cosmic radiation. It has its origins in the sun and other stars. Other sources of radiation are soil, rocks, and even vegetation and water. Their radiation often comes from elements such as uranium which are decaying and therefore emitting radiation. The level of this radiation varies from place to place and depends on the amount of decaying elements like uranium that are in an area. Finally, in our bodies, there are very low levels of radiation from, um, potassium, carbon, and lead isotopes. Those are the primary natural sources of radiation.

And how about manmade sources of radiation . . . ? Let me see . . . The cigarettes that some people smoke contain radiation. So does electronic equipment such as TVs and smoke detectors. You can receive a dose of radiation when you get X-rayed at the hospital. It's not a dangerous dose, but, if you work as an X-ray technician, you need to take safety measures to prevent yourself from being overexposed to radiation. Nuclear power plants are one obvious source of radiation if there's a reactor leak. There's also radiation that's, um, given off by radio towers, microwave transmitters, and any kind of communication device that uses waves on the electromagnetic spectrum. As you can see, we're surrounded by radiation.

W Student: Aren't all of these types of radiation dangerous?

M: Honestly, yes, but only if a person receives a significant dose. And as you should be able to guess by now, the amount needed to harm someone varies depending on the type of radiation they're exposed to. Alpha particles are the most dangerous, so a small dose of them can be quite harmful. In contrast, X-rays are much less dangerous so therefore require a larger dose. Finally, radio waves, which have fairly long wavelengths, pose little danger at all. Hmm . . . Why don't I be a little more specific? X-rays . . . If you were X-rayed 1,000 times in a single year, you'd run the risk of getting a dangerous dose of radiation. That's a lot of X-rays you know. How many have you had in your entire life? Not many, I'd wager.

We measure exposure to radiation in units called rads. That's spelled R-A-D-S. It's an acronym for radioactively absorbed dose. The more rads a person gets, the greater the danger the person is in. Another, um, smaller, unit of measurement is the gray. One rad equals 100 grays.

The biggest effect radiation has on living organisms is that it causes cell damage, which can lead to the onset of cancer. In extreme cases of short-term high exposure, such as the atomic bomb blasts at Hiroshima and Nagasaki, Japan, and the nuclear power plant accident at Chernobyl, which was in the Soviet Union at that time, people can die within days or weeks of exposure. But individuals exposed to long-term low doses may not get cancer for decades. And many suffer no harm at all.

6 **Gist-Content Question** | The professor mostly talks about the origins of radiation and the various types of it.

7 **Making Inferences Question** | The professor notes, "As wavelengths decrease in length, uh, starting with ultraviolet waves and microwaves, the danger to living organisms increases. Finally, at the end of the spectrum are X-rays and gamma rays, which have very short wavelengths. They pose significant danger to living organisms." Since X-rays and gamma rays "pose significant danger to living organisms" and they are at the end of the spectrum, then ultraviolet waves and microwaves must be less dangerous than them.

8 **Connecting Content Question** | The professor states, "Their radiation often comes from elements such as uranium which are decaying and therefore emitting radiation." Since uranium emits radiation, it must be a radioactive element.

9 **Understanding Organization Question** | Throughout the lecture, the professor asks several questions. However, the professor, not the students, answers his own questions.

10 **Detail Question** | The professor says, "We measure exposure to radiation in units called rads."

11 **Understanding Function Question** | When the professor remarks, "I strongly suggest that you check it out as your final exam grade may depend on it," he is hinting that the students will be tested on the material on the class website. His tone of voice is important. He is giving the students a clue about how important the material is.

Lecture 06-05

p.135

M Professor: Today, the Netherlands is a small, yet wealthy, nation. This has been true for the majority of its history dating back to the seventeenth century. This was when the Dutch Golden Age, as historians refer to it, took place. During that period, the Dutch people were global leaders in trade, science, and the arts. There were several reasons the Dutch managed to experience such success. Among them were a highly skilled labor force, an abundant supply of cheap energy, and good internal communication and transportation systems of roads and canals. The Dutch further possessed a large fleet, had skilled naval commanders, and were beginning to establish an overseas colonial empire. These factors all combined to create an enormous amount of wealth, which then supported the advancement of the sciences and arts there.

Be aware that when I talk about the Netherlands in the past, I'm referring to the land covered by the modern-day countries Belgium and the Netherlands. They were once a single political entity. That nation comprised seventeen provinces. During the sixteenth century, there were two important events in Dutch history. The first happened when the Spanish, under King Charles the Fifth, managed to gain control of the land. The second was that the Protestant Reformation took place and was successful in converting the majority of the people in the seven northernmost provinces. Catholic Spain, under Charles's son Phillip the Second, tried to restore the Catholic religion in those provinces by resorting to force. Those seven Protestant provinces rebelled and came together to form the United Provinces.

The ten southern provinces remained Catholic. So in 1568, a war began. The war lasted for eighty years. Yes, eighty. Sure, a lot of the fighting was off and on, but it was still a long war. During the war, the ten southern provinces remained possessions of Spain. But many people in them converted to Protestantism and departed for the northern provinces. These individuals were often highly skilled craftsmen, sailors, soldiers, and merchants. Many would contribute to the eventual success of the Dutch in winning their independence from Spain by 1648. Despite being long, the war united the Dutch people and marked the beginning of their golden age.

As I stated, one reason the Dutch enjoyed such prosperity during the seventeenth century was their power sources. In the pre-Industrial Revolution era, power came from humans, animals, and a few natural sources, namely wind and falling water. The Dutch obtained much of their energy from wind power. They used windmills to give them enough energy to pump out seawater to reclaim land. Uh, remember that a large percentage of the Netherlands lies below sea level. Areas once submerged by the North

Sea became dry land thanks to the remarkable Dutch system of pumps and levees that removed the water and kept it from returning. These windmills also powered the machinery in mills for grinding grain as well as sawmills.

The Dutch additionally used the relatively small size of their country and their high population density to their advantage. Since their country was so small, they were able to develop efficient road and canal systems. These enabled people to move and items to be transported both easily and quickly.

Since the Dutch were master sailors and had a large commercial fleet, their ships carried Dutch exports to many parts of Europe. The ships further returned laden with imports that the Dutch required. These included raw materials such as wool for their weaving industry and timber, pitch, and rope for their shipbuilding industry.

Abroad, Dutch explorers—thanks in part to their strong navy—established colonies in North America, Africa, India, Japan, and, uh, Indonesia. Amsterdam and the other great ports of the Netherlands became trading hubs in Europe, and many people in these cities became fabulously wealthy. In 1602, the Dutch founded the world's first large shareholding corporation, the Dutch East India Company. They also established the world's first stock market in Amsterdam. The Dutch East India Company would remain the world's largest trading company for almost two centuries. The amount of wealth that corporation created was, well, uh, it was phenomenal.

This wealth also helped contribute to various Dutch scientific and artistic achievements. For instance, it was three Dutchmen who invented the world's first telescope. Other Dutchmen contributed to advances in the fields of optics, mathematics, physics, and biology. Great artists such as Rembrandt and Vermeer established themselves as world-class painters.

W Student: It sounds like a great period of time. So why didn't it last?

M: In some ways, the Dutch were victims of their own success. Being rich and powerful brought them into the great power games of Europe. Spain caused them constant problems. So did France, which was right next to the Netherlands. At that time, France was the most powerful country in Europe, and its leaders dreamed of expanding their territory. This included taking over the Netherlands. The English also came into conflict with the Dutch at times. England and the Netherlands actually fought three wars with each other in the seventeenth century.

12 **Gist-Content Question** | The professor mostly talks about the Dutch Golden Age of the 1600s.

13 **Making Inferences Question** | The professor notes, "Be aware that when I talk about the Netherlands in the past, I'm referring to the land covered by the modern-day countries Belgium and the Netherlands. They were once a single political entity." So the Netherlands in the past was larger than it is today.

14 **Detail Question** | During the sixteenth century, the professor notes, "The Spanish, under King Charles the Fifth, managed to gain control of the land. The second was that the Protestant Reformation took place and was successful in converting the majority of the people in the seven northernmost provinces."

15 **Understanding Attitude Question** | The professor declares, "Areas once submerged by the North Sea became dry land thanks to the remarkable Dutch system of pumps and levees that removed the water and kept it from returning."

16 **Understanding Attitude Question** | The professor states, "Abroad, Dutch explorers—thanks in part to their strong navy—established colonies in North America, Africa, India, Japan, and, uh, Indonesia. Amsterdam and the other great ports of the Netherlands became trading hubs in Europe, and many people in these cities became fabulously wealthy. In 1602, the Dutch founded the world's first large shareholding corporation, the Dutch East India Company. They also established the world's first stock market in Amsterdam. The Dutch East India Company would remain the world's largest trading company for almost two centuries. The amount of wealth that corporation created was, well, uh, it was phenomenal." He is recognizing the importance of trade in the Netherlands in talking about the company.

17 **Connecting Content Question** | According to the lecture, one cause of the Dutch Golden Age was that the Netherlands gained its independence from Spain. Another was that Dutch ships transported goods to many ports in Europe. As for the effects, the Dutch spent a lot of money on the arts, and England and the Netherlands fought three wars in the 1600s.

Actual Test 07

p.139

Answers

PART 1

1 (C) 2 (C) 3 (A) 4 (B) 5 (A)
6 (C) 7 (D) 8 (A) 9 Fact: [1], [3], [4]
Not a Fact: [2] 10 (B) 11 (D)

PART 2

1 (B) 2 (A) 3 (C) 4 (A) 5 (C)
6 (C) 7 (B) 8 (D) 9 (C) 10 (C)
11 (B)

PART 3

1 (C) 2 (B) 3 (A) 4 [3], [4] 5 (C)
6 (A) 7 (C) 8 (B) 9 Ptolemy: [1], [4]
Nicolas Copernicus: [2], [3] 10 (B) 11 (D)
12 (A) 13 (B) 14 (C) 15 (A) 16 (D)
17 (A)

Scripts & Explanations

PART 1

Conversation 07-01

p.142

M Professor: Good afternoon, Jodie. I got your email about wanting to have a meeting with me today. What can I do for you?

W Student: Well, sir, if it's all right with you, I would like to go over the paper that you gave back to me in class yesterday.

M: Sure. Pardon me, Jodie, but I can't remember your paper exactly. I wish I could, but there are just too many students in that class for me to recall individual papers. You didn't happen to bring it with you, did you?

W: Actually, sir, I've got it right here. Would you like to see it?

M: Please. That would be a tremendous help.

W: Here you are . . .

M: Ah, yes . . . I remember this paper.

W: You do? Then would you mind telling me why exactly I got a C on it? I mean, uh, I put a lot of effort into writing that paper. [4]I thought I was going to get an A- or a B+ at worst, but then you gave me this grade.

M: **First of all, Jodie, I didn't give you a grade. You earned a grade.** There is a distinction you know. It also doesn't really matter how many hours you put into the writing of the paper. What matters is the final product. Honestly, I couldn't care less if you spent thirty minutes or thirty hours on it. I'm only interested in what was on the paper that you handed in.

W: But you didn't think that what I handed in was any good?

M: Not particularly. No. Sorry if that upsets you.

W: Well, uh, could you be more specific, please? I'd like to know what I'm doing wrong, and, um, you didn't leave too many comments on this paper.

M: Sure. I can go over this paper with you.

W: Thanks.

M: First of all . . . You didn't write an introduction. You started the paper by citing some statistics and then describing them. So, uh, I really had no idea what your paper was going to be about. You need to provide an introduction to let the reader know what the topic of your paper is and what you're going to argue in the paper.

W: Okay. What else?

M: Let's see . . . Ah, right. You got a lot of your facts wrong. Notice these passages that I have circled in red. Here's one . . . And here's another . . . These circled passages all contain factual mistakes. You really have to check your facts much better, Jodie.

W: Is there anything else?

M: You needed to provide a conclusion as well. The paper just, uh, it just suddenly ended. You need to explain what you have proved in your conclusion. That's crucial for any paper.

W: I see. Okay. Uh, thanks.

M: [5]You know . . . I allow rewrites in my class. If you were to resubmit the paper, oh, three days from now, I would be glad to look it over again. **Perhaps your grade will change.**

W: Is that so? I had no idea. Thanks for the good news, sir. I'll be sure to fix my paper, so it will be much better by then.

1 **Gist-Purpose Question** | At the beginning of the conversation, the student tells the professor, "Well, sir, if it's all right with you, I would like to go over the paper that you gave back to me in class yesterday."

2 **Detail Question** | The student says she put a lot of effort into writing the paper, so she thinks that her grade should have been higher.

3 **Understanding Attitude Question** | The student asks the professor if her paper was any good, and he responds by saying, "No."

4 **Understanding Function Question** | The professor says, "I didn't give you a grade. You earned a grade." So he is criticizing the student's choice of words.

5 **Making Inferences Question** | When the professor says, "Perhaps your grade will change," he is hinting that, if she does a rewrite of her paper, she might be able to get a better grade.

Lecture 07-02

p.144

M Professor: Let's turn our attention to the commodities market, which is also known as the futures market. I'm sure you've all heard those terms before, right? But do you know what happens on the commodities market . . . ? Hmm . . . Perhaps not. Okay, let me tell you. When you trade on the futures, uh, commodities market, you're not really buying or selling anything. What you're doing is speculating on the direction that the price of a certain commodity is going to take in the future. So if you think that the price is going to increase, then you make a purchase. Naturally, if you feel that the price will drop, then you sell. In that regard, the commodities market is like the stock market. But one key aspect of the commodities market is that while every trade has a buyer and seller, neither party actually has to own the commodities they are dealing with.

I know that sounds a little strange. I was confused the first time I ever heard that. However, if you'll be patient, I think I can explain this to you in a way that should make sense. To do that, I need to go back to the past and give you a quick history lesson on the origins of the commodities market. In the 1840s, Chicago, Illinois, had become a thriving commercial center in the United States. With its railroad lines, which connected the Midwest and parts of the West with the East Coast, it was a vital transportation hub. Midwestern farmers frequently grew wheat as a major cash crop back then. After they harvested their wheat, they went to Chicago to find dealers to buy it. The dealers then used Chicago's railroad lines to ship the wheat all over the country. Sounds easy, right?

But one problem the farmers encountered was that when they went to Chicago hoping to make quick sales, the dealers had the upper hand. You see, Chicago had few storage facilities in which the wheat could be kept. There was also no established procedure for handling the farmers and their wheat when they wanted to sell it. Finally, the farmers mostly wanted to sell their wheat and get back to their farms, where there was always work to do. These factors all left the farmers at the mercy of the dealers, who could merely hold out until the farmers settled for the lower prices they were being offered.

Then, in 1848, a central place opened where farmers and dealers could meet and where dealers could immediately accept the delivery of wheat in return for cash. From this modest beginning was born the futures contract where, uh, farmers and dealers—acting as sellers and buyers—could commit to future exchanges of wheat and other grains in return for money. This pleased everyone since the farmers knew upfront how much they'd be getting for their crops while the dealers knew what their buying costs would be as well.

This type of transaction quickly became common. When written down in contractual form, futures contracts were even accepted as collateral for bank loans. Soon, these contracts began changing hands before their due dates. For instance, one farmer might decide that he didn't want to sell his crop, so he'd find another farmer to take over his delivery obligation. The same went for dealers. They too bought and sold contracts they'd made with other farmers. Eventually, this gave birth to speculators. These are people who don't intend to buy or sell commodities but merely make contractual transactions out of the desire to buy low and to sell high.

Just a minute ago, I brought up the stock market and noted a similarity between it and the commodities market. However, there's one critical way in which the two are different: Products bought and sold on the commodities market have finite lives. Once the wheat, corn, or other commodities are brought to the market, the contracts for them are over. So, um, speculators closely scrutinize the near future as they try to earn quick profits. There's not much long-term thinking that goes on in the commodities market as, uh, as opposed to the stock market.

Because of the nature of the commodities market, a few important things occurred. First, the commodities being sold were standardized. That way, there was no confusion about what the buyers and sellers were trading. Next, all of the perishable commodities being traded had to have adequate shelf lives since the sales of the items were being put off into the future. Finally, the commodities' prices weren't fixed. They were allowed to fluctuate enough so that uncertainty was created. This gave people the opportunity either to gain or lose on every transaction. And that, I think, is one of the allures of the commodities market. There's potential to reap enormous profits, but, at the same time, people run the risk of losing fortunes. Sharp daily price movements are common and have a tremendous effect on investors in commodities.

6 **Gist-Content Question** | The professor explains how the commodities market operates during his lecture.

7 **Understanding Organization Question** | The professor talks about Chicago to explain why it was there that the commodities market was founded.

8 **Detail Question** | The professor states, "Eventually, this gave birth to speculators. These are people who don't intend to buy or sell commodities but merely make contractual transactions out of the desire to buy low and to sell high."

9 **Detail Question** | According to the lecture, the first commodities market was founded in Chicago. In addition, the goal of its founding was to make buying and selling easier. Finally, all of the commodities sold are standardized. However, it is not true that more items are traded on the commodities market than on the stock market.

10 **Connecting Content Question** | The professor tells the class, "When you trade on the futures, uh, commodities market, you're not really buying or selling anything. What you're doing is speculating on the direction that the price of a certain commodity is going to take in the future. So if you think that the price is going to increase, then you make a purchase. Naturally, if you feel that the price will drop, then you sell. In that regard, the commodities market is like the stock market."

11 **Understanding Attitude Question** | The professor notes, "This gave people the opportunity either to gain or lose on every transaction. And that, I think, is one of the allures of the commodities market. There's potential to reap enormous profits, but, at the same time, people run the risk of losing fortunes."

PART 2

Conversation 07-03

p.148

M1 Professor: Jim, you are just the person I was looking for. Please come in here for a second. I would like to have a word with you.

M2 Student: Oh, hi, Professor Samson. Sure. I've got a bit of time to talk to you. I don't have class for another half an hour. What do you need?

M1: Are you still looking for some part-time work?

M2: Huh? How did you know about that?

M1: Ah, I had lunch with Professor Douglas this afternoon, and he told me that you were trying to find some part-time work somewhere on campus. I hope that you don't mind us talking about you like that.

M2: Not at all. I'm actually kind of flattered that I was the topic of discussion amongst a couple of professors. That's pretty cool now that I think of it.

M1: Well, what's even cooler, I think, is the opportunity that I have for you. You know I run the chemistry laboratory on the fourth floor, right?

M2: Yes, I think I heard that from someone. I've never been in that lab before, but I've been by it a few times. That's the lab for freshmen and sophomores, isn't it?

M1: That's correct. And even though you haven't been in it, at least you know where it is. Anyway, one of my lab assistants had to drop out of school last week. He had some personal issues that . . . Well, it's not important why he left school. The point is that he's gone, and I'm looking for a new person to help out in the lab.

M2: All right. What exactly would you need for me to do?

M1: The vast majority of it is pretty mundane stuff. You would mostly need to keep the lab clean and make sure that we have enough supplies—chemicals and all that.

M2: I see. Would I get a chance to lead any of the labs that the students take?

M1: Well . . . Not this semester. No. Sorry. I know that you're definitely qualified to do it, but those positions are completely filled. It wouldn't be fair for me to bump anyone in favor of you.

M2: Yes, I can see your point. That's fine.

M1: But . . .

M2: But what?

M1: You would get a chance to be a part of those labs while they are being taught. So you would be able to observe how the other lab assistants teach and interact with the students. That would get you a lot of hands-on experience I think, and then you'll be in a good position to get your own lab class next semester. That is, uh, if you're interested in the job.

M2: I'm definitely interested. You can count me in.

M1: Great. I was hoping you'd say that. In that case, let me know the hours when you are available to work in the lab. I've got enough funding to let you work twenty hours a week if you are interested in working that much.

M2: Twenty hours a week? Excellent. That's precisely the number of hours that I was hoping for.

M1: It looks like it was a good thing that Professor Douglas and I had lunch together today, doesn't it?

1 **Gist-Content Question** | The professor has a job that he wants the student to do, so that is what they mostly talk about.

2 **Making Inferences Question** | The professor says, "Ah, I had lunch with Professor Douglas this afternoon, and he told me that you were trying to find some part-time work somewhere on campus. I hope that you don't mind us talking about you like that." Since the student's desire for a job is a personal matter, it can be inferred that Professor Douglas speaks with the student about his personal matters.

3 **Making Inferences Question** | The professor declares, "Anyway, one of my lab assistants had to drop out of school last week. He had some personal issues that . . . Well, it's not important why he left school. The point is that he's gone, and I'm looking for a new person to help out in the lab."

4 **Understanding Function Question** | The professor states, "You would mostly need to keep the lab clean and make sure that we have enough supplies—chemicals and all that." He is explaining the duties to let the student know what kind of work needs to be done in the laboratory.

5 **Making Inferences Question** | The student comments positively about the job. He also responds that he wants to work twenty hours a week, which is how many hours the professor says that he can work. So the student will probably accept the professor's offer.

Lecture 07-04

p.150

W Professor: One of the staples of science-fiction works is time travel. You know, uh, the ability to move either forward or backward in time. According to Albert Einstein, time travel isn't possible because it would require a person to move faster than the speed of light. Since Einstein believed it was impossible for anything to exceed the speed of light, he declared that time travel was impossible. However, Einstein also believed that time was relative. In his view, depending upon how fast a person was moving, time could either speed up or slow down. For instance, as a person's speed approached that of light, time for that person would slow down. Thus, uh, as a single day elapsed for that person, several days might pass for people moving at regular speeds.

[11] While I suppose that could be regarded as a form of time travel, Einstein still felt that it was impossible for a person to move forward or backward in time by using a, uh, time machine or similar sort of contraption. **Most science-fiction authors, meanwhile, don't find themselves constrained by the laws of physics like Einstein was.** In fact, in many science-fiction stories, time travel is an important plot device. Today, I'd like to mention a couple of these stories in brief and describe the methods the people in them used to travel in time.

Most authors that write about time travel use one of two primary methods. The first is having some sort of machine that enables a person to travel in time. The second involves, hmm . . . I guess you could say natural means. In other words, there's no machinery involved.

Let me describe a couple of stories that involve machinery first . . . Um, one of the first—and arguably the most famous—works involving time travel was H.G. Wells' masterpiece *The Time Machine*. Most of you, I imagine, are familiar with the story. If not, you will be soon since we're going to read it next week and then discuss it in detail. I think you'll enjoy the book. It's one of my personal favorites. Anyway, without spoiling the story, the main character, known only as the Time Traveler, creates a time machine that's basically a chair. The Time Traveler sits in the chair, which creates a time bubble that takes him forward into the future. During the story, the Time Traveler uses his time machine to travel millions of years into the future and then back to his regular time.

Another well-known story that uses time travel is *The Door into Summer*, which was written by a true master of science fiction, Robert Heinlein. The main character gets put into suspended animation and is then awakened many years in the future without having aged. Then, while he's in the future, the main character learns about a scientist who has invented a time machine that can send people or objects either into the past or the future. The main character uses the time machine to go back into the past and to make sure that his future life turns out well.

The Time Machine and *The Door into Summer* are typical of science-fiction stories that use machinery to let characters travel in time. The author may describe some aspects of the machine, yet the technical details are kept to a minimum. But the machine itself is usually a crucial part of the story.

In other science fiction stories, time travel happens through different means. Are any of you familiar with Mark Twain's novel *A Connecticut Yankee in King Arthur's Court*

. . . ? Hmm . . . Only a few of you. Well, I guess that book isn't taught in schools too much anymore. In Twain's story, the main character, named Hank Morgan, goes back in time after he gets hit on the head. That's it. Twain didn't really concern himself with the actual process of time travel. And that's what's important about stories that rely on the, uh, natural means of time travel. The authors don't really care that much about how it happens. It just does.

There's also another more modern story . . . It's the book *Replay* by Ken Grimwood.

M Student: Oh, I love that book. I've read it three or four times.

W: Ah, I'm glad to see we have at least one fan of *Replay*. Um, for those of you that haven't read it, let me fill you in. The main character in the novel dies of a heart attack only to wake up many years in the past. He goes through life again, has another heart attack at the exact same time as the previous one, and then wakes up again in the past but, uh, at a different time than before. The character keeps replaying his life—hence the book's title—as he dies, wakes up, and lives a new life. If you're not familiar with it, I recommend that you check it out.

6 **Gist-Content Question** | The professor's lecture focuses on some works of literature that have stories involving time travel.

7 **Detail Question** | The professor says, "Anyway, without spoiling the story, the main character, known only as the Time Traveler, creates a time machine that's basically a chair. The Time Traveler sits in the chair, which creates a time bubble that takes him forward into the future."

8 **Gist-Purpose Question** | About *A Connecticut Yankee in King Arthur's Court*, the professor states, "Twain didn't really concern himself with the actual process of time travel. And that's what's important about stories that rely on the, uh, natural means of time travel." So the time travel in this book does not rely on machinery to happen.

9 **Understanding Attitude Question** | About *Replay*, the student exclaims, "Oh, I love that book. I've read it three or four times."

10 **Understanding Organization Question** | The professor gives several examples of different ways that people time travel in works of literature.

11 **Understanding Function Question** | The professor makes this comment to add some humor to her lecture.

PART 3

Conversation 07-05

p.154

M Student: Hello. I'm having some trouble with my dorm room, and my dormitory RA told me I should visit this office to solve the problem.

W Housing Office Employee: Sure. What's wrong with your room?

M: The door won't open.

W: Um . . . Do you mean that it's stuck?

M: Oh, no. Not that. I mean that there's a problem with the lock. When I place my ID on the keyless lock and then input my PIN, nothing happens. The door won't open. And I know that the lock works properly because my roommate doesn't have any problems at all getting into the room.

W: I see. Hmm . . . Are you able to use your ID card to access the main entrance to the dorm as well as any other buildings on campus that you may be allowed into?

M: Um . . . Honestly, I don't know. The problem just started this morning. I went to the bathroom around 8:00, and when I returned to the room, I couldn't get back in. I had to wait for my roommate to come back from breakfast to let me in. I tried to open the door multiple times, but nothing happened. And, uh, once I left my dorm . . . Well, I haven't gone back there yet because I've been in classes the entire day. So . . . I just don't know if the problem is the lock or my card.

W: Could I see your ID card, please?

M: Of course . . . Here you are.

W: Okay. Let me call up your name here on the computer screen . . . Jason Whitman. W-H-I-T-M-A-N.

M: Find anything?

W: Hmm . . . Yes, I think I see the problem. You haven't paid your tuition yet.

M: Huh?

W: There's a note which has been attached to your file. Apparently, you haven't paid your tuition for this semester, and the deadline to do that was yesterday. Every semester, the Bursar's office sends us a list of students with unpaid bills, and, uh, those individuals get locked out of their dorm rooms until their bills are paid.

M: [5]There must be some kind of mistake.

W: What do you mean?

M: **I'm here on a full scholarship.** I'm a member of the school's basketball team, so my tuition as well as my room and board are completely paid for. I shouldn't owe anything.

W: Hmm . . . It sounds to me like there must be some kind of a mix-up, but I can't do anything to help you at this moment. I suggest that you go to the Bursar's office at once and clear up this problem. It's three o'clock now, so if you go there, you should be able to solve your problem within the next hour. Once that happens, return here, and then I can make sure that you can get back into your dorm room. We close at half past five, so you have a bit of time to do everything you need to do. Oh, you might also call your coach and have him talk to somebody at the Bursar's office. That's likely the fastest way to resolve this issue.

M: Ah, that's good advice. I'll head to the Bursar's office just as soon as I make this call. Thanks for your assistance.

1 **Gist-Content Question** | The student tells the woman that he is unable to unlock the door to his dormitory room.

2 **Understanding Function Question** | The student tells the woman about his morning activities in response to a question that she asks him.

3 **Making Inferences Question** | When the woman states, "Every semester, the Bursar's office sends us a list of students with unpaid bills, and, uh, those individuals get locked out of their dorm rooms until their bills are paid," it can be inferred that she has seen other people with the same problem that the student has.

4 **Detail Question** | The woman tells the student, "I suggest that you go to the Bursar's office at once and clear up this problem," and then she says, "Oh, you might also call your coach and have him talk to somebody at the Bursar's office."

5 **Understanding Function Question** | In stating, "I'm here on a full scholarship," the student is implying that he does not owe the university any money.

Lecture 07-06

p.156

M Professor: Throughout history, several individuals have proposed various models of the universe. During this time, there have been many theories on Earth's place in the universe. However, for much of history, there were two main ones: The first stated that Earth was the center of the universe. This was the most commonly accepted model of the universe up until around, um, around the sixteenth century or so. That's when Nicolas Copernicus proposed his new model of the universe, one in which Earth, like the other planets, revolved around the sun.

[11] I'd like to begin by describing what's known as the geocentric theory of the universe. ***Geo* is the Greek word for Earth, so you should be able to guess that "geocentric" refers to the notion that Earth is the center of the universe.** People began proposing the geocentric theory back in ancient times, including Greece and Rome. One of the most famous proposals was that of Ptolemy, a Greek who lived in Egypt from the years 90 to 168 A.D. At that time, Egypt was a part of the Roman Empire, so Ptolemy was a Roman citizen. Like many educated men in ancient times, Ptolemy had been schooled in a wide range of subjects, one of, uh, of which was astronomy. His famous work, the *Almagest*, covered what Ptolemy knew—or believed he knew I should say—about the universe.

The *Almagest* contained thirteen sections that covered various aspects of the movements of the sun, moon, planets, and stars. Bear in mind that during Ptolemy's time, the only known planets were Jupiter, Saturn, Mars, Venus, and Mercury. Well, the *Almagest* contained a veritable wealth of information, but a great deal of that information was, um, to put it delicately, was incorrect. First, Ptolemy believed that Earth was at the center of the cosmos. Second, he had everything else in the universe revolving around Earth. Third, in his universe, Earth was stationary and didn't move at all. Fourth, the universe was spherical in shape. Fifth, the moon, the sun, the planets, and the stars all moved in separate spheres around Earth. Of these spheres, the moon's sphere was the closest to Earth. It was followed by Mercury, Venus, the sun, Jupiter, Saturn, and the stars in that order. With slight variations, Ptolemy's model of the universe became the accepted view for nearly 1,500 years.

W Student: Why did it last for so long when it was obviously wrong?

M: Well . . . it may be obvious to me and you today, but it wasn't apparent in the past. Remember that knowledge spread and advanced slowly in those days. Books were copied by hand, which took a long time, so they were quite rare. Ptolemy's *Almagest* was actually one of the few books to be copied quite often, so the knowledge in it spread to numerous lands. The Arabs accepted his work as the truth as did people in many other places. During the Middle Ages in Europe, Ptolemy's views became accepted as well.

However, as time passed and people started learning more about science, some individuals began to question Ptolemy and the validity of his model of the universe. They realized that Ptolemy's theories didn't explain many of the motions of the heavenly bodies in a logical manner. Of course, we now know the reason was that, in Ptolemy's model, Earth didn't move, yet it does in actuality. But nobody in the past was aware of that. They only knew that something wasn't right with Ptolemy's universe.

Still, it wasn't until 1543, when Nicolas Copernicus published his work on heavenly bodies, that someone proposed a strong competing model of the universe. Copernicus believed in a heliocentric, or sun-centered, universe. The book Copernicus wrote was called *On the Revolutions of Heavenly Spheres*. In it, Copernicus argued that the sun, not Earth, was the center of the universe. Copernicus's universe contained eight spheres—one for the stars, one for the sun, and one for each of the six known planets. The moon lacked its own sphere as it orbited the Earth, not the sun. Copernicus believed the sun didn't move and that the planets and stars all moved in perfect circles around the sun.

Take a look up here at the screen. You can see Ptolemy's and Copernicus's universes here . . . Note that they have some similarities . . . Both have one stationary object at the center. Both believe the orbits are perfect circles rather than the elliptical paths we know the planets actually make. And both rely on complex theories and formulas to account for inconsistencies in the movements of the heavenly objects.

Copernicus's book was widely read, and his theory became well known in scientific circles. While it was resisted by some, including the Church, many scientists, including Galileo Galilei, made their own contributions to the heliocentric model of the universe. Thanks to telescopes, which were first used to explore the night sky by Galileo, scientists began proving that certain aspects of Ptolemy's universe were wrong while parts of Copernicus's universe were right. Now, before we stop for a break, let's move on to the contributions that Galileo made.

6 **Gist-Content Question** | The professor describes two different ancient models of the universe in his lecture.

7 **Understanding Organization Question** | The professor says, "The *Almagest* contained thirteen sections that covered various aspects of the movements of the sun, moon, planets, and stars." Then, he describes the information in the *Almagest*.

8 **Detail Question** | The professor responds, "Well . . . it may be obvious to me and you today, but it wasn't apparent in the past. Remember that knowledge spread and advanced slowly in those days," when a student asks him a question.

9 **Connecting Content Question** | According to the lecture, Ptolemy's model of the universe claimed that Earth did not move. In addition, the moon was in the closest sphere to Earth in his model. As for Nicolas Copernicus, he had a heliocentric, or sun-centered, universe. He described his universe in the book *On the Revolutions of Heavenly Spheres*.

10 **Making Inferences Question** | The professor says, "Now, before we stop for a break, let's move on to the contributions that Galileo made."

11 **Understanding Function Question** | The professor talks about the origins of the word "geocentric" to explain from where it was derived.

Lecture 07-07

p.159

M Professor: In our last few minutes, let me discuss one more thing before we call it a day. I'd like to examine that role that biofilm plays in various environments. And by biofilm, er, I'm not talking about a movie biography of a famous person. If you want to study that, Professor Ford's cinema class is right down the hall. [16]The biofilm we're studying is a thin sheet of biological matter which clings to the surface of something that can be either natural or manmade. Biofilm can be found in virtually any natural environment, but it requires moisture, uh, like water, to survive. **As for manmade environments, biofilm has been observed on pipes, shower walls, glass windows, and the bottoms of ships, to name just a few places.**

Biofilm is formed of biological matter. It's mostly bacteria although other microorganisms, including fungi and algae, may be present at times. These microorganisms initially attach themselves to surfaces at random. They can cling to these surfaces due to something known as a van der Waal's force. As the microorganisms remain attached to the surface, they begin to change. They develop their own ways of clinging to the surface of the structure. Soon, they attract other microorganisms, and, over time, a layer builds up. The biofilm constantly adds new layers. All of these are very thin and are practically invisible to the naked eye.

While the layers are increasing in number, they excrete a substance called EPS. That stands for extracellular polymeric substance. The EPS connects the individual microorganisms to one another and allows them to sort of, uh, communicate with each other. Not by talking of course. But they communicate biologically. For instance, the upper layers of the biofilm assume a greater importance than the other layers as they assume protective duties. They maintain something of a defensive shield until a new layer builds up. Then, that new layer takes over the defensive role.

It should come as no surprise to you that most biofilm is harmful and can be blamed for many of the infections that people get as well as the spread of various illnesses. Because of the protective upper level of the biofilm, the microorganisms beneath that top layer can survive even the toughest antibacterial lotions and disinfectants that people apply to try to kill them. In fact, some studies suggest that after, um, over time, some biofilm develops a resistance to antibacterial cleaning products. As a result, in some cases, biofilm actually clings to supposedly sterile medical equipment, restaurant tables, household pipes, and other places of importance. [17]This can result in a person being infected by biofilm even in places such as hospital operating rooms.

W Student: Are you trying to say that biofilm is everywhere? Even in the cleanest homes and hospitals?

M: **No, not at all. I had no intention of implying that.** I am, however, saying that biofilm is present in some of those places. But biofilm is most assuredly not found on every surface. Please also note that not all biofilm is fatal . . . or even dangerous for that matter. For example, um, take dental plaque. It's classified as a biofilm. Yet, if it were fatal, I don't think any of us would be alive, would we? And remember that the human body has numerous ways to protect itself against infections.

All right. So we've established that biofilm isn't always deadly. However, its effects are costly. Every year, billions of dollars worldwide are lost due to biofilm. Here are a few ways that happens . . . Biofilm can grow on plants, so it causes diseases that can wipe out entire fields of crops. It can cause damage to pipes and other kinds of equipment. It causes the equipment to corrode, so pipes may burst for instance. Biofilm can also form of the bottoms of ships. When that happens, the biofilm attracts other organisms such as barnacles. As barnacles begin to accumulate on a ship's hull, the speed of the ship can be reduced significantly. This causes the ship to burn more fuel, which is an extra expense for the owner. Because of biofilm, ships need to be put in dry dock at times so that their bottoms can be scrubbed clean of these organisms. Oh, biofilm can also reduce the structural integrity of a ship's hull, which thereby reduces the ship's lifetime.

Interestingly, not all biofilm is bad. Some can actually be useful. At sewage treatment plants, for example, biofilm is purposely grown on filters through which raw sewage passes. The biofilm extracts the organic material from the sewage, which helps to, uh, break it down. Likewise, some biofilm is used to clean up oil spills in the ocean. The bacteria in some biofilm can degrade the hydrocarbon molecules in oil, thereby removing it from the water. As you would expect, scientists are working hard to come up with other ways to utilize biofilm.

12 **Making Inferences Question** | At the beginning of the lecture, the professor tells the class, "In our last few minutes, let me discuss one more thing before we call it a day." So he implies that the class is going to end soon.

13 **Detail Question** | The professor remarks, "While the layers are increasing in number, they excrete a substance called EPS. That stands for extracellular polymeric substance. The EPS connects the individual microorganisms to one another and allows them to sort of, uh, communicate with each other."

14 **Connecting Content Question** | The professor notes, "In fact, some studies suggest that after, um, over time, some biofilm develops a resistance to antibacterial cleaning products. As a result, in some cases, biofilm actually clings to supposedly sterile medical equipment, restaurant tables, household pipes, and other places of importance." So it is likely that if the same disinfectant is applied to biofilm for a long period of time, the biofilm will become resistant to it.

15 **Detail Question** | The professor informs the class, "Likewise, some biofilm is used to clean up oil spills in the ocean. The bacteria in some biofilm can degrade the hydrocarbon molecules in oil, thereby removing it from the water."

16 **Understanding Attitude Question** | When the professor says, "to name just a few places," he means that he has not told the students everywhere where biofilm may exist.

17 **Understanding Function Question** | When the professor says, "I had no intention of implying that," he is trying to reduce the student's level of concern since she sounds very worried.

TOEFL® MAP
ACTUAL TEST

New TOEFL® Edition

Michael A. Putlack
Stephen Poirier
Angela Maas
Maximilian Tolochko

Listening 1

Translations

DARAKWON

TOEFL® MAP
ACTUAL TEST

New TOEFL® Edition

Listening 1

Translations

DARAKWON

Actual Test 01

PART 1

Conversation p.16

학생: Higgins 교수님, 약속이 2시라는 점은 알고 있지만, 어, 조금 일찍 와도 괜찮은 거죠? 안 되나요?

교수: 물론 되죠, Allen. 10분 일찍 오는 것은 상관없어요. 게다가 학생이 오기를 기다리고 있던 중이라서 지금 온 것이 제게는 도움이 되는 걸요.

학생: 다행이군요. 감사합니다.

교수: 좋아요… 학생이 어제 수업 후에 오늘 만나자고 요청을 했죠. 정확히 무엇에 관해 이야기를 해야 하나요? 수업 내용을 이해하는데 문제라도 있나요?

학생: 오, 전혀 그렇지 않아요. 아시겠지만, 이번 수업은 꽤 어려워서 결국 수강 신청을 철회하게 될지도 모른다고 생각했는데, 수업 내용을 상당히 잘 이해하고 있는 편이에요.

교수: 제 기억이 맞는다면 학생은 중간고사에서 97점을 받았기 때문에 학생의 말에 동의할 수밖에 없겠네요. 그러면 수업 내용은 아니군요. 그렇다면, 어, 무엇이죠?

학생: 보고서입니다.

교수: 보고서요?

학생: 네, 기말에 제출해야 하는 중요한 보고서요. 이미 주제는 정해 놓았고, 이제 조사를 하려고 하고 있어요.

교수: 잘 되었군요. 저는 학생들이 의욕을 보이는 것이 좋아요.

학생: 어, 감사합니다. 막판까지 기다렸다가 보고서를 쓰고 싶지는 않아서요. 2년 전 신입생 때 그렇게 하려다가… 오. 얼마나 결과가 좋지 못했는지 믿지 못하실 거예요.

교수: 사실 믿을 수도 있을 것 같아요. 제가 지도를 담당하고 있는 학생이 몇 명 있는데, 매 학기마다 그런 일들이 일어나는 걸 보게 되죠. 다행히 그 중 일부는 문제를 깨닫고 정신을 차리지만요. 학생도 그런 것 같군요.

학생: 저도 그렇게 믿고 싶어요. 1학년 때 이후로 성적이 꾸준히 상승했거든요. 어쨌든, 어, 보고서 이야기로 돌아가시죠.

교수: 그래요.

학생: 저는 아프리카의 대형 포유 동물들의 이동 패턴에 초점을 맞추기로 했어요. 아시겠지만, 날씨 패턴에 따라 어떻게 이동을 하는지… 이동 중 어떤 문제들에 직면하는지… 어디에서 새끼를 낳고 기르는지… 그런 것들이죠. 하지만, 어…

교수: 너무 많군요, 그렇지 않나요?

학생: 맞아요.

교수: 우선, Allen, 학생의 의욕이 높은 것은 좋아요. 하지만 학생이 제시하려는 것은 10페이지짜리 보고서가 아니라 박사 과정의 논문처럼 들리는군요. 대학원에 갈 생각이라면 그것을 1년짜리 프로젝트를 위한 연구 과정으로 삼을 수 있을 거예요. 하지만 제 수업에서 그러한 주제로 보고서를 쓰려면 정말로 종합적인 접근을 해야 할 거예요. 그리고 그건 제가 바라는 것이 아니에요.

학생: 그러면 제가 어떻게 해야 할까요?

교수: 쉬워요. 주제를 좁히도록 해요. 우선 이동하는 하나의 동물에만 초점을 맞춰 봐요. 어떤 동물인지는 상관없어요. 하나만 선택해요. 그 다음에는 이동 습성 중 한 가지 측면만을 살펴봐요. 그 후에는 그에 대해 최대한 깊이 조사하고요.

학생: 좋아요. 이해가 가는군요.

교수: 어떤 동물을 선택할 건지 알고 있나요? 그러면 제가 학생의 조사에 확실히 도움이 될 몇 권의 책을 추천해 줄 수 있어요.

학생: 아직 확실한 것은 아니지만 염두에 둔 동물은 두어 개 있어요. 그에 대해 생각을 해 보고 내일 수업 후에 말씀을 드릴게요. 그때, 교수님께서 괜찮으시면, 조사 자료에 관해서 교수님의 도움을 받도록 할게요.

WORD REMINDER

schedule 예정하다 drop 들리다 wind up -ing 결국 ~으로 끝나다 assessment 주장, 진술 turn in 제출하다 initiative 솔선, 진취적 기상 last minute 최후의 순간, 막바지 work out 결국 ~이 되다 advisee (지도 교수의) 과목 선택의 지도를 받는 학생 see the light 묘안을 얻다 shape up 발전하다 encounter 우연히 만나다 overwhelming 압도적인 master's thesis 박사 논문 graduate school 대학원 pare down 줄이다, 절감하다 positive 확실한 pick one's brain ~의 지혜를 빌리다

Lecture • Environmental Science p.18

교수: 전 세계 바다의 해수면은 매일 올라갔다가 내려갑니다. 이러한 활동은, 여러분들이 이미 확실히 알고 있는 것처럼, 조수라고 불립니다. 일반적으로 조수는 하루에 두 번 발생하지만, 일부 지역에서는 하루에 한 번만 일어날 수도 있습니다. 조수는 보통 여러 시간에 걸쳐 일어납니다. 해수면이 올라가기 시작할 때나 내려가기 시작할 때는 조수의 변조라고 불립니다. 조수가 올라가고 내려가는데 걸리는 시간은 지역에 따라 다르지만, 방금 말씀을 드렸다시피, 대부분의 지역에서 하루에 네 차례의 변화를 겪습니다. 또한 한 차례의 썰물이 다른 썰물보다 수위가 낮으면 이를, 어, 저저조라고 부릅니다. 아시겠죠…? 좋습니다.

그러면, 어, 왜 조수가 발생할까요…? 조수는 중력 때문에 일어납니다. 달은 지구의 조수에 커다란 영향을 끼칩니다. 생각해 보세요… 달의 중력이 지구를 달 쪽으로 끌어당기지만 성공하지는 못합니다. 하지만 지구의 물은 지구의 나머지 부분만큼 저항력이 높지가 않습니다. 따라서 물은 달 쪽으로 이동합니다. 물론, 어, 지구도 자체적인 중력을 갖고 있기 때문에 물이 우주로 솟구쳐 올라가지는 않고, 중력으로 인해 물은 계속해서 지구에 남아 있게 됩니다. 그럼에도 불구하고 물에 미치는 달의 중력은 해안가 지방에서 뚜렷하게 볼 수 있으며, 이는 조수의 형태로 드러납니다.

태양 또한 달과 거의 동일한 방식으로 조수를 일으킵니다. 그러나, 태양의 크기가 더 크지만, 달이 지구에 훨씬 더 가까이 있다는 사실 때문에 지구의 조수에는 달이 더 큰 영향을 미칩니다. 혹시 궁금하실 것 같아 말씀을 드리면, 지구의 조수에 미치는 태양 중력의 영향은 달 중력의 영향의 50퍼센트보다 작습니다. 하지만 이 둘이 같은 방향에 있으면 조수에 엄청난 영향을 미칠 수 있습니다. 예를 들겠습니다… 보름달이나 초승달이 뜨면, 달, 태양, 그리고 지구가 모두 같은 방향에 있습니다. 즉, 어, 모두가 일직선 상에 있는 것이죠. 이러한 때에는 달과 태양의 중력이 합쳐져 매달 가장 높이가 높은 조수가 만들어집니다. 이를 한사리라고 부르며, 이는 한 달에 두 번 발생합니다.

학생: 질문이 있습니다. 초승달과 보름달 사이의 중간쯤에는, 어, 조수의 높이가 더 낮다는 의미인가요?

교수: 상당히 빨리 알아차렸군요, Melissa. 그래요, 달의 네 단계 중 첫 번째와 세 번째 단계에서 등장하는, 태양과 달이 약 90도를 이루는 시기에는 조수가 크게 변하지 않습니다. 이를 소조라고 부르며, 이 역시 한 달에 두 번 나타납니다. 또 다른 질문이 있나요?

학생: 네, 있습니다. 소조와 한사리, 그리고 보통의 조수들 간의 수면의 높이 차이는 어느 정도인가요?

교수: 음… 그 질문에는 간단히 대답할 수가 없군요. 대략, 오, 말하자면, 약 20퍼센트 정도 차이가 난다고 할 수 있을 것 같아요. 하지만 지역에 따라 수위가 다르기 때문에 정확한 수치는 아닙니다. 그 이유는 조수에 영향을 미치는 다른 힘들도 있기 때문입니다. 예를 들면… 지구의 회전, 자전축의 기울기, 해저의 상태, 해류, 해수면의 깊이, 그리고 해안가의 형태가 있습니다. 이러한 모든 요인들이 만조와 간조의 높이에 영향을 미칩니다. 오, 그래요, 그리고 달이 지구를 회전하면서 이들 간의 거리가 약간씩 달라진다는 점을 기억하세요. 달이 지구와 얼마나 가까이에 있는지, 혹은 얼마나 멀리 떨어져 있는지에 따라 조수에 미치는 달의 영향이 달라질 수 있습니다.

해안가의 형태가 조수에 어떻게 영향을 미칠 수 있는지 살펴봅시다. 스크린의 여기 위쪽에 캐나다 노바스코샤의 펀디 만의 한 항구의 모습이 있습니다. 시간의 경과를 나타내기 위해 속도를 빠르게 한 이 동영상에서 볼 수 있는 것처럼 조수의 변화가 얼마나 급격한지에 주목해 주십시오. 일부 지역에서는 거의 20미터의 차이가 나는데, 이는 세계에서 가장 큰 폭의 조수의 변화 중 하나입니다. 조수가 얼마나 크게 변하는지 보세요… 놀랍습니다, 그렇지 않나요?

자, 이 펀디 만의 지도를 보세요. 펀디 만이 기다랗고 폭이 좁다는 점과 깔때기처럼 생겼다는 점에 주목하세요. 이것이 바로 조수의 높이가 그처럼 높은 이유입니다. 이곳에 중력이 미칠 때 만에 있는 물은 빠져 나갈 곳이 없습니다. 물이 넓은 대양으로 나갈 수가 없기 때문에 높이가 매우 높은 조수가 만들어집니다.

학생: 그곳에는 틀림없이 많은 조력 발전소들이 있겠군요.

교수: 그렇게 생각할 수도 있겠지만 제가 알기로는 펀디 만에 단 한 기의 소규모 조력 발전소만 있습니다. 발전소가 환경에 부정적인 영향을 미칠 수 있다는 일부 사람들의 우려 때문에 대규모 발전소들은 아직까지 지어지지 않고 있습니다. 보다 빨리 공사가 시작되면 좋겠군요. 조력은 저렴하고 깨끗하죠. 어쨌든 그에 대한 이야기로 주의를 돌리고 싶지는 않습니다. 조수에 대한 논의로 되돌아갑시다.

WORD REMINDER

turning of the tide 조수의 변조 lower low tide 저저조 resistant 저항하는, 저항력이 있는 spiral 솟아 오르다 manifest 명백해지다 in conjunction 함께 be lined up 일직선이 되다 spring tide 한사리 neap tide 소조 estimate 추산하다, 추정하다 figure 수치 play a role 역할을 하다 orbit 궤도를 따라 돌다 funnel 깔때기 tidal power 조력 get distracted 주위가 산만해지다

PART 2

Conversation

p.22

학생: Dave 조교님, 조교님과 이야기해야 할 문제가 두어 가지 있어요. 일이 분 정도 시간을 내 주실 수 있나요?

기숙사 조교: 물론이죠, Susan. 무엇을 도와 줄까요?

학생: 음, 어, 이틀 후인 추수감사절 휴일에 집에 가려고 계획 중이에요. 여름 방학 때에는 여기에서 수업을 듣느라 집에 갈 기회가 없었고, 부모님들께서는 정말로 단 며칠 동안이라도 저를 보고 싶어하시죠. 어쨌든 모든 가족들이, 고모들과 삼촌들을 포함해서, 올해 모이게 될 거예요.

기숙사 조교: 잘 되었군요. 그런 이야기를 들으니 기쁘네요.

학생: 그래요, 그렇기 때문에, 어, 수요일 오전에 공항으로 가서 비행기를 타려고 해요. 하지만 아시다시피 공항은 학교에서 꽤 멀리 떨어져 있잖아요.

기숙사 조교: 확실히 그렇죠. 저기, 제 차로 거기까지 데려다 주겠다는 제안을 하고는 싶지만 제가 화요일 밤에 집으로 가야 해서, 학생이 공항에서 밤을 보내기를 원치 않는 경우, 제가 도움을 줄 수는 없을 것 같아요.

학생: 오, 조교님도 집에 가시는군요? 가시는 줄 모르고 있었어요.

기숙사 조교: 저도 가족들을 본지가 한참 되었기 때문에 집에 가야 할 것 같았어요. 하지만 제가 거의 이 나라의 반대편에서 살고 있기 때문에 그곳에 도착하려면 야간 비행편을 이용해야만 하죠.

학생: 잘 되었군요. 어쨌든, 제안은 고맙지만 저는 수요일 오전에 공항으로 갈 거예요. 그래서, 어, 이제 질문을 할게요.

기숙사 조교: 어떤 질문이요?

학생: 공항까지 가는 버스가 있나요? 제 말은, 보통 친구 중 한 명과 함께 그곳에 가지만 제가 아는 사람 중 누구도 저와 같은 시간에 공항에 갈 사람은 없더군요. 그리고 택시로 공항까지 가는데 40달러 정도 들 수 있다고 들었어요. 제 예산의 범위를 벗어나는 금액이죠.

기숙사 조교: 실은, 캠퍼스에서 출발해서 공항까지 직행으로 가는 버스가 한 대 있어요.

학생: 그럴 리가요. 농담 아니시죠?

기숙사 조교: 그에 관해서는 농담할 생각 없어요. 새로 생긴 서비스죠. 그래서 아마도 학생이 들어보지 못했을 거예요. 학생 서비스 빌딩에서 출발해요. 그곳에 가면 직원에게서 버스 시간표를 받을 수 있을 거예요.

학생: 정말 잘 되었군요. 전혀 모르고 있었어요. 알려 주셔서 정말 고마워요.

기숙사 조교: 천만에요.

학생: 오, 잠깐만요. 그러면 그 버스가 다시 공항에서 학생들을 태워서 학교로 데려다 주나요?

기숙사 조교: 맞아요. 하지만 몇 시에 돌아올 예정이죠?

학생: 일요일 자정을 조금 넘긴 시간에요. 왜 물으시죠?

기숙사 조교: 아, 버스는 밤 11시에 운행을 중단해요. 학교로 돌아오기 위해서는 택시나 기차 중 하나를 타야 할 거예요. 모르고 있는 경우를 위해 미리 말을 하면, 기차는 밤새 운행하지만 오후 10시 이후에는 운행 횟수가 줄어들어요.

학생: 알겠어요. 알려 줘서 고마워요. 나중에 학생 서비스 빌딩에 가서 버스표를 예매할 수 있는지 등에 대해 알아볼게요. 그리고 기차 시간표도 알아보고 어떻게 하면 이곳으로 돌아올 수 있는지도 알아볼게요.

기숙사 조교: 문제 없을 거예요. 오, 그리고 학생이 떠나기 전에 학생을 보지 못할 경우를 대비해서 미리 말하자면, 휴일 잘 보내요.

WORD REMINDER

head 향하다, 가다 redeye 야간 비행편 pull one's leg 속이다, 놀리다 make a reservation 예약하다 figure out 알아내다

Lecture • Physics

p.24

교수: 레이저는 더 이상 공상 과학 소설이나 공상 과학 영화에서만 볼 수 있는 상상 속의 존재가 아닙니다. 오늘날 레이저는 실제로 존재하며 다양한 방법으로 이용되고 있습니다. 예를 들어 몇 가지의 용도만 말하자면, CD 및 DVD 플레이어, 여러 가지의 유형의 수술, 그리고 전자 통신의 전송 과정에서 레이저가 사용되고 있습니다.

레이저란 무엇일까요? 레이저는 일종의 빛이지만, 한 방향으로만 나아가는 빛입니다. 또한 레이저의 모든 빛 입자들은 하나의 색을 띠는데, 이는 빛 입자들이 동일한 파장을 가지고 있다는 점을 의미합니다. 아시다시피 어떤 것이 하나의 색을 띨 때에는 단색성을 갖는다고 말합니다. 레이저가 만들어지는 과정에 대해 이야기를 하면… 음, 레이저는 광자가 자극을 받아 방출된 결과입니다. 광자에 어떤 일이 일어나는지는… 어, 광자란 빛의 기본 단위인데… 광자가 여기 상태에 있는 원자와 부딪치게 됩니다. 이로써 원자는 또 다른 광자를 방출하게 되는데, 이 광자는 첫 번째 광자와 동일합니다. 두 광자는 같은 방향으로 이동합니다. 이들은 다른 원자들과 충돌해서 더 많은 광자들이 방출됩니다. 그 다음에는 일종의 연쇄 반응이 일어나 레이저 빔이 만들어집니다. 이것이 실제 우리가 레이저라는 명칭을 사용하는 이유입니다. 유도 방출 복사에 의한 빛의 증폭(light amplification by stimulated emission of radiation)의 머리글자를 딴 것이죠. 스펠링은 L-A-S-E-R입니다. Janice, 손을 든 건가요?

학생: 네, 교수님. 누가 레이저를 — 아마 발명했다고 해야 할 것 같기도 한데 — 발견했나요?

교수: 좋은 질문이군요. 흠… 레이저에 숨겨진 원칙들은 1917년 알버트 아인슈타인의 논문에서 처음으로 소개되었습니다. 그 후 전 세계의 몇몇 과학자들이 실제 레이저를 만드는 연구를 했지만, 1960년대가 되어서야 최초의 레이저가 만들어졌습니다. 미국에서 만들어졌지만 한 사람이 만들어 낸 것은 아니었어요. 대신 여러 사람들과 Bell Labs라는 기업이 레이저를 실제로 만드는데 중요한 역할을 했습니다. 실제 레이저를 만드는데 있어서 그들이 직면했던 주된 문제는 먼저 원자를 여기 상태로 만드는 것과 그 다음에 광자들을 한 방향으로 위치시키는 방법을 찾아내는 것이었습니다. 아시다시피, 어, 하나의 물질에 낮은 에너지 상태에 있는 원자보다 여기 상태에 있는 원자가 더 많으면 소위 반전 분포가 만들어집니다. 이 여기 상태에 있는 원자들을 반전 분포로 가져가기 위해서는 전기와 같은 동력원뿐만 아니라 이득 매체가 들어 있는 광공진기도 필요합니다. 이해가 가나요…?

학생: 죄송하지만, 교수님, 전혀 알아들을 수가 없어요.

교수: 좋아요… 여러분 중 몇몇이 약간 혼란스러워 하는 것처럼 보이는군요. 그러면 여러분들을 위해 이들 용어를 설명해 드리죠. 먼저, 광공진기입니다. 이것은 단순히 폐쇄된 공간입니다. 광공진기 내부에는 이득 매체라 불리는 것이 들어 있습니다. 원자들이 반전 분포 단계에 들어갈 수 있도록 원자들로 하여금 에너지를 증가시키도록 만드는 물질입니다. 전형적인 물질로는 크리스탈, 기체, 그리고 특별한 종류의 유리가 있습니다. 광공진기에는 또한 두 개 이상의 거울이 들어 있는데, 이들은 이득 매체를 통해 빛을 서로 반사시켜 원자가 여기 상태에 들어가 광자를 방출하도록 만듭니다. 광공진기의 한 쪽 면은 다른 쪽에 비해 보다 투명합니다. 이러한 면은 집광된 광선이 — 바로 레이저죠 — 광공진기로부터 방출되는 방향이 됩니다. 이러한 신기한 장치 전체에는 동력원이 필요한데, 거의 대부분 전기가 사용됩니다. 이 에너지원은 에너지 펌프라고 불리며 에너지를 적용시키는 과정은 펌핑이라고 불립니다. 이제 모두들 이해가 가나요…? 그럼 계속하죠.

중요한 점으로서 에너지 펌프가 충분치 않다면 레이저는 발진되지 않을 것입니다. 왜냐고요? 음, 이득 매체를 통과하는 빛이 충분한 여기 상태를 만들어 내지 못해서 충분한 수의 원자가 반전 분포에 이르지 못하기 때문입니다. 간단히 말해, 충분한 에너지가 광공진기로 펌핑되지 못하면 레이저 빔이 발진되지 않을 것입니다. 레이저를 발진시킬 수 있을 정도의 충분한 에너지가 있는 상태를 레이저 동작 임계치라고 부릅니다. 그건 그렇고, 레이저 동작 임계치는 어떤 종류의 이득 매체가 사용되느냐에 따라 달라집니다. 그리고 아시겠지만, 제가 설명한 모든 것들은 극도로 빠르게 이루어집니다… 실제로 눈 깜짝할 사이죠.

많은 종류의 레이저가 존재하며, 레이저는 여러 가지 방법으로 만들어집니다. 레이저의 강도는 증가시키거나 감소시킬 수 있습니다. 또한 이동 거리에 따라서도 달라집니다. 예를 들면, 짧은 거리에서는 대부분의 레이저 빔이 연필만큼 얇은 형태로 집광되며 강도가 꽤 높습니다. 보다 긴 거리에서는 동일한 빔이라도 빛이 산란되어 보다 폭이 넓어지는데, 이로써 강도는 더 약해집니다. 또한 레이저는 연속적일 수도 있고, 짧은 폭을 가질 수도 있습니다. 연속파 레이저 빔은 끊김없이 작동하는 반면, 펄스 레이저 빔은 일정한 간격으로 끊어집니다.

오늘, 제가 몇 분 전에 알려 드린 대로, 레이저는 다양한 방법으로 이용되고 있습니다. 열을 발생시킬 수 있기 때문에 수술이나 산업에서 절단 기구로 사용될 수 있습니다. 하지만 오늘날 가장 일반적으로 사용되는 레이저는 레이저 다이오드입니다. 전기 장치에서 사용되는 작고 단순한 형태의 레이저이죠. 이제 이러한 전기 장치 중 하나의 작동 방식에 대해 짧게 설명을 드리도록 하겠습니다.

WORD REMINDER

exclusively 배타적으로, 독점적으로 reality 실체 a multitude of 다수의 to name but a few 몇 가지만 예를 들면 wavelength 파장 monochromatic 단색의 photon 광자 excited state 여기(勵起) 상태 chain reaction 연쇄 반응 acronym 두문자어, 약어 population inversion 반전 분포 optical cavity 광학 동공, 광공 진기 gain medium 이득 매체 go over one's head 키가 넘는 물속에 들어가다, 힘이 미치지 못하다 contraption 새 고안물, 기묘한 장치 simply put 간단히 말해서 lasing threshold 레이저 동작 임계치 diffuse 방산되다, 흩어지다 pulse 맥이 뛰다, 고동하다

PART 3

Conversation

p.28

교수: Jeff, 오늘 오전 수업이 끝날 무렵에 저와 이야기해야 한다고 말했죠. 무슨 일인가요?

학생: 오늘 수업에서 강의하신 내용 중에 약간 혼란스러운 부분이 있는 것 같아서요.

교수: 그래요? 그게 무엇인가요?

학생: 수업 중 외래종과 침입종에 대해 말씀하신 부분이었어요. 제가 제대로 기억하고 있다면 교수님께서는 소와 닭이 외래종이라고 말씀하셨죠. 음… 그것이 어떻게 가능한가요? 외래종이란, 어, 열대 지방 같은 곳에서 온 식물이나 동물들로 알고 있었거든요.

교수: 아, 어떤 부분이 혼란스러운지 알겠군요. 그래요, 많은 사람들이 외래종의 식물이나 동물을 열대의 섬과 같이 멀리 떨어진 곳에서 온 존재라고 말하죠.

학생: 맞아요.

교수: 하지만 그것이 과학적인 정의는 아니에요.

학생: 그러면 과학적인 정의가 무엇인가요?

교수: 간단해요. 외래종이란 원산지가 아닌 지역으로 유입된 동물과…

학생: 잠깐만요. 그건 침입종이라고 알고 있었는데요.

교수: 끝까지 들어보세요, Jeff.

학생: 어… 죄송해요. 말씀하세요.

교수: 외래종은 원산지 밖의 생태계로 유입된 것이에요. 하지만 — 매우 중요한 점인데 — 그 생태계에 해를 끼치지는 않죠. 침입종에 대해 말하자면, 음, 이들은 새로운 지역으로 유입된 식물과 동물, 혹은 기타 유기물로서 일정한 방식으로 해를 끼쳐요. 침입종이 해를 끼칠 수 있는 이유는 이들에게 천적이 없기 때문인데, 이로써 칩임종은 매우 빠르게 번식할 수가 있어요. 칡과 같은 식물의 경우, 이들은 어디에서나 자랄 수 있기 때문에 토종 식물들을 전멸시킬 수도 있죠.

학생: 오… 그러면 교수님께서 소와 닭이 외래종이라고 말씀하셨을 때 이들이 원산지가 아닌 곳에서 현재 살고 있다는 의미였군요. 맞나요?

교수: 정확해요.

학생: 알겠어요, 이해가 가는군요. 그 밖의 외래종도 말씀해 주실 수 있나요?

교수: 물론이죠. 고양이와 개도 외래종이에요. 어, 식물의 사례도 알고 싶다면 파리지옥풀도 외래종이죠.

학생: 그러면 침입종은요?

교수: 조금 전에 침입종으로 칡을 언급했어요. 거대한 크기의 뱀인 버마왕뱀은 플로리다 에버글레이드에 커다란 위협이 되고 있죠. 빠르게 번식을 해서 그곳 토종 동물들을 몰살시키고 있어요. 사실, 어, 그것을 주제로 학생이 중간고사용 보고서를 쓰면 좋을 것 같아요, Jeff. 외래종과 침입종을 비교했으면 해요. 각각 두 개를 고른 후 그들이 유입된 곳에 어떠한 영향을 끼치고 있는지에 대해 써 보세요. 그들이 새로운 환경의 토종 생물이 아니기 때문에, 혹시 있다면, 우리가 그에 대해 할 수 있는 일이 무엇인지에 대해서도 잊지 말고 제안해 보세요.

학생: 좋을 것 같아요, 교수님. 설명해 주셔서 정말 고맙습니다. 시간을 내주셔서 명확히 알려 주신 점에 대해 정말 고맙게 생각해요.

교수: 천만에요. 다른 질문이 있으면 주저하지 말고 제게 이메일을 보내도록 해요. 제가 댈러스에서 열리는 컨퍼런스에 참석할 예정이라 주 후반에는 교내에 없을 거예요. 실은 몇 분 후에 공항으로 출발해야만 하죠.

학생: 오, 기다리게 해서 죄송해요. 다음 주 수업에서 뵐게요. 다시 한번 감사드립니다.

WORD REMINDER

exotic species 외래종 invasive species 침입종 tropics 열대 refer to A as B A를 B로 지칭하다 ecosystem 생태계 kudzu 칡 Venus flytrap 파리지옥풀 Burmese python 버마왕뱀 menace 위협, 위협적인 존재 wipe out ~을 파괴하다, 몰살시키다

Lecture • History

p.30

교수: 오늘날 아일랜드는 독립국이지만, 한때는 전 영토가 대영 제국에 속해 있었습니다. 이 섬은 1801년 연합법에 의해 공식적으로 영국의 일부가 되었습니다. 그 전에는 아일랜드에 자체 의회가 있었지만, 연합법이 통과된 후 아일랜드 의회는 폐쇄되었고, 아일랜드인들은 영국 의회의 의원 선출권을 얻게 되었습니다. 그 다음 세기에 걸쳐, 아일랜드에 소위 자치권을 부여하려는 다양한 시도들이 이루어졌습니다. 이는 기본적으로 아일랜드 의회가 복원될 것이며, 그 결과 아일랜드인들에게 어느 정도의 자치권이 부여될 것이라는 점을 의미했습니다. 안타깝지만 자치권 확보를 위한 모든 시도는 실패로 끝났습니다. 이는 결국 아일랜드 내의 보다 급진적인 세력들로 하여금 무장 봉기를 일으켜 아일랜드에서 영국인들을 쫓아내도록 만들었습니다.

자유를 위한 아일랜드인들의 투쟁 중에서 가장 중요한 사건은 1차 세계 대전이 정점에 이르렀던 1916년에 일어났습니다. 이는 '부활절 반란' 혹은 '부활절 봉기'로 알려지게 되었습니다. 1916년 4월 24일, 부활절이었던 월요일에 아일랜드 민족주의자들이 수도인 더블린에서 몇 군데의 중요한 거점을 장악했습니다. 그 후 7일 동안 영국이 통제력을 되찾을 때까지 더블린 각지에서 전투가 벌어졌습니다. 즉각적인 결과로 반란은 진압되었고, 반란 지도자들은 붙잡혀, 많은 경우, 반역죄로 사형을 받았으며, 아일랜드의 독립의 기회는 사라진 것처럼 보였습니다. 하지만 부활절 봉기는 아일랜드 내의 독립 운동에 불을 붙였고 이는 곧 보다 큰 규모의 독립 전쟁으로 이어졌는데, 이로 인해 아일랜드 민족주의자들은 1922년까지 대부분의 목적을 달성하게 되었습니다.

1916년 부활절 봉기에 대해 말을 하면… 많은 파벌들이 관련되어 있었습니다. 너무나 많아서 일일이 나열한다면 여러분들은 엄청난 양의 이름과 조직 속에서 헤어나오지 못할 것입니다. 그 이야기로 여러분들을 어지럽게 만들지는 않겠습니다. 이들 모든 파벌들이 서로 협력한 것은 아니며, 모든 파벌들이 부활절 봉기에 관여한 것도 아니었다는 점만 말씀드리도록 하죠. 흥미롭게도 이러한 단체 중 다수가 독일의 도움을 구했습니다. 1차 세계 대전 때 독일은 다른 나라 중에서도 특히 영국과 싸우고 있었기 때문에, 유럽 본토로부터 영국의 주의를 돌리기 위해 독일인들이 아일랜드 문제에 개입한 것은 신중한 행동으로 비춰졌다는 점을 기억하세요. 따라서 독일인들은 무기와, 무기를 아일랜드까지 운반할 수 있는 선박을 제공해 주었습니다. 독일인들과 아일랜드 민족주의자들은 모르고 있었지만, 영국인들은 독일의 비밀 암호를 해독하여 그 선박이 아일랜드로 향하고 있다는 점을 알아냈습니다. 4월 20일 영국 해군이 이 선박을 나포했으나 항구에 닿을 때쯤 승무원들이 배를 침몰시켜 버렸습니다. 확실하게 무기들은 배와 함께 바닷속으로 가라앉았죠.

이러한 손실은 아일랜드인들로 하여금 사실상 자신들의 계획을 포기하게 만들었지만, 어쨌든 아일랜드인들은 계속 밀고 나갔습니다. 4월 23일 부활절 일요일에서 그 다음날로 행동을 늦출 뿐이었죠. 바로 그날, 약 1,200명의 무장 병력들이, 우체국을 포함하여, 더블린의 중요 지역들을 장악했고, 우체국은 그들의 사령부가 되었습니다. 그 후 아일랜드 민족주의자들은 아일랜드 공화국의 독립을 선포했습니다. 하지만 아일랜드인들은 중요한 한 곳을 얻는데 실패했습니다: 바로 더블린 성이었죠. 이곳은 아일랜드 전체에서 영국의 권력이 집중되어 있던 곳으로, 영국에 대한 증오의 상징으로 여겨졌습니다. 성을 지킴으로써 영국은 더블린에서 어느 정도의 통제력을 유지할 수 있었습니다.

학생: 반란이 일어나고 있다는 점을 영국인들이 알고 있지 않았나요? 독일 선박에 대해 알고 있었으니까 틀림없이 반란에 대해서도 알고 있었을 텐데요.

교수: 음, 무언가 진행되고 있다는 점은 알았지만, 부활절이었기 때문에 그 날은 아무 일도 일어나지 않을 것이라고 생각했어요. 하지만 영국인들이, 독립 운동을 이끄는 것으로 생각되는 많은 사람들을 체포할 계획은 가지고 있었으나, 런던으로부터 체포를 승인하는 명령은 봉기가 이미 시작된 후에야 도착을 했습니다. 그래서, 맞아요, 영국인들은 깜짝 놀랐고, 첫날 있었던 일부 충돌에서, 어, 십자 포화 속에 있던 몇몇 민족주의자들 및 시민들과 함께 많은 영국 군인들이 목숨을 잃었습니다.

그 다음에는 어떤 일이 일어났을까요? 음, 영국인들은 신속하게 폭동을 진압했습니다. 의도치 않게 아일랜드인들의 도움을 받았는데, 이들은 항구 시설 및 주요 기차 역을 장악하지 못했습니다. 분명 반란 지도자들은 군사적인 분야에 대해 많이 알고 있지 못했을 것입니다. 어쨌든 이러한 전술적 실패로 영국인들은 중포병 부대를 포함하여 병력을 증강시킬 수 있었습니다. 지역 사령관이 계엄령을 선포했고, 이후 영국인들은 천천히, 그렇지만 확실하게, 더블린에 대한 통제권을 되찾기 시작했습니다. 이후 며칠 동안 치열한 전투가 벌어졌습니다. 영국인들은 주로 포격으로 아일랜드인들을 격퇴시켰습니다. 보병 간의 전투도 있었는데, 이때는 아일랜드인들이 영국군을 밀어붙이면서 영국군에 수많은 사상자를 안겨다 주었습니다. 하지만 그 다음 일요일에 아일랜드인들은 항복을 해야만 했죠.

많은 아일랜드 지도자들이 목숨을 잃었습니다. 살아남은 사람들은 대부분 포로가 되어 재판을 받은 후 징역형이나 사형에 처해졌습니다. 하지만 반란의 불꽃은 꺼지지 않았습니다. 아일랜드인들은 독립을 쟁취하기 위해 정치적 및 군사적 수단을 모두 사용하려고 했습니다. 이제 그들이 그 다음에 무엇을 했는지에 대해 이야기하도록 하겠습니다.

WORD REMINDER

formally 형식적으로, 공식적으로 parliament 의회 home rule (지방) 자치 autonomy 자치, 자율 radical 급진적인 armed insurrection 무장 봉기 nationalist 민족주의자 seize 포위하다, 붙잡다 reestablish 재건하다, 복구하다 execute 사형을 집행하다 treason 반역 bid 입찰; 기회 doomed 운이 다한, 불운한 fraction 조각, 파편 suffice it to say ~이라고만 말해두자 pit 싸움을 붙이다 among others 그 중에서도 특히 prudent 신중한 code 암호 intercept 가로채다 abandon 폐지하다, 폐기하다 press on (단호하게) 밀고 나아가다 clash 충돌, 대립 crossfire 십자 포화, 교차 사격 suppress 억압하다, 진압하다 tactical 전술적인 reinforcement 지원병, 증원 부대 heavy artillery 중포병 부대 bloody 치열한, 피비린내 나는 wear down 격퇴시키다 casualty 사상자

Lecture • Zoology

p.33

교수: 수백만 년 전 인간과 다른 영장류들이 동일한 조상을 가지고 있었다는 증거는 반박할 수 없는 것처럼 보입니다. 하지만, 우리 인간은 언어를 사용하는 능력을 얻은 반면, 다른 영장류들은 그렇지 못했습니다. 음, 어, 적어도 우리가 이해할 수 있는 어떤 음성적인 커뮤니케이션은 익히지 못했던 것이죠. 하지만 흥미로운 질문을 하나 드리겠습니다. 영장류들은 — 특히 고릴라와 침팬지는 — 인간이 가지고 있는 DNA의 95% 이상을 가지고 있기 때문에 그들이 인간처럼 커뮤니케이션하는 법을 배울 수는 없을까요? 실제로 우리와 의사소통을 할 수 있도록 그들을 가르칠 수도 있지 않을까요? 최근 몇십 년 동안 일부 학자들이 영장류들을 테스트해서, 몇몇 경우, 이들에게 인간과 의사소통을 하는 법을 가르쳤다고 보고했습니다. 그럼에도 불구하고 그 결과에 대해서는 다소 논란의 여지가 있습니다.

영장류들은, 어, 앵무새와 같이 단어를 발음할 수가 없으므로 영장류들이 인간과 어떻게 이야기를 나눌 수 있는지 먼저 설명을 드려야 할 것 같군요. 그 대신 학자들은 의사소통을 하기 위해 두 개의 주요한 방법을 사용합니다. 첫 번째는 수화와 관련이 있습니다. 아시겠지만, 청각 장애인과 언어 장애인들이 다른 사람과 의사소통을 할 때 사용하는 것이죠. 수화는 세 가지 이유 때문에 영장류들과의 커뮤니케이션 수단으로 가장 먼저 제안되었습니다. 첫째, 여러 학자들은 음성 언어를 사용할 정도의 충분한 지능이 영장류에게 없다고 생각했습니다. 둘째, 영장류들은, 인간의 아이들이 그러는 것과 달리, 들은 소리를 흉내 낼 수 없을 것으로 생각한 학자들도 있었죠. 셋째, 학자들은 신체적으로 영장류의 성대가 인간의 발성을 내지 못할 것이라고 생각했습니다. 두 번째 방법에 대해 이야기하면, 이는 그림 문자로 된 키보드를 사용합니다. 그건 그렇고, 그림 문자란 단어를 나타내기 위해 사용되는 기호입니다. 칠판에 두어 개를 적어 보도록 하죠… 이것을 보세요… 이것도요… 여기에 또 있습니다… 이것들이 무엇을 의미하는지 여러분들도 알 수 있으리라 생각합니다. 꽤 간단합니다. 그림 문자는 1970년대 초에 처음으로 만들어진, 비교적 새로운 것입니다. 어쨌든, 그림 문자 키보드를 사용함으로써 — 그림 문자가 들어있는 키보드죠 — 영장류들은 인간과 의사소통을 할 수 있습니다.

학자들은 두 가지 방법 모두에서 성공을 이루었습니다. 두 개의 성공 사례에 대해 말씀을 드리죠. 첫 번째는 Washoe라는 이름의 암컷 침팬지와 관련이 있습니다. 1970년대 초 Washoe는 미식 수화를 익혔습니다. 사육사들은 이 침팬지를 마치 인간의 아이처럼 길렀고, 수화만을 사용했습니다. 말을 하면 침팬지가 혼란스러워하고 수화 학습의 진도가 지체될 수 있다고 생각했기 때문에 사육사들은 Washoe 앞에서 말을 하지 않았습니다. 몇 년간의 훈련 끝에 Washoe는 수화를 사용하기 시작했습니다. 마침내 350개 정도의 단어를 익혔습니다. 흥미롭게도 Washoe는 이들 기호들을 조합하여 사용하는 법도 익히게 되었는데, 이는 결코 가르친 적이 없는 것이었습니다. 그렇게 함으로써 Washoe는 자발적으로 단어를 가지고 문장을 만드는 능력을 보여주었습니다. 얼마 후 Washoe는 때때로 조련사보다 더 빠른 속도로 수화를 할 정도로 수화에 능숙해졌고, 종종 조련사들이 자신의 말을 이해할 수 있도록 자신의 수화 속도를 늦춰야만 했습니다.

Kanzi라는 수컷 보노보 침팬지에 관련된, 현재 진행 중인 실험이 있습니다. Kanzi는 그림 문자 키보드를 사용하여 커뮤니케이션을 합니다. 몇 년 전 한 학자가 Kanzi의 어미에게 그림 문자 키보드의 사용법을 가르치려고 했는데, 이때 Kanzi는 그냥 지켜보고만 있었습니다. 어느 날 Kanzi가, 어, 그림 문자 키보드를 사용하여 커뮤니케이션을 하기 시작했습니다. 빠르게 10개의 단어를 익혔고, 그 이후로 수천 개의 새로운 단어들을 알게 되었습니다. 문장을 만들 수 있고, 지시를 따르고, 심지어는 발성도 합니다. Kanzi와 관련된 최근의 몇몇 연구에 따르면 Kanzi는 키보드에서 한 단어에 해당되는 버튼을 누름과 동시에 발성을 하는데, 그가 만들어내는 발성은 그 특정한 심볼을 나타냅니다.

학생: 죄송하지만, Kanzi가 실제로 말을 하고 있다는 말씀이신가요?

교수: 음, 그래요, 자신만의 특별한 방법으로 하고 있죠. Kanzi를 다루는 연구팀은 그가 영어 단어를 발음하려고 노력 중일 수도 있다고 생각합니다. 하지만 그 음역이 너무 높아서 무슨 말을 하는지는 이해할 수가 없는 것이고요. 만약 그러한 가설이 사실로 판명된다면, 그것은, 음, 영장류와 인간간의 커뮤니케이션에 있어서 주목할 만한 획기적인 사건이 될 것입니다.

많은 사람들이 — 그 중 다수는 언어 학자들인데 — Washoe 및 Kanzi와 같은 사례는 사례일 뿐이라고 주장합니다. 어, 그러니까, 그러한 사례들이 영장류에게는 인간과 같이 의사소통할 수 있는 지능이 없다는 일반 원칙에 대한 예외라는 것이죠. 이러한 주장은 학자들이 가르치려고 했던 다수의 영장류 중 극히 일부만이 커뮤니케이션에 성공했다는 점에서 어느 정도 타당성이 있습니다. 그리고 제가 말씀드린 두 가지 사례는 그 중에서도 가장 성공적인 사례입니다. 일부 회의론자들은 이러한 성공 사례에도 의문을 제기합니다. 이들은 영장류들이 수화나 키보드로 약간의 단어들을 표현할 수는 있지만, 이는 언어를 구사하는 것이라기 보다 자신이 본 행동을 흉내 내는 것일 뿐이라고 주장합니다. 영장류들은, 자신의 생각과 감정을 전달하는 대신, 사육사들을 기쁘게 해 주려고 그렇게 하는 것이라고 주장합니다. 또한 이러한 회의론자들은, 비교적 수월하게 언어를 배우는 인간의 아이들과 비교해 볼 때, 학습 곡선상 영장류들은 상당히 뒤떨어진다는 점에 주목합니다. 그것은

분명 사실입니다. 하지만 이것이 영장류들은 전혀 커뮤니케이션을 할 수 없다는 점을 의미하지는 않습니다. 사실 저는 미래에 Washoe 및 Kanzi와 같은 성공 사례들이 더 많아질 것으로 확신합니다.

WORD REMINDER

irrefutable 반박할 수 없는 verbal 말의 controversial 논란의 여지가 있는 vocalize 목소리로 내다, 발음하다 sign language 손짓 언어, 수화 verbal language 음성 언어 vocal cord 성대 vocalization 발성 lexigram 그림 문자 figure out 알아내다 combination 조합, 결합 spontaneous 자발적인 proficient 능숙한 ongoing 진행 중인 pick up 익히다 instruction 지시 (사항) articulate 분명히 발음하다, 또박또박 말하다 vocal range 음역 breakthrough 획기적인 사건 validity 타당성 the best of the bunch 엄선한 것, 가장 뛰어난 것 skeptic 회의론자, 의심 많은 사람 lag 뒤떨어지다 learning curve 학습 곡선

Actual Test 02

PART 1

Conversation

p.40

학생: Marconi 교수님, 수업 프로젝트에 관한 제 제안을 어떻게 생각하셨나요?

교수: 제안이요? 어떤 제안이요?

학생: 오늘 오전 교수님께 이메일로 보내 드린 것이요. 받지 못하셨나요? 틀림없이 주소가 잘못되었거나 한 것 같아요.

교수: 아, 미안하지만, Kelly, 어젯밤 이후로 이메일을 확인해 보지 못했어요. 일 때문에 정신이 없어서 오늘 인터넷에 접속할 기회가 없었네요. 하지만 학생이 여기에 왔으니까 어떤 제안을 했는지 말해 줄래요? 어떤가요?

학생: 좋아요. 감사합니다.

교수: 그래요. 그러면, 음, 프로젝트에서 무엇을 하고 싶은가요?

학생: 캠퍼스 근처에 새로 생긴 병원을 알고 계시나요?

교수: 어떤 병원이요?

학생: Baker 홀의 맞은 편 거리에 있어요. 병원 이름이 Dr. Brown's Family Health Clinic이죠. 건물 앞에 꽤 커다란 간판이 있어요. 그곳을 지나가신다면 틀림없이 보시게 될 거예요.

교수: 아, 그렇군요. 어떤 병원을 말하는지 알겠어요. 흠… 궁금하군요. 그 병원이 학생의 프로젝트와 어떤 관련이 있죠?

학생: 음, 저는 그 병원이 지역 신문 등 뿐만 아니라 교내에서도 광고를 하고 있다는 점에 주목했어요. 그래서 Dr. Brown's의 마케팅 기법이 정확히 얼마나 효과적인지 살펴보겠다고 생각을 했죠.

교수: 정확히 어떤 기법들인가요?

학생: 우선 환자들이 몸이 좋지 않을 때 예약을 할 필요가 없어요. 바로 찾아가서 몇 분 안에 진찰을 받을 수가 있죠. 또한 병원에서 건강 보험을 인정해 주지는 않지만 진료비가 매우 저렴해요. Brown 의사 선생님 말씀에 따르면, 보험 업무 처리에 필요한 많은 양의 서류 작업을 할 사람들을 고용할 필요가 없기 때문에 그렇게 해도 수익이 날 수 있다고 하더군요.

교수: 흠… 흥미롭게 들리는군요. 그 병원이 얼마나 인기가 많은지 알고 있나요?

학생: 어, 네. 실은 병원에 직접 가 보았어요. 그리고 제가 아는 많은 사람들도 다녀왔고요. 제가 말을 해 본 사람들 모두가 크게 만족해 했어요.

교수: 좋아요. 나중에 저도 직접 확인해 봐야겠군요.

학생: 그러면 제 제안이 괜찮다는 말씀이신가요?

교수: 우선은, 그래요. 하지만 학생이 어떤 식의 접근법을 취할 것인지는 알고 싶어요. 또한 마케팅 기법이 얼마나 효과적이었는지를 알아내기 위해 Brown 선생님과 인터뷰를 할 수 있기를 바라요. 그리고 잊지 말고 가능한 많은 환자들을 — 만족해 하는 환자들과 만족해 하지 않는 환자들 모두 — 인터뷰하세요.

학생: 걱정하지 마세요, 교수님. 제 제안서에 그러한 모든 것들을 어떻게 할 것인지 설명해 두었어요. 그리고 실제로 이번 주말에 Brown 선생님과의 인터뷰 약속도 잡아 두었고요.

교수: 훌륭하군요. 결과가 정말 기대되네요.

학생: 고맙습니다.

교수: 오늘 늦게라도 이메일을 확인해 보고 오늘밤 답장을 해서 확실히 된다, 안 된다를 알려 줄게요. 하지만 그 대답은 '된다'가 될 것 같군요. 또한 학생에게 피드백도 줄게요. 알겠지만, 어, 학생이 물어봐야 할 질문 같은 것에 대한 의견이죠.

학생: 좋아요. 그렇게 해 주시면 정말 좋을 것 같아요. 어쨌든, 음, 그러면 다시 일을 하실 수 있도록 저는 이만 일어나도록 할게요. 지금은 교수님께서 무척 바쁘신 것 같아요.

교수: 좋아요. 그럼 나중에 이야기하죠, Kelly.

WORD REMINDER

proposal 제안 submit 제출하다 up to one's eyeballs with ~에 얽매인, ~ 때문에 정신이 없는 clinic 진료소, 개인 병원 have to do with ~와 관련이 있다 pay 보답하다 a bunch of 한 무리의 tentatively 임시로 feedback 반응, 피드백

Lecture • Zoology

p.42

교수: 여기 화면 위쪽에 또 다른 종의 개미가 있습니다… 팽창되어 있는 복부를 주목해 주세요… 얼마나 부풀어 있는지를요. 너무 커서 포도나 체리 알 정도의 크기로 보입니다. 여러분들이 보고 있는 것은 꿀개미입니다 — 음, 적어도 꿀개미 종의 하나인 것이죠. 꿀개미는 특이한 능력을 지니고 있습니다. 개미집에 있는 다른 개미들이 나중에 사용할 수 있도록 배에 음식물을 저장할 수가 있습니다.

하지만 모든 꿀개미들이 이렇게 할 수 있는 것은 아닙니다. 특정 암컷들만이 할 수가 있죠. 몇몇 개미들이 밖으로 나가서, 다양한 곳에서 음식을 얻은 후, 이를 다시 개미집으로 가지고 옵니다. 그런 다음 이 음식을 특정 암컷들에게 건네는데, 이들이 자신의 몸 속에 음식물을 오랫동안 보관합니다. 이 암컷 개미들은 개미집의 안쪽 천장에 매달려 있습니다. 하나의 개미집 안에 수백 마리의 — 심지어 수천 마리의 — 개미들이 다른 개미들을 위해 음식을 저장할 것입니다. 이 개미들이 더 많은 음식을 모으면 복부가 거대해질 때까지 부풀어 오릅니다. 실제로 음식물을 저장하는 꿀개미의 배는 보통 너무나 크게 부풀어서 이 개미들은 개미집을 떠날 수도 없고, 심지어는 그 때문에 개미집의 굴조차 빠져나갈 수 없게 됩니다. 하지만 시간이 지남에 따라 신체 내부에 저장해 둔 음식이 게워진 후 개미집 내의 다른 개미들이 이를 소화시키

면 개미의 복부는 작아집니다.

여기를 주목해 주세요··· 배가 부풀어 있는 개미 중 일부는 황색을 띕니다··· 반면에 다른 개미들은 보다 하얀색을 띄죠. 곧 터질 것 같이 보이지만, 사실 개미의 복부는 믿을 수 없을 정도로 튼튼합니다.

학생: Popper 교수님, 이 개미들은 무엇을 먹나요?

교수: 꿀개미는 다양한 먹이를 먹습니다. 꽃의 즙에서 나오는 당질의 탄수화물을 즐겨 먹습니다. 또한 진디가 만들어 내는 꿀도 먹습니다. 이 당질의 음식 때문에 음식을 저장하는 꿀개미의 불룩한 복부가 대부분 황색을 띄는 것이죠. 또한 꿀개미들은 자라나는 애벌레, 아, 새끼 개미들에게 단백질을 공급해 주어야 합니다. 이러한 단백질을 얻기 위해 먹이를 구하러 간 개미들이 종종 죽은 곤충의 시체를 개미집으로 끌고 오기도 합니다. 때로는 무리를 형성해서 다른 곤충들을 공격하기까지 하죠. 꿀개미들은 다른 여러 개미들처럼 침을 가지고 있지는 않지만, 가성 소다와 비슷한 물질을 뿌릴 수가 있습니다. 이 물질은 다른 곤충들을 마비시켜 꿀개미들이 곤충을 죽일 수 있게 만듭니다. 그 후 죽은 곤충들은 음식을 저장하는 꿀개미에게 보내집니다. 마지막으로, 소수의 저장 개미들이 물을 섭취하여 이를 저장하면 복부에 하얀색 색깔이 나타납니다.

꿀을 저장하는 개미의 복부는 다소 특이합니다. 복부에는 복부의 단단한 외피, 즉 체절 안쪽에 감추어진 여러 겹의 부드러운 막이 있습니다. 꿀개미가 음식을 집어 넣기 시작하면 외피가 움직이고 부드러운 막이 팽창하기 시작합니다. 유연하다는 점과 많은, 어, 많은 양의 음식을 저장할 수 있도록 커다랗게 부풀어 오를 수 있다는 점에서 개미의 복부는 포유 동물의 위와 비슷합니다. 하지만 음식이 소화되지는 않는데, 음, 포유 동물의 위에서는 소화가 이루어집니다. 그 대신 다른 개미들이 이용할 수 있도록 저장되는 것이죠.

흥미롭게도 이들 꿀개미들은 종종 공격을 받습니다. 저장 개미들은 예컨대, 어, 오소리와 같은 몇몇 포식자들에게 별미로 여겨지며, 심지어 인간도 이들을 먹는 것으로 알려져 있습니다. 농담이 아닙니다. 언제가 한번 드셔 보세요. 꽤 맛이 좋습니다. 다른 포유들은 그렇게 하지만··· 통째로 먹지는 마시고요. 대신 단맛이 나는 즙을 드시면 되는데, 즙은 배를 짜면 나옵니다. 마치, 흠··· 당밀 맛이 난다고 말씀드리고 싶군요. 좋아요, 여러분 중 일부가 약간 언짢아 하는 것 같아 이만하기로 하죠. 아, 하지만 한 가지가 더 있는데··· 꿀개미들은 종종 다른 꿀개미의 개미집을 공격해서 음식을 저장하는 개미들을 포획하려고 합니다. 승자들은 저장 꿀개미들을, 마치 전리품인 양, 자신의 개미집으로 끌고 갑니다.

음식을 모으고 저장하는 것 이면에 어떠한 동기가 있는지 궁금해 하실 것 같군요, 그렇죠? 그렇게 복잡한 것은 아닙니다. 많은 꿀개미 종들은 미 남서부와 같은 건조한 기후에서 살아갑니다. 사막과 같은 환경에서는 때때로 음식을 구하기가 힘들죠. 그래서 저장 꿀개미들에 의해 보관되는 음식으로 개미집의 다른 구성원들이 생존할 수 있습니다. 저장 꿀개미의 혜택이 없다면 많은 종의 꿀개미들은 현재 멸종되었을 가능성이 높습니다.

좋아요. 오늘 다루어야 할 내용은 충분히 다룬 것 같군요. 다음 수업 전까지 여러분 모두 교재의 10장을 읽으면 좋겠습니다. 거미류 종에 대한 부분인데, 다음 두 차례의 강의에서는 거미류에 대해 알아볼 것입니다. 수업 시간의 토론이 기대만큼 잘 되고 있지 못하기 때문에 반드시 읽어 오시기 바랍니다. 질문이 있나요···? 좋아요. 아무 말 없으면 질문이 없는 것으로 알겠습니다. 그러면 다음 금요일에 뵙죠. 모두들 남은 하루 잘 보내세요.

WORD REMINDER

distend 넓히다, 부풀다 abdomen 복부 regurgitate 게우다, 토하다 amber 호박(색), 황색 honeydew (진디가 분비하는) 꿀 aphid 진디 account for ~을 설명하다 stinger 침 caustic acid 가성 소다 membrane 막 segment 체절, 환절 gorge 게걸스럽게 먹다, 쑤셔 넣다 be subject to ~을 받다 delicacy 맛있는 것, 진미 badger 오소리 squeeze 짜내다 molasses 당밀 squeamish 신경질의 spoils of war 전리품 arachnid (거미, 전갈 등의) 거미류의 동물

PART 2

Conversation

p.46

생활관 직원: 안녕하세요. 어떻게 도와 드릴까요?

학생: 안녕하세요, 선생님. 제 이름은 Lisa Carter이고, 이곳 학교의 신입생이죠. 저는 다른 두 명의 룸메이트와 함께 Patterson 홀에서 살고 있어요. 하지만 방에 두어 가지 문제가 있어서요. 그래서, 어, 선생님께서 도와 주셔서 문제를 해결해 주셨으면 해요.

생활관 직원: 최선을 다하도록 할게요. 그러면, 기숙사에 어떤 문제가 있는지 제게 말씀해 주실래요?

학생: 좋아요. 첫 번째 문제는 지붕이 샌다는 점이에요. 저희는 기숙사 건물 7층에서 살고 있어요. 꼭대기 층이죠. 그리고, 어, 이틀 전에 비가 어떻게 내렸는지 기억하시나요?

생활관 직원: 오, 그래요. 확실히 폭풍우가 쳤죠, 그렇지 않나요?

학생: 바로 그거예요. 음, 어, 천장 일부가 젖어 있기 때문에 지붕에는 분명 아직도 많은 물이 남아 있을 것이고, 심지어 몇 군데에서는 바닥으로 물이 떨어지고 있어요. 물을 받기 위해 양동이들을 방에 가져다 놓았지만··· 아시다시피 저희 방에 곰팡이가 피게 될 텐데, 그것은 정말 저희들이 원치 않는 일이거든요.

생활관 직원: 분명 원치 않겠죠. 게다가 아직까지 위쪽에 물이 많으면 지붕이 무너져 내릴 수도 있어요.

학생: 오··· 그 점은 생각하지도 못했네요.

생활관 직원: 좋아요. 전화를 걸어서 작업팀이 확인할 수 있도록 그들을 학생의 기숙사로 바로 보내 드릴게요. 잠시도 지체할 수가 없는 일이군요. 몇 호실에서 산다고 했죠?

학생: Patterson 홀 705호에서 살아요. 그리고, 어, 방에 물이 샌다고 불평하는 말을 다른 학생들에게서도 들은 것 같으니 작업하시는 분들께 다른 학생들의 방도 방문해 달라고 하시면 좋을 것 같아요.

생활관 직원: 흠··· 전혀 좋은 일이 아니군요. 좋아요. 알려 줘서 정말 고마워요.

학생: 천만에요. 그럼, 두 번째 문제에 대해 말씀을 드리면···

생활관 직원: 두 번째 문제요?

학생: 예, 죄송해요. 어쨌든, 음, 두 번째 문제는 저희 방에 개미가 있다는 점이에요. 그리고, 물으시기 전에 먼저 말씀을 드리면, 저희는 먹지 않는 음식을 바닥에 놔두지 않아요.

생활관 직원: 알겠어요. 제가 학생에게 물어보려고 했던 첫 번째 질문이었어요.

학생: 그러실 줄 알았어요. 하지만 저희가 방을 최대한 깨끗하게 사용하고

있기 때문에 왜 개미가 있는지 잘 모르겠어요. 벽장 한 곳에도 있고, 가끔은 바닥에서 보이기도 해요.

생활관 직원: 흠… 마찬가지로 좋지 않군요. 다른 사람을 시켜서 문제를 확인하도록 할게요. 오늘 오후 정도가 될 것 같은데… 어, 세 번째 문제는 없나요, 있나요?

학생: 없어요, 선생님. 그게 다예요.

생활관 직원: 음, 다행이군요. 좋아요. 한 시간 내로 사람들이 방문할 거예요. 이제 기숙사 방으로 돌아갈 거죠, 그렇죠? 사람들이 안으로 들어가기 위해서는 누군가 그곳에 있어야 해요. 아무도 없으면 방에 들어갈 수가 없죠.

학생: 아, 그건 괜찮을 거예요. 제가 오늘 수업이 없기 때문에 방으로 돌아가서 일하시는 분들이 모든 걸 살펴볼 때까지 그곳에 있을게요.

WORD REMINDER
leak 누수 mold 곰팡이 mildew 흰곰팡이 closet 벽장

Lecture • Art History

p.48

교수: 19세기의 운동으로 넘어가서 미국 미술에 대해 계속 살펴보도록 하겠습니다. 지난 수업의 내용을 기억하시면 좋겠는데, 10세기 식민지 당시의 미국 화가들은, 풍경화 및 기타 회화들을 그리는 화가들도 있었지만, 주로 초상화에 집중을 했습니다. 또한 당시 미국의 많은 화가들이 유럽에서 배울 수 있는 회화 기법을 익히기 위해 유럽으로 가기도 했습니다. 이러한 화가들은, 짐작할 수 있듯이, 유럽 양식으로부터 많은 영향을 받았습니다. 유럽의 다양한 학파들, 예컨대, 어, 인상주의가 미국 화가들에게 막대한 영향을 끼침에 따라 이러한 경향은 19세기 동안 계속되었죠. 하지만 미국의 화가들은 고유한 양식을 만들어 냈고, 19세기에는 확실히 미국 미술이 독자적인 양식으로 발전하기 시작했다고 말할 수 있습니다.

허드슨 리버파는 19세기의 중요한 미술 운동 중 하나였습니다. 그 이름에서 추측할 수 있듯이, 이 화가들은 뉴욕 동부에 위치한 허드슨 강 계곡과 관련이 있었습니다. 이 운동의 화가들이 그린 회화 작품 중 대부분은 강 계곡의 자연적인 풍경 뿐만 아니라, 인근의 캐츠킬 산맥 및 아디론댁 산맥의 풍경도 묘사를 했습니다. 그리고, 덧붙이자면, 이곳은 미국에서 가장 아름다운 지역 중 하나입니다. 만약 여기에 방문해 보신 적이 있다면 왜 그곳이 당시 그렇게 많은 화가들을 매료시켰는지 아실 수 있을 것입니다. 허드슨 리버파의 선구자로 널리 알려진 토마스 콜에게 실제로 일어났던 일이죠. 1825년 그는 허드슨 강을 따라 보트 여행을 했습니다. 그는 곧바로 그 지역의 풍경을 그리기 시작했습니다. 콜과 동시대에 살았던 많은 화가들이 그가 그린 풍경에 주목했고, 당연한 이야기라고 말하고 싶은데, 그의 작품을 따라 하기 위해 그곳을 여행하기 시작했습니다.

허드슨 리버파의 화가들 중 다수는 영국의 J.M.W 터나와 존 컨스터블과 같은 풍경화가들의 영향을 받았지만, 또한 새로운, 음, 미국만의 새로운 것을 만들어 내기 위해 노력했습니다. 자, 허드슨 리버파의 화가들이 그린 작품들을 몇 개 보여 드리죠. 이야기를 계속하면서 화면을 넘기겠습니다. 먼저, 그들의 작품이 파노라마 양식으로 그려졌다는 점과 허드슨 강 계속 및 인근 산맥들의 자연 경관을 보여 준다는 점에 주목하세요… 그들의 그림은 낭만주의 버전의 풍경화였고… 그리고 종종 자연과 신을 연결시키려는 시도이기도 했죠. 화가들은 종종 빛을 이용해서 그림을 보다 극적으로 보이게 했는데… 여기를 보시면… 그리고 여기도요. 이는 루미니즘이라고 불립니다. 루미니즘은 주로 19세기 후반에 사용되었습니다. 루미니즘을 이용한 그림은 물과 빛이라는 요소를 사용해서 평온한 분위기를 나타냈습니다. 전형적으로는 약간의 안개가 낀 풍경을 묘사했으며, 수면에 빛이 반사되는 모습을 그렸습니다.

학생: 마치 인상주의처럼 들리는군요.

교수: 일부 측면에서는 그렇지만, 허드슨 리버파는 사실 인상주의 운동보다 시기적으로 앞서 있습니다. 또한 허드슨 리버파의 화가들은 루미니즘을 활용하여 붓터치를 감추고자 했지만, 인상주의 작품에서는 붓터치가 뚜렷하게 보일 수 있습니다.

자, 토마스 콜 이외에도, 허드슨 리버파에는 다른 유명한 화가들도 있었습니다. 프레드릭 처치는, 이 사람은 콜의 제자 중 한 명이었는데, 자신의 힘으로 유명해졌습니다. 토마스 더우티, 샌포드 기퍼드, 그리고 조지 인스도 주목할 만한 화가들입니다. 허드슨 리버파는 1870년대까지 미국에서 영향력을 발휘했습니다. 대략 그때쯤에 미국 화가들은 다시 한번 유럽의 영향을 받기 시작했습니다.

이러한 영향의 대부분은 인상주의자들이 끼친 것이었습니다. 인상주의는, 1860년대에 시작되어 1870년대에 보다 유명해졌는데, 빛과 무거운 붓터치로 인상을, 혹은, 어, 자연계의 이상적인 풍경을 나타냈습니다. 이 운동은 두 가지 방식으로 미국에 전파되었습니다. 첫째, 1880년대에 미국 전역의 도시에서 인상주의 미술 전시회가 열렸습니다. 둘째, 몇몇 미국인 화가들이 미술을 공부하기 위해 유럽으로 갔는데, 이들은 인상주의 화가들로부터 직접적인 영향을 받았습니다.

시어도어 로빈슨이 첫 번째 주요 미국인 인상주의 화가였습니다. 그는 프랑스에서 8년 동안 살았고, 화가인 클로드 모네 밑에서 그림을 배웠습니다. 미국으로 돌아오자마자 로빈슨은 생계를 위해 미술 교사로 일을 했는데, 그 결과 인상주의의 아이디어가 학생들에게 전파되었습니다. 여기 위쪽, 몇몇 로빈슨 작품에 주목해 주세요… 멋집니다, 그렇죠…? 여기 이 로빈슨의 작품을 보면… 그리고 이것은 모네의 그림인데… 모네가 그에게 미친 영향을 확실히 알 수 있습니다.

19세기 미국 미술의 또 다른 주제는 미 서부와 미 서부의 사람들을 그린 작품과 관련되어 있었습니다. 조지 캐틀린과 프레드릭 레밍턴과 같은 화가들은 드넓은 미 서부 개척지의 극적인 풍경을 그렸습니다. 또한 미 원주민들과, 새로운 삶을 시작하기 위해 서부로 온 정착민들의 이미지도 그렸습니다. 그들의 작품은 허드슨 리버파 화가들의 작품이나 인상주의자들의 작품보다 더욱 사실적이었습니다. 이제 그들의 작품을 몇 개 보도록 합시다.

WORD REMINDER
examine 검증하다, 조사하다 portrait painting 초상화 surmise 추측하다 captivate 매료시키다 take note of ~에 주목하다 emulate 흉내를 내다, 모방하다 strive 노력하다, 애쓰다 flash 번쩍이게 하다; 순간적으로 전달하다 serene 고요한, 차분한 hazy 안개가 낀, 흐릿한 brushstroke 붓놀림 in one's own right 자신의 권리로, 자신의 힘으로 dramatic 극적인

Lecture • Meteorology

p.51

교수: 좋아요. 저것은 대기의 층입니다. 자, 대기가 어떻게 순환하는지를 살펴보도록 하죠. 대기는 정지해 있지 않습니다. 대신 항상 움직이고 있습니다. 대기가 순환한다는 사실은 기온뿐만 아니라 날씨에도 막대한 영향을 미칩니다. 대기가 왜 순환하는지를 이해하기 위해서는 먼저 대기가 태양에 의해 어떻게 가열되는지를 이해해야 합니다. 햇빛은 위도에 따라 서로 다른 각도로 지구에 도달합니다. 적도에서는 일 년 내내 햇빛이 거의 직접적으로 지구에 닿습니다. 그 결과로 적도는 다른 지역 보다 더 많은 햇빛과 더 많은 열 에너지를 받습니다. 적도에서 멀어져 극지방에 가까이 갈수록 태양과 지구가 이루는 각도가 바뀌기 때문에 지구의 표면은 보다 적은 햇빛과 보다 적은 열

에너지를 받습니다.

이러한 점 때문에 적도 부근의 대기는 지구의 북쪽 및 남쪽에 있는 대기보다 더 따뜻합니다. 학습한 바와 같이 따뜻한 공기는 위로 상승하여 팽창하는데, 이로써 밀도는 낮아지게 됩니다. 반면, 차가운 공기는 아래로 가라앉고 수축하여 밀도가 높아지게 되죠. 적도의 따뜻한 공기는 상승해서 북쪽과 남쪽으로 이동합니다. 이러한 공기가 적도에서 멀어지면 온도가 떨어져 결국 아래로 가라앉고 차가워집니다. 그러면 새롭게 차가워진 공기는 다시 적도 쪽으로 이동하게 되는데, 적도에서는 공기가 다시 따뜻해지고 상승해서 북쪽이나 남쪽으로 가고, 차가워져서 가라앉은 후 다시 적도 쪽으로 돌아오게 됩니다. 여러분들도 알 수 있듯이 순환하는 것이죠. 이러한 이동은 움직이는 공기로 이루어진 대류 세포를 만들어 냅니다. Christina, 질문이 있나요?

학생: 있습니다. 적도의 따뜻한 공기가 가라앉지 않고 남극과 북극까지 가나요?

교수: 그렇지는 않습니다. 또 다른 요인이 관련되어 있기 때문에 그런 일은 일어나지 않아요. 바로 지구의 자전입니다. 지구가 자전을 하기 때문에 소위 코리올리의 효과가 만들어집니다. 이는 욕조나 화장실에서 물이 빠져나갈 때 물을 회전하게 만드는 효과입니다. 코리올리의 효과는 이동 중인 거대한 기단을 옆으로 이동하게 만듭니다. 또한 따뜻한 공기의 흐름을 깨서 적도의 북쪽과 남쪽 지역에 보다 작은 형태의 대류 세포를 만들어 냅니다. 여러분 교재 73페이지에 있는 그림을 보고 있나요…? 자, 그 그림은 우리가 생각하는 대류 세포의 모습이 이상적인 형태로 그려져 있다는 점을 명심하세요. 실제로는 대부분의 경우 보다 무질서하고 예측 불가능한 형태가 될 것입니다. 하지만 그림을 보면 어떤 일이 일어나고 있는지를 머리 속으로 그려 볼 수 있을 것입니다.

그래서, 어, 적도에서 가장 가까이 있는 대류 세포는 적도 위아래 쪽으로 약 0도에서 30도의 위도 내에 있습니다. 이 두 대류 세포는 — 하나는 북쪽에 그리고 하나는 남쪽에 있는데 — 해들리 세포라고 불립니다. 해들리 세포 다음에는 또 다른 두 개의 대류 세포들이 있습니다. 이들은 페렐 세포라고 불립니다. 해들리 세포와 페렐 세포 모두 그들이 존재한다는 이론을 제시한 과학자의 이름에서 유래되었습니다. 끝으로, 각 극지방의 상공에는 또 다른 두 개의 대류 세포들이 있습니다. 이들은, 적절하게도, 극 세포라는 이름으로 불립니다.

각 세포에서 대류는 서로 다른 방식으로 순환합니다. 지금은 북반구에만 초점을 맞추도록 하죠. 해들리 세포에서 적도의 따뜻한 공기는 위로 상승하여 북쪽으로 약 30도 정도 이동합니다. 그런 다음 차가워지고 가라앉아 다시 남쪽으로 이동합니다. 극 세포의 공기도 동일한 방식으로 움직입니다. 오, 극 세포는 대략 북위 60도에서 90도까지의 지역에 걸쳐 있습니다. 어쨌든 그곳에서는 따뜻한 공기가 상승하여 북쪽으로 이동해 가라앉은 다음, 다시 남쪽으로 이동하게 됩니다. 극 세포와 해들리 세포 모두 완전한 대류 세포로 간주됩니다.

반면, 페렐 세포는 다르게 작동합니다. 페렐 세포는 북위 30도와 60도 사이에 놓여져 있습니다. 그곳에서는 따뜻한 공기가 지구 표면을 따라 북쪽으로 이동합니다. 그런 다음 상승해서 차가워지고 남쪽으로 이동합니다. 남쪽에서는 가라앉고 다시 북쪽으로 이동하는 과정이 반복됩니다. 왜 이 세포 내의 공기는 다른 두 세포와 반대 방식으로 이동할까요? 한 가지 주요한 원인은 제트 기류입니다. 이 기류는 따뜻한 공기가 북쪽으로 이동하는데 중요한 역할을 합니다. 하지만 페렐 세포는 극 세포나 해들리 세포와 달리 완전한 순환 운동을 하지 않는다는 점을 지적하고 싶군요. 때때로 페렐 세포 내의 공기는, 다른 두 세포의 경우와는 다르게, 원활하게 이동하지를 못합니다. 또한 페렐 세포는 극 세포와 해들리 세포 사이에서 일종의 완충 장치 역할을 합니다. 마치 일종의… 흠, 다른 두 안정적인 대류 세포 사이에서 불안정하게 튀는 볼 베어링과 같죠. 또 다른 차이로, 극 세포와 해들리 세포 모두에서는 날씨 패턴을 꽤 정확하게 예측할 수 있지만, 페렐 세포의 날씨는 불안정하고 예측하기가 어렵습니다.

그래서 코리올리의 효과와 함께 이러한 순환 공기의 모든 활동이 지구의 바람과 날씨 패턴을 만들어 냅니다. 이는 또한 해류가 이동하는 방식에도 영향을 미칩니다. 서로 다른 세포 사이에는 주로 높지만 때때로 낮은 기압 구역이 놓여 있습니다. 이러한 요인들이 모두 합쳐져 지구의 날씨를 만들어 내는 역할을 하는데, 이에 대해서는, 더 이상 시간이 없으므로, 다음 수업 시간에 알아보도록 하겠습니다.

WORD REMINDER

circulate 순환하다 static 정적인, 움직이지 않는 profound 심대한, 심오한 latitude 위도 convection cell 대류 세포 chaotic 혼돈의, 무질서한 visualize 시각화하다, 마음 속에 그리다 buffer 완충 장치 in tandem with ~와 함께

Actual Test 03

PART 1

Conversation

p.58

학생: Wilkinson 선생님, 저와 이야기를 하셔야 하나요?

학생 회관 직원: 네, Susan. 그래요. 어, 하지만 먼저, 어, 학생의 근무 시간이 끝났나요? 일하느라 바쁜데 방해하고 싶지는 않거든요.

학생: 오늘 일은 끝났어요. 5분 전쯤에 마무리를 했죠. 그래서 이야기가 끝나면 기숙사로 돌아가서 다음 수업이 시작되기 전까지 두 시간 정도 있을 수 있어요.

학생 회관 직원: 그런 말을 들으니 다행이네요. 좋아요, 어, 이야기하는데 그렇게 오래 걸리지는 않을 거예요. 이번 학기에 학생이 일할 수 있는 시간대가 더 있다는 점을 알려 주고 싶어요. 제 기억으로는 학생이 이번 학기에 12시간 근무를 하고 싶어한다고 제게 말했던 것 같아요. 현재, 어, 학생은 9시간 근무를 하는 것으로 알고 있고요. 맞죠, 그렇지 않나요?

학생: 네, 선생님, 그래요. 그러면, 음, 일할 수 있는 시간대가 또 있다고요? 잘 되었네요. 언제인가요?

학생 회관 직원: 여기 리스트를 확인해 볼게요… 금요일 11시부터 2시까지군요. 어떤가요? 사실상 주말이긴 하지만, 어, 제가 할 수 있는 최선이에요.

학생: 금요일이라… 오, 안 돼요, 할 수 없어요.

학생 회관 직원: 그래요? 왜죠?

학생: 11시 30분에 끝나는 러시아 역사 수업이 있어요. 게다가 캠퍼스의 반대편에서 진행되는 수업이라 12시까지 여기에 올 수는 없을 것 같아요. 음, 제 앞에 근무하는 사람이 12시까지 있을 수는 없을까요? 그러면 제가 적어도 2시간 더 일을 할 수 있을 것 같은데요. 어떻게 생각하시나요?

학생 회관 직원: 미안하지만, Susan, 그건 정말로 불가능해요. 사실 Calvin은 수업에 늦지 않기 위해 11시가 되기 몇 분 전에 자리에서 일어나죠. 그가 더 늦게 있을 수는 없어요. 할 수 없죠, 다른 사람을 찾아봐야겠네요.

학생: 음…

학생 회관 직원: 네?

학생: 근무하는 다른 두 명의 학생에게 제가 말을 해 보면 어떨까요? Peter와 Rajiv를 생각하고 있어요. 그 중 한 명을 설득해서 그 시간에 일을 하도록 하고 그들의 근무 시간대 중 하나를 저와 바꾸면 괜찮지 않을까요?

학생 회관 직원: 솔직히 말해 어떤 학생이 어떤 시간에 일을 하는지는 제게 전혀 문제가 되지 않아요. 제가 관심을 갖는 것은 모든 근무 시간이 채워지도록 만드는 일이죠.

학생: 좋아요. 그러면 두 명 모두와 이야기를 할 수 있도록 제게 30분을 주시는 것이 어떨까요? 제가 그들 중 한 명을 설득해서 바꿀 수 있다면… 어, 물론 그들의 스케줄이 괜찮다는 가정 하에서요.

학생 회관 직원: 그렇게 해요. 전화 번호를 가지고 있나요?

학생: 갖고 있어요. Peter와 저는 기숙사의 같은 층에 살고 있고 Rajiv와 저는 물리학 수업의 실험실 파트너이죠. 실제로 두 명 다 꽤 잘 알고 있어요.

학생 회관 직원: 오, 제가 몰랐네요. 좋아요. 그러면 학생이 제 문제를 해결해 줄 수 있을 것 같군요. 하지만, 어, 두 명 중 아무도 그 시간대에 들어 올 수 없는 경우에는 제가 학생 고용 사무실에 채용 공고를 내야만 해요. 그러니까 잊지 말고 가능한 빨리 제게 연락을 줘야 해요. 괜찮죠?

학생: 문제 없어요, Wilkinson 선생님. 30분 이내에 사무실로 전화를 드릴게요.

학생 회관 직원: 잘 되었군요. 그래요. 전화를 기다리고 있을게요.

학생: 네. 조금 있다가 말씀을 드릴게요.

WORD REMINDER

shift 근무 시간, 교대조 **finish up** 끝마치다, 마무르다 **switch** 교환하다, 교체하다 **handle** 다루다, 처리하다 **get back** 대답하다, 답장을 주다

Lecture • Literature

p.60

교수: 1800년대는, 특히 당시 살고 있던 사람들에게 꽤 멋진 시대였습니다. 사회에서 온갖 종류의 변화가 일어나고 있었죠. 예를 들면 많은 식민지들이 독립을 했고 전 세계 여러 나라에서 혁명이 일어났는데, 이는 특히 유럽에서 두드러졌습니다. 국가들이 자유를 얻고 있었을 뿐만 아니라, 서구에서 노예제가 종식됨에 따라 사람들도 자유를 얻고 있었습니다. 산업 혁명이 진행 중이었고, 수많은 실용적인, 그리고, 어, 혁신적인 발명이 이루어지고 있었습니다. 또한 과학 분야에서도 대단한 발견이 있었습니다.

오늘 저의 관심을 끄는 것이 바로 과학입니다. 1800년대에 사람들은 보다 과학적으로 세상을 바라보기 시작했습니다. 과학의 비밀이 풀리기 시작했죠. 이러한 사실은 사람들을 매료시키는 동시에 두려움도 가져다 주었습니다. 이에 대한 증거는 1800년대에 쓰여진 문학 작품에서 찾아볼 수 있으리라 생각합니다. 당시 만들어진 장르가 있었습니다… 소위 공상 과학, 사이언스 호러, 혹은 일반적인 공포물도 될 수 있을 것 같은데… 이들은 과학에 초점을 맞추어 줄거리를 이어 나갔습니다. 많은 경우, 작가들은 과학의 위험성과 과학을 남용함으로써 비롯될 수 있는 나쁜 — 혹은 심지어 악한 — 점들을 강조했습니다. 하지만 작가들이 과학에 대해 보다 긍정적인 견해를 취하고, 과학이 적절하게 사용된다면 과학에 막대한 가능성이 있다고 본 경우도 있었습니다. 이 새로운 장르의 주요 작가로 세 명이 있었습니다. 메리 셸리, 로버트 루이스 스티븐슨, 그리고 쥘 베른이 그들입니다.

메리 셸리는 그녀의 소설 *프랑켄슈타인: 현대의 프로메테우스*로 가장 잘 알려져 있습니다. 오늘날에는 보통 줄여서 *프랑켄슈타인*이라고 부르죠. 메리 셸리는 영국 출신으로, 시인이었던 퍼시 비쉬 셸리의 아내였습니다. 자, 프랑켄슈타인에 기반을 둔 수많은 영화들 때문에 소설에 관한 몇 가지 오해가 생겼습니다. 그래서 그러한 오해에 대해 짧게 다루도록 하겠습니다. 글의 구성은 빅터 프랑켄슈타인 박사의 삶과 그가 만들어 낸 괴물에 초점을 맞추고 있습니다. 그리고, 아니죠, 소설에서 괴물의 이름은 프랑켄슈타인이 아니었습니다. 할리우드 덕분에 잘못된 것이에요.

어쨌든, 어떤 일이 있었는지 알려 드리겠습니다. 한 대학에서 연구를 하고 있던 프랑켄슈타인 박사는 죽음으로부터 생명을 만들어 낼 수 있다는 생각에 매료되었습니다. 오늘날에는 사이비 과학이라 부르겠지만 메리 셸리가 살았던 당시 이러한 생각은 꽤 널리 퍼져 있었어요. 생명을 만들어 낼 수 있을 것으로 생각되던 방법은 직류 전기 요법이라고 불렸습니다. 당시 사람들은 음, 인간이나 기타 동물의 사체에 전기를 통과시키면 사체가 다시 살 수 있을 것이라고 믿었습니다. 이러한 존재는 기본적으로 다시 활기를 얻게 됩니다. 여하튼 프랑켄슈타인은 시체들의 조각을 조합해서 거기에 전기를 흐르게 합니다. 그것은 살아났지만, 기형이었고 끔찍한 외모를 가지고 있습니다. 그것을 본 다른 모든 사람과 마찬가지로 프랑켄슈타인 박사도 괴물에 혐오감을 느낍니다. 괴물은 — 처음에는 순진했는데 — 점차 원한을 품게 되고, 조롱거리가 되고 무시를 당하게 되자 프랑켄슈타인 박사와 그와 가장 가까운 사람들에게 복수를 하려고 합니다. 결국 프랑켄슈타인의 목숨을 빼앗고 그의 아내와 몇몇 가족들을 살해하죠.

셸리의 작품은 잘못된 사람의 손에 들어간 과학이 비극적인 결과를 가져올 수 있다는 점을 분명하게 경고하고 있습니다. 물론 직류 전기 요법이 실제 과학은 아니지만, 셸리가 살았던 당시에는 알려져 있지 않았습니다. 자, 로버트 루이스 스티븐슨은 자신의 작품 *지킬 박사와 하이드 씨의 이상한 사건*에서 과학의 오용이 가져올 수 있는 위험성에 대해 글을 쓴 또 다른 작가였습니다. 지킬 박사는, 여러분들도 짐작할 수 있듯이, 과학자입니다. 착한 사람인 그는 자신의 보다 어둡고 악한 측면을 연구하는데 관심을 갖게 됩니다. 연구를 위해 그는 자신을 또 다른 사람으로 바꾸어 놓는 약을 만듭니다: 바로 그 사람이 하이드 씨입니다. 하이드는 줄거리상 지킬의 분신으로서 활동합니다. 지킬은 선한 존재를 상징하지만 하이드는 악의 화신입니다. 하이드로 변하기 위해 지킬은 약을 마셔야 합니다. 하지만 하이드는 때때로 사람들을 무작위로 공격하고, 심지어 런던 거리를 걸으면서 사람들을 살해하기도 합니다.

결국 하이드가 지킬을 지배하기 시작하고 때때로 약을 먹지 않은 경우에도 지킬은 하이드로 변하게 됩니다. 자기 자신으로 돌아오기 위해 지킬은 보다 많은 양의 약을 복용해야만 합니다. 말할 필요도 없이 이 이야기는 지킬이 완전히 사라지고 결국 — 아마 자기 자신의 손에 의한 — 하이드 씨의 죽음으로 끝이 납니다. *프랑켄슈타인*의 셸리와 마찬가지로 스티븐슨은 과학이 야기하는 위험에 대해 경고하고 있습니다. 즉, 어, 지킬 박사가 자신이 만들어 낸 약에 대해 완전히 이해하고 있지는 않다는 점을 스티븐슨은 명백히 보여줍니다. 자신은 모르고 있었지만 그의 첫 1회분 약에는, 그를 다시 자기 자신으로 돌아오게 만드는, 불순물이 포함된 화학 물질이 들어 있었습니다. 하지만 이 특정 화학 물질을 다 쓰자 지킬은 이를 더 구입하는데, 새로 구입한 것은 순수한 형태였습니다. 순수한 화학 물질이 약에 더해지자 지킬은 실제 자신으로 쉽게 되돌아올 수가 없습니다. 스티븐슨의 세계에서, 이는 완전히 이해되지 않는 것들이 뒤엉켜 발생한 하나의 결과입니다.

셸리와 스티븐슨이 과학의 사용에 대한 경고를 나타낸 반면, 쥘 베른은 경우는 달랐습니다. 그는 과학에 대해 그들과는 반대되는 견해를 가지고 있었고, 종종 인간이 과학을 이용하여 어떻게 혜택을 누릴 수 있는지에 대한 글을

썼습니다.

WORD REMINDER

notably 뚜렷하게, 명백히 come to an end 끝나다 realm 영역 plain 평범한 plot (글의) 구성 misconception 오해, 잘못된 생각 pseudoscience 유사 과학, 사이비 과학 galvanism 직류 전기 요법 galvanize 직류 전기로 자극하다, 갑자기 활기를 띄게 하다 spare part 예비 부품 misshapen 기형의 hideous 끔찍한, 오싹한 repulse 혐오감을 주다, 불쾌감을 주다 vengeful 복수심에 불타는, 원한에 쌓인 concoct 섞다 potion (약의) 1회 분량 alter ego 분신 embody 구체화하다, 구현하다 epitome 척도, 전형 randomly 무작위로 unbeknownst to ~에 알려지지 않은 batch 1회분

PART 2

Conversation

p.64

교수: 얼굴에 낙심한 기색이 있는 건 무엇 때문인가요, Bruce? 좋지 않은 일이 있었던 것 같네요. 무슨 문제라도 있나요?

학생: 정말 좋지가 않아요, 교수님. 저는, 어, 저는 오늘 좋지 못한 소식을 들었어요.

교수: 좋지 못한 소식이요? 이런, 부모님께서는 괜찮으신가요? 그분들에게 아무 일도 없기를 바라요.

학생: 부모님이요? 오, 아니에요. 그런 건 아니에요. 제 부모님께서는 정말로 괜찮으세요.

교수: 좋아요. 안심이 되는군요. 음, 저쪽에 앉아서 무슨 일이 있는지 제게 이야기해 볼래요?

학생: 네, 교수님.

교수: 여기… 커피 한 잔 마셔요. 여기에 있는 커피 머신으로 제가 만들었어요. 이 커피 한 잔이 어느 정도 도움이 될 거라고 생각해요.

학생: 친절에 감사드립니다, 교수님. 정말로 고마워요.

교수: 좋아요, 그러면…

학생: 아, 네. 제 문제요. 여기… 제가 몇 분 전에 받은 이 시험지를 봐 주세요…

교수: 64점? 어… 시험 공부를 하지 않았나요, Bruce? 학생이 이처럼 낮은 점수를 받은 것은 본 적이 없는 것 같은데요. 그리고, 어, 지도 교수로서 학생의 학점은 전부 보고 있죠. 무슨 일이 있었나요?

학생: 바로 그것이 문제예요, 교수님. 무슨 일이 있었는지 모르겠어요.

교수: 설명해 보세요. 정확히 무슨 말인가요?

학생: 음, 저는 이번에 등록한 천문학 수업이 꽤 재미있을 것이라고 생각했어요. 아시겠지만, 학교 천문대도 갈 수 있고, 밤하늘의 별을 볼 수도 있고, 그리고 그와 같은 다른 재미있는 것들도 할 수 있을 것으로 생각했죠… 하지만 이 수업은 제가 상상했던 것과 완전히 달라요. 지루한 강의가 반복되는 수업일 뿐이죠. 그뿐만 아니라 수업에서 어떻게 해야 할지 전혀 모르겠어요. 예전에 하던 것보다 훨씬 더 수학을 많이 해야 해요. 어, 지난 학기를 기억하신다면, 수학은 제가 정말로 취약한 부분이죠. 그리고 제가 시험 공부를 하지 않은 것도 아니었어요. 3일 연속으로 공부를 했죠. 그리고 최악인 부분을 아시나요?

교수: 모르겠어요. 무엇이죠?

학생: 왜 제가 이 모든 문제를 틀렸는지 아직도 이해가 가지 않아요. 천문학 교수님께서 수업 시간에 답을 확인해 주셨지만, 저는… 저는 이해가 가질 않았어요.

교수: 이번 일에 대해 어떻게 생각하고 있나요?

학생: 음… 저한테 최선책은 수강을 철회하는 것이라고 생각해요. 제 말은, 어, 과학 관련 필수 과목들은 이미 이수했기 때문에, 이 수업은 단지 선택 과목일 뿐이죠. 그리고 제가 그 수업을 계속 듣는다면 이번 학기의 우등생 명단에 들어갈 수 있는 방법이 없어요. 그러면 제가 대학을 마친 후 좋은 대학원에 들어갈 수 있는 기회도 없어질 것이고요.

교수: 이미 마음 속으로는 수강 신청 철회를 결정해 둔 것처럼 들리는군요. 음, 잘 되기를 빌게요. 하지만 잊지 말고 내일까지 그렇게 하세요. 성적표에 기록이 남지 않고 수강 철회를 할 수 있는 마지막 날이니까요.

학생: 오, 알려 주셔서 감사해요. 그런 경우라면 수강 신청 철회 용지를 받아서 지금 바로 Danielson 교수님께 가 봐야겠어요. 지금 사무실 근무 시간으로 알고 있기 때문에 분명 그곳에 계실 거예요.

WORD REMINDER

dejected 낙심한, 낙담한 observatory 천문대 go over 검토하다 fulfill 이행하다, 수행하다 elective course 선택 과목 slip 종이 조각, 종이 쪽지

Lecture • Anthropology

p.66

교수: 네안데르탈인은 약 2십 만년에서 3만년 전 유럽과 아시아 및 중동의 일부 지역에서 살았습니다. 몇 해 동안 우리는 이들에 대해 많이 알고 있지 못했습니다. 사실상 완전한 형태의 네안데르탈인 유해가 1856년 독일 뒤셀도르프 근처 네안더 계곡의 석회암 채석장에서 최초로 발견되자 상황이 바뀌었습니다. 이곳은 "네안데르탈"이라는 이름이 유래된 곳입니다. 그리고 궁금하실 것 같아 말씀을 드리면, *thal*은 독일어로 "계곡"을 의미합니다. 어쨌든, 이 유인원의 유해는 조심스럽게 보관되어 연구되고 있습니다. 이를 연구한 학자들은 곧 이것이 현생 인류와 다른, 독특한 견본이라는 점을 깨닫게 되었습니다.

학생: 네안데르탈인이 현생 인류와 정확히 어떻게 다른가요, Watson 교수님?

교수: 많은 방면에서 다릅니다. 첫째, 네안데르탈인의 뼈는 현생 인류의 것보다 더 단단하고 컸습니다. 평균적으로 손과 팔도 현생 인류의 것보다 훨씬 더 튼튼했죠. 또한 상당히 강력한 다리를 가지고 있었습니다. 신장에 대해 말씀을 드리면, 남성 네안데르탈인들은 평균 165센티미터의 신장을 가지고 있었고, 반면에 여성 네안데르탈인은 평균적으로 남성들보다 약, 음, 약 10센티미터 정도 키가 작았습니다. 네안데르탈인의 머리 형태 또한 현생 인류와 달랐습니다. 여러분 교재에 네안데르탈인의 두개골 사진이 있는 것으로 알고 있습니다. 하지만 정확한 페이지 번호는 생각나지 않는군요…

학생: 324페이지입니다, Watson 교수님.

교수: 오늘 집중력이 좋군요, Tom. 고마워요… 아, 그래요, 모두들 지금 보고 있나요…? 그 옆에 있는 인간의 두개골과 어떻게 비교되는지 주목해 주세요. 보시다시피 네안데르탈인의 두개골이 보다 기다랗고… 코 주변의 얼굴은 더 튀어나와 있으며… 그리고 턱 부분 또한 더 큽니다. 하지만 이마와 아래턱은 튀어나와 있지 않다는 점에 주목하세요. 대신 이마가 뒤로 경사져 있으며 아래턱은 뒤쪽으로 물러나 있습니다. 마지막으로 네안데르탈인의 뇌는 현생 인류의 뇌보다 약간 더 컸습니다. 이러한 점은 네안데르탈인들이 현대 인류보다 더 지능이 뛰어났다는 점을 의미하는 것일까요…? 흠… 대답하기가 어

렵습니다. 아무도 확실히는 모릅니다.

네안데르탈인의 신체적인 측면에 대해서는 충분히 다룬 것 같군요. 이제 그들의 행동으로 넘어가 봅시다. 첫째, 모든 초기 인류와 마찬가지로 네안데르탈인들도 수렵 채집민이었습니다. 긁개와 같은 간단한 석기 도구를 만들었고, 무기로는 창을 사용했습니다. 쇠퇴기에 접어들었을 때 이들이 동물의 뼈와 뿔로 도구를 만들었다고 생각되지만, 그러한 주장의 타당성을 입증해 줄 정보는 아직 충분하지가 않습니다. 하지만 네안데르탈인들은 불에 대해 알고 있었고 불을 사용했습니다.

인류학자들은 네안데르탈인들이, 오늘날의 가족과 상당히 비슷한, 소규모 사회 집단을 이루고 살았다고 믿습니다. 그들은 집단 내의 연장자들과 환자들을 돌보았다고 생각됩니다. 이에 대한 증거는 동굴에서 발굴된 일부 유해들이 다소 나이가 많은 네안데르탈인의 유해로 보인다는 사실에 기반하고 있습니다. 일부 유골에는 상처가 치료되었다는 증거와… 어, 부러진 뼈 등등… 그리고 질병에 대한 증거도 있습니다. 네안데르탈인이 시체를 매장했다는 증거가 있기는 하지만, 증거가 다소, 음, 빈약하기 때문에 모든 이들이 이에 동의하는 것은 아닙니다. 인류학자들이 확실히 알지 못하는 또 다른 점은 네안데르탈인이 말을 할 수 있었는지의 여부와, 말을 했더라면, 언어를 가지고 있었는지에 대한 것입니다. 그들의 뇌는 지능을 가지고 있었을 정도로 충분히 컸기 때문에 말과 언어 모두 존재했을 가능성이 있습니다. 또한 일부 네안데르탈인의 유해에서 설골이 발견되었습니다. 이는 후두에 붙어 있는 목청의 뼈로, 주로 말을 하는데 사용되는 것입니다.

자, 네안데르탈인은 확실히 멸종했습니다. 무엇 때문에 이들이 사라졌는가는 전문가들 사이에서 큰 논란을 불러 일으키고 있는 문제입니다. 여러분들도 짐작할 수 있듯이 네안데르탈인에 대한 많은 질문들은 답을 얻지 못하고 있습니다. 어쨌든, 그들의 멸종에 대해 또 다른 유인원 종, 즉 크로마뇽인들이 주요한 역할을 했다는 이론이 있습니다. 현생 인류의 조상인 이 유인원들은 아프리카에서 처음 출현하여 약 4만 년 전 유럽에 도착했습니다. 약 1만 년 동안 크로마뇽인들과 네안데르탈인들은 유럽에서 상당히 가까운 거리를 두고 살았습니다. 하지만 네안데르탈인은 사라진 반면 크로마뇽인들은 번성했습니다. 무슨 일이 있었을까요? 자원 경쟁에서 크로마뇽인이 네안데르탈인들을 물리쳤을까요? 크로마뇽인들이 고의적으로 네안데르탈인을 살해했을까요? 또 다시, 그에 대한 답은 확실하지 않습니다. 우리가 알고 있는 것은 약 기원전 3만년 경 네안데르탈인이 사라졌고, 크로마뇽인들이 유럽 대부분의 지역에서 지배적인 종이 되었다는 점입니다.

학생: 네안데르탈인이 현생 인류와 관련이 있나요?

교수: 아, 그것 역시 아직까지 답이 확실하지 않은 질문입니다. 네안데르탈인과 크로마뇽인은 수천 년 동안 함께 살았던 것으로 보입니다. 그들이 섞여서 자손을 낳았을까요? 음, 우리가 네안데르탈인과 관련이 있다는 점을 암시해 주는 어떤 신체적인 특징도 현대 인류에게 존재하지 않습니다. 하지만 현대의 DNA 검사로 인해 그 답을 찾게 되었습니다. 유럽인과 아시아인의 DNA 중 약 1%에서 4%는 네안데르탈인에게서 유래된 것입니다. 이러한 점은 크로마뇽인이 아프리카를 떠나고 얼마 후에 그 일부가 네안데르탈인과 함께 자손을 낳았다는 점을 암시합니다. 흥미롭게도, 아프리카 사람들에게는 네안데르탈인의 DNA가 없는데, 이는 그러한 교류가 유럽 지역에 한정되었다는 이론을 뒷받침해 줍니다.

WORD REMINDER

quarry 채석장 hominoid 사람과 비슷한 것, 유인원 specimen 견본, 표본 on average 평균적으로 on the ball 빈틈이 없는; 사정을 잘 아는 protrude 튀어나오다 chin 턱 recede 물러나다, 뒤쪽으로 기울다 wane (달이) 이지러지다, 쇠퇴하다 antler (사슴 등의) 뿔 unearth 발굴하다 scanty 부족한, 빈약한 hyoid bone 설골 larynx 후두 outcompete 능가하다, 경쟁에서 이기다 comingle 혼합하다 lend weight to ~을 뒷받침하다, 입증하다

Lecture • Geology

p.69

교수: 전 세계에는 말 그대로 수십만 개의 섬들이 존재합니다. 하지만 모든 섬들이 똑같다고 생각하지는 마세요. 일부 사람들이 저지르는 실수이죠. 사실, 몇 가지 유형의 섬들이 존재합니다. 섬들이 실제로 어떻게 형성되었는지를 말씀드리는 것입니다. 이제 섬들이 만들어지는 다섯 개의 주요한 방식에 대해 간단히 살펴보도록 하겠습니다. 그런 다음, 몇몇 섬들의 생성 과정을 보다 자세하게 알아보도록 하죠.

아시겠지만, 지구가 생긴 이후로 계속해서 지구의 모습은 극적으로 변해 왔습니다. 우리는 이미 판 구조론에 대해 배웠고, 시간이 지나면서 지구의 표면이 어떻게 이동했는지에 대해서도 논의했습니다. 팡게아뿐만 아니라 한때 존재했던 기타 초대륙에 대해서도 이야기를 했습니다. 대륙이 바쁘게 움직임에 따라, 이러한 모든 움직임 때문에 때때로 보다 큰 땅덩어리로부터 비교적 작은 땅덩어리들이 분리되는 결과가 만들어졌습니다. 대부분의 지질학자들이 믿기로는 다수의 거대한 섬들… 몇 가지만 이야기하면, 뉴기니아, 영국 제도, 뉴펀들랜드, 그리고 배핀 아일랜드… 어, 이 섬들은 한때 보다 큰 대륙의 일부였을 것입니다. 단지 떨어져 나온 것이죠.

학생: Davidson 교수님, 오스트레일리아도 그러한 유형의 섬에 속하나요?

교수: 음, Mary, 엄밀히 말하면 호주는 대륙이지 섬이 아닙니다. 제 말은, 그래요, 까다롭게 하고자 하면, 유라시아-아프리카 대륙을 섬이라고 할 수도 있을 거에요, 그렇죠? 그리고 북미와 남미 대륙에 대해서도 똑같이 말을 할 수 있을 것이고요. 어쨌거나 두 대륙 모두 물로 둘러싸여 있는 육지니까요, 그렇지 않나요? 하지만 그렇게 부르지는 않는데, 그 이유는, 어, 지구본에서 어떻게 보이더라도 오스트레일리아를 섬이라고 생각하지 않기 때문이죠. 오스트리아는 대륙입니다. 하지만 좋은 질문이었어요. 이야기를 꺼내게 해 줘서 고마워요.

섬이 형성된 두 번째 방식은 수천 년 전 마지막 빙하기가 끝날 때 이루어졌습니다. 빙하기가 끝날 당시 많은 양의 물이 얼음에 갇혀 있었습니다. 얼음이 녹자 전 세계의 해수면이 상승하게 되었습니다. 그러한 결과 중 하나로서 갑작스럽게 물이 찬 저지대로 둘러싸인 고지대에서 섬이 형성되었습니다. 동시에 커다란 빙붕, 어, 빙하들이 땅을 움푹 패이게 만들었고, 여기에 물이 들어오자 이들은 호수와 내해가 되었습니다. 하지만 빙하가 고르게 땅을 패이게 만든 것은 아니었기 때문에 호수와 바다의 수면은 서로 달랐습니다. 많은 지역에서, 이러한 호수 및 바다에 있는 고지대들은 갑작스럽게 섬이 되었습니다.

섬이 형성된 세 번째 방식은 대양의 화산 활동이었습니다. 해수면 아래의 화산이 마그마를 분출했고, 마그마가 식어서 수중에 단단한 암석이 형성되었습니다. 시간이 지남에 따라… 어, 수만 년 동안… 몇몇 화산들이 계속해서 폭발했습니다. 마침내 충분한 양의 화산암이 축적되어 해수면을 뚫고 나온 곳이 생겼고 섬이 형성되었습니다. 아이슬란드가 이러한 방식으로 형성되었습니다. 인도네시아와 같은 주요 군도들도 마찬가지입니다. 전 세계에 화산섬과 열도들이 산재해 있지만 대부분은, 짐작할 수 있듯이, 지구의 더운 지방을 따라 발견됩니다. 이러한 곳들은 화산 활동과 지진이 가장 빈번하게 발생

하는 지역입니다. 태평양은 많은 화산 섬이, 특히 환태평양 화산대라고 알려진 지역에 있는 섬들이 만들어진 곳입니다.

때때로, 화산에 의해 만들어진 이 열도들은 지구의 판이 움직임에 따라 이동하는 열점의 산물이기도 합니다. 하와이 열도가 이러한 방식으로 만들어졌다고 생각됩니다. 아시겠지만 지각의 약한 부분에서 마그마가 밑으로부터 솟아오릅니다. 이처럼 약한 지역이 있는 판이 수천 년에 걸쳐 동쪽으로 이동하면서, 상당한 규모의 화산 활동이 있을 때마다, 새로운 섬들이 형성되었습니다. 잠시 하와이 지도를 봐 주세요. 열도들이 서쪽에서 동쪽으로 어떻게 뻗어 있는지 아시게 될 것입니다.

섬이 형성되는, 특히 태평양 섬들이 형성되었던 다섯 번째 방식은, 음, 산호에서 비롯됩니다. 환초를 말씀드리는 것입니다. 이들은 죽은 산호의 잔해로 만들어진 섬입니다. 산호는, 그건 그렇고, 얕은 해저 바닥에 붙어사는 생물입니다. 시간이 지나면서 산호는 단단해지는 칼슘 물질을 분비합니다. 산호가 죽으면 이 물질들이 합쳐져 단단한 물질의 덩어리가 됩니다. 대부분의 산호초는 원형이며, 석호라고 불리는 내수를 둘러싸고 — 혹은 거의 완전하게 둘러싸고 — 있습니다. 이 석호에는 한때 바다 속으로 가라앉은 화산 섬이 포함되어 있다고 생각됩니다. 과학자들은 이러한 믿음의 근거를 대부분의 산호초들이 섬에서 가까운 곳에 형성되었다는 사실에 두고 있습니다. 여기에 어떤 일이 있었는지가 나오는데… 바다에서 화산 섬이 올라옵니다. 시간이 지나면 그 주변에 산호초가 형성되고요. 그런 다음 시간이 지남에 따라 지구에서 일어나는 활동들에 의해 화산이 물속으로 가라앉게 됩니다. 하지만 산호는 남아서 점차적으로 환초로 변하게 되죠.

WORD REMINDER

fussy 까다로운, 복잡한 supercontinent 초대륙 ice sheet 빙붕 depression 함몰, 움푹한 땅 spew 내뿜다, 분출하다 breach 돌파하다 archipelago 군도, 다도해 presume 가정하다 bubble up 끓어오르다 secrete 분비하다 coral atoll 환초 incorporate 통합하다 lagoon 석호

PART 3

Conversation

p.74

학생: Crow 교수님, 지금 사무실 근무 시간이시죠, 아닌가요?

교수: 음, 30분 전에 끝나긴 했지만 오늘 이후 시간에 예정된 회의나 수업은 없어요.

학생: 잘 되었군요. 그러면 제가 잠깐 들어가도 괜찮을까요?

교수: 물론이에요, Stuart. 보고서 점수에 대해서 이야기하려고 여기에 온 것으로 생각하면 될까요?

학생: 네, 교수님. 맞아요. 저는, 어, 저는 사실 교수님에게서 보고서를 돌려 받고서 크게 놀랐어요. 보고서 점수로 C-를 받아본 적이 없는 것 같거든요. 그리고, 솔직히 말씀드리면, 왜 그런 일이 일어났는지 이해가 가지 않아요.

교수: 사실 꽤 간단해요. 학생은 보고서와 관련해서 제가 수업 시간에 알려준 지시 사항을 따르지 않았어요.

학생: 예? 제가 지시 사항을 따르지 않았다고요? 하지만… 하지만…

교수: 지시 사항이 무엇이었는지 제게 얘기해 보세요.

학생: 그럴게요. 교수님께서는 저희에게 종이 어떻게 멸종할 수 있는지, 아니면 어떻게 개체수가 크게 감소할 수 있는지에 대한 글을 쓰라고 지시하셨죠. 그리고 그것이 제가 한 일이고요.

교수: 흠… 그것은 제가 말한 지시 사항이 아니었어요. 저는 분명히 — 칠판에 지시 사항을 적기까지 했고 많은 학생들이 이를 스마트폰 카메라로 찍은 것으로 알고 있는데 — 저는 분명히 모든 학생들에게 어떤 종이 멸종하거나 멸종 위험에 처할 수 있는 몇 가지 방법에 대한 글을 쓰라고 말했어요. 학생은 제 지시 사항을 따르지 않았고, 그것이 낮은 점수를 받게 된 이유예요.

학생: 하지만… 저는 인간이 어떻게 그처럼 많은 동물들을 멸종시켰는지, 그리고 다른 종들을 멸종 위험에 처하게 만들었는지에 대한 글을 썼는걸요. 그것이 왜 잘못된 건가요?

교수: Stuart, 실제로 인간이 특정 종들을 멸종 위험에 빠뜨리거나 멸종시키는 유일한 원인이라고 생각하지는 않죠, 그렇죠?

학생: 음, 물론이에요.

교수: 좋아요, 저는 학생이 지난 2주 동안의 읽기 과제를 전혀 하지 않았다고 생각할게요. 만약 읽었다면 이러한 일이 일어날 수 있는 수많은 방법들을 학생이 알고 있었을 거예요. 예를 들어 공룡은 수백만 년 전 운석이 지구와 충돌하여 멸종한 것으로 널리 알려져 있어요. 마찬가지로 수많은 질병으로 인해 식물과 동물이 모두 멸종하거나 개체수가 크게 감소하기도 했고요. 역사를 통틀어 초화산 폭발과 쓰나미 때문에 해당 지역의 식물 및 동물들의 개체수가 감소하기도 했죠.

학생: 오… 그래요, 무슨 말씀인지 알 것 같아요. 저는, 어, 저는 인간이 현재 많은 동식물들에게 일으키고 있는 문제에 초점을 맞추고자 했어요.

교수: 그 점은 이해하지만 학생은 지시 사항을 따르지 않았어요. 학생이 써야 하는 것을 쓰지 않았기 때문에, 사실 보고서에서 낙제 점수를 받지 않은 것은 다행스러운 일이죠.

학생: 아, 그래요… 음, 교수님께서 알려 주신 지시 사항을 따르지 않은 점은 정말로 죄송해요. 제가 보고서를 다시 쓰는 일 같은 것도 가능할까요? 제 말은, 음, 이번에 받은 낮은 점수 때문에 제가 수업에서 A를 받지 못하는 것은 원치 않거든요.

교수: 저는 제 수업에서 리라이팅을 허용하지 않아요. 하지만 너무 걱정하지는 말아요. 이번 보고서 점수가 최종 성적에서 차지하는 비중은 적으니까요. 그러니 남은 두 번의 시험과 한 번의 보고서에서 잘 하면 이번 학기 학생의 최종 성적은 만족할만한 것이 될 거예요.

WORD REMINDER

to be frank 솔직히 말하면 eliminate 제거하다 go extinct 멸종하다 asteroid 운석 supervolcano 초화산

Lecture • Linguistics

p.76

교수: 교육을 연구하는 사람들이 곤란해 하는 한 가지 문제는 — 특히 언어 학습 분야의 연구자들의 경우 — 아이가 특정 언어를 배울 수 있는 능력을 타고 나는 것인지, 혹은 아이의 환경에 다양한 영향을 미침으로써 아이가 어떠한 언어를 배우도록 프로그램될 수 있는 것인지에 관한 것입니다. 이러한 주제를 다룬 두 명의 위대한 지성인이 미국인인 B.F. 스키너와 노암 촘스키입니다. 흥미롭게도 위와 같은 학습의 측면에 대해 이들의 의견은 크게 다릅니다. 이들의 논쟁은 1950년대 이후 행태주의와 언어학이라는 분야를 탄생시켰습니다. 두 사람 및 두 사람의 이론 모두 지지자들과 반대자들을 가지고 있으며, 각각의 이론들은, 음… 각각의 이론에는 타당한 측면도 있지만 문제점 또한 존재합니다. 학계에서 흔히 있을 수 있는 일이죠. 어쨌든, 저는 두 이론에 대해 균형 잡힌 설명을 드리고자 하며, 어떤 이론이 더 그럴 듯한 것인지는 여러분의 판단에 맡기겠습니다.

언어 학습에 대한 스키너의 아이디어로 시작해 보겠습니다. 스키너는 아이들이 언어를 지각할 수 있는 능력을 가지지 않은 채 태어난다고 믿었습니다. 그의 견해에서는 아이들의 머리가 깨끗한 판과 같습니다. 점차 주위 환경과 상호 작용을 함으로써 아이들은 언어를 배우기 시작합니다. 이러한 학습은 부모의 지도와 기타 외부 자극에 의해 도움을 받습니다. 스키너의 견해는 그가 언어적 행동이라고 지칭한 것의 발달로 이어졌습니다. 언어적 행동에서 언어 활동은 타인의 반응으로 이어집니다. 스키너 이론의 핵심적인 측면은 그가 강화 이론이라고 명명한 것입니다. 예를 들면 한 아이가 단어를, 음… 물이라는 단어를 배운다고 가정해 봅시다. 좋아요. 어린 여자 아이가 "물"이라고 말하자 부모들이 아이에게 물을 한 잔 가져다 줍니다. 아이는 "물"이라는 단어를 실제의 것과 연관시키고, 시간이 지남에 따라, 이러한 연관성은 강화됩니다. 나이가 들면서 아이는 보다 많은 어휘를 익히게 되고, 단어열을 조합하여 문장을 만들 수 있게 되며, 그리고 문법적인 구조도 이해할 수 있게 됩니다. 이러한 모든 것들은 아이의 조건 반사를 형성시키고, 환경 및 아이가 말을 할 때마다 부모로부터 받는 반응에 의해 강화됩니다.

학생: 스키너가 믿기에 특정 가족에 태어난 아이는 그 가족의 언어를 배우게 된다는 말씀이시죠, 맞나요?

교수: 스키너의 견해에 따르면 그렇습니다. 그리고 수차례에 걸쳐 계속해서 옳다고 입증되었죠. 어떻게요? 음, 오늘날 이루어지고 있는 국제 입양을 생각해 보십시오. 한 러시아 아이가 영어를 말하는 미국인 부모에게 입양되었다고 가정해 봅시다. 이 아이는 러시아어가 아닌 영어를 배우게 되며, 그가 수년 동안 러시아어를 공부한다고 해도 결코 친부모의 언어를 숙달하지는 못할 것입니다. 물론, 스키너의 이론에는 문제가 있습니다. 많은 사람들은 언어를 완벽하게 익힐 수 있는 유일한 시기가 — 아동기인 — 어렸을 때뿐이며, 나이를 먹으면, 설사 수년 동안 언어를 배우기 위해 해당 언어의 문화에 완전히 몰입한다고 해도, 언어를 학습할 수 있는 능력이 감퇴한다고 믿습니다. 스키너에 의하면 인간이 그러한 환경에 놓이고 기타 자극을 받게 되면 언어를 익힐 수 있어야 하죠. 하지만 항상 그런 것은 아닙니다, 그렇죠?

촘스키의 이론은 어떨까요? 1957년 스키너가 *언어적 행동*이라는 제목의 책을 발간하자 촘스키는 이를 반박하는 책을 썼습니다. 촘스키는, 여러분이 모르고 있는 경우를 대비해 말씀을 드리면, 문법 구조에 정통한 언어학자입니다. 그는 모든 사람들이 어떤 언어라도 그 고유한 문법적 구조를 이해하고 배울 수 있는 능력을 타고난다고 믿었습니다. 여러분이 태어났을 때 여러분의 머릿속에 블랙 박스가 있다고 상상해 보세요. 이 블랙 박스에는 언어로 프로그램되기를 기다리는 코드가 들어 있습니다. 바로 그것이 촘스키가 생각한 것입니다. 어, 물론 실제 블랙 박스는 아닙니다. 그러한 개념을 말씀드리는 것입니다. 자, 어, 촘스키는 아이가 자라고 배움에 따라 이러한 타고난 능력을 발견해서, 시간이 지나면, 자신의 언어에 대한 문법적 구조를 충분히 발전시키게 될 것이라고 생각했습니다.

촘스키는 더 나아가 아이들이 빠르게 언어를 습득하는 것을 스키너의 이론은 설명하지 못한다는 점에 주목했습니다. 특정 단계에 이르면 아이들은 급속도로 언어를 배우게 됩니다… 종종 어떠한 외부적 요인에 의해 강화된 언어 능력 없이도 그런 것처럼 보입니다. 이로써 언어를 배우는 타고난 능력이 있다는 촘스키의 이론이 보다 그럴 듯하게 보입니다.

촘스키는 더 나아가 사람이 처음 언어를 습득한 이후에는 결코 완전하게 제2언어를 숙달할 수 없다고 믿었는데, 그 이유는 인간의 뇌가 내장된 하드웨어와 같아서 처음 배운 언어의 구조만을 완벽하게 이해하기 때문입니다. 물론 두 개, 세 개, 혹은 더 많은 언어에 숙달한 사람들이 많기 때문에 여기에는 많은 예외들이 존재합니다. 제가 생각하기에 이는 촘스키 이론의 명백한 오류입니다. 또한 다른 문화권으로 입양된 유아들은 어떨까요? 그들의 뇌에는 친부모의 언어를 습득할 수 있는 능력이 있을까요, 아이를 입양한 부모의 언어를 습득할 수 있는 능력이 있을까요, 아니면 두 언어 모두를 습득할 수 있는 능력이 있을까요? 입양된 아이들에 관한 사례 등을 관찰해 보면 사전에 할당되어 있는 언어라는 것은, 음, 없는 것 같아 보입니다. 선천적인 학습 능력만이 있을 뿐이죠. 아이가 어떤 언어를 배우게 될 것인지는 아이가 태어나서 처음 몇 년 동안 어떤 것을 듣느냐에 달려 있습니다. 따라서 아이의 환경에서 비롯되는 외부 자극은, 어, 스키너의 주장대로, 언어 습득에 필수적인 것으로 보입니다.

WORD REMINDER

detractor 가치를 폄하하는 사람 **academia** 학문적인 세계, 학계 **appealing** 호소력이 있는 **string word** 단어열 **condition** 조건 반사를 일으키게 하다 **time and time again** 몇 번이고, 되풀이하여 **diminish** 감소하다 **immerse** 담그다; 몰입하다 **inherent** 고유한 **by leaps and bounds** 껑충껑충 뛰어서, 급속도로 **plausible** 그럴듯한 **hard-wired** 하드웨어에 내장된

Actual Test 04

PART 1

Conversation

p.82

학생: 안녕하세요. 여기가 도서 연체료를 내는 곳이죠, 그렇지 않나요?

사서: 맞아요. 연체료가 있나요? 정말 유감이네요.

학생: 예, 저도 그래요. 반납 기한이 지난 도서들의 연체료가 많이 나오지 않기를 바랄 뿐이죠.

사서: 저도 그랬으면 좋겠네요. 음, 확인해 보죠, 그럴까요? 혹시 학생증을 가지고 있나요? 학생의 이름을 컴퓨터로 확인하려면 제가 봐야 할 것 같아서요.

학생: 오, 네. 맞아요… 여기 있어요.

사서: 좋아요… 학생의 이름이 Rebecca Mills군요, 맞죠?

학생: 저예요. 그리고 이틀 전에 두 권의 도서를 반납한 것 같아요.

사서: 맞아요. 책들이… F.A. 하이에크의 *치명적 자만*… 어, 그건 8일이 연체되었고, 그리고… 제임스 버크의 *지식의 그물*… 미안해요. 그 책 역시 8일 연체된 것으로 보이네요.

학생: 네, 제가 반납한 책이 그 두 권이에요. 미리 연장 신청을 하지 않았다니 믿을 수가 없네요. 요즘 너무 바빠서 도서관에 들릴 시간이 없었거든요.

사서: 실은, 어, 연장 신청을 하기 위해 반드시 도서관에 들릴 필요는 없어요. 이용할 수 있는 두어 가지 방법이 있죠. 봅시다… 도서관이 문을 연 경우라면 언제든지 전화를 해서 연장 신청을 할 수가 있어요. 그리고 온라인으로 연장 신청을 할 수 있는 새로운 프로그램도 도입되어 있고요. 그래서 기숙사에서 편리하게 연장 신청을 할 수가 있죠. 물론 원한다면 언제든지 이곳 대출대에 들릴 수도 있어요. 많은 학생 및 교직원들이 선호하는 방식이죠.

학생: 예. 저도 그게 익숙한 것 같아요. 어쨌든 알려줘서 고마워요. 인터넷으로 도서 연장 신청을 할 수 있는지는 모르고 있었네요. 한번 해 봐야 할 것 같군요.

사서: 좋아요. 저희도 많은 학생들이 해 보기를 바라고 있어요.

학생: 그러면, 어, 어쨌거나… 제가 얼마를 내야 하죠?

사서: 아, 네. 권당 2달러를 내야 해요. 그러면 전부 4달러군요. 지금 지불하시겠어요, 아니면 학기 말에 청구서를 통해 내시겠어요?

학생: 음, 부모님께서 처리하시도록 하고 싶지만, 연체된 도서에 대해 돈을 내는 것은 달가워하지 않으실 것 같네요. 여기 5달러 드릴게요.

사서: 정말 고마워요. 그리고 여기 잔돈이요.

학생: 오, 어, 실은… 여기에 온 김에 제가 대출한 도서들에 대해 지금 연장 신청을 할 수 있을까요? 5권을 빌린 것 같은데요.

사서: 전혀 문제 없죠. 그리고… 네, 학생 말이 맞네요. 5권을 빌렸군요. 책 제목들을 알아야 하나요?

학생: 괜찮아요. 어떤 책들인지 알고 있어요.

사서: 오, 이런… 그 책들 중 한 권은 4일이 연체되었네요. 연장해 줄 수 있지만 연체료를 내야 해요. 지금 처리하고 싶다면 제가 다시 1달러를 돌려 받아야 해요.

학생: 믿을 수가 없네요. 제 기억력이 정말 좋지 않군요. 여기 1달러요. 그리고 앞으로는 잊지 말고 인터넷 연장 신청 시스템을 확인해야겠어요.

WORD REMINDER

library fine 도서 연체료 overdue 기한이 지난 beforehand 앞질러, 사전에 circulation desk (도서관의) 대출대 faculty 교수진, 교직원들 tempt 유혹하다 from now on 지금부터는, 앞으로는

Lecture • Zoology

p.84

교수: 사막의 모든 동물 중에서 가장 유명한 동물은 분명 낙타일 것입니다. 그곳에 사는, 가장 쓸모가 많은 동물이죠. 사막에서 낙타는 이동 수단으로, 운송 수단으로, 식량 자원으로, 그리고 심지어는 돈이나 물품을 얻기 위해 거래되는 상품으로서 기능합니다.

생리학적인 측면에서 낙타는 짝수 발굽을 지닌 유제 동물입니다. 유제 동물은 발에 짝수의 발굽이 있는, 포유류의 과(科)입니다. 아, 그 수는 일반적으로 둘이나 넷입니다. 낙타의 경우에는 발에 두 개의 커다란 발굽이 있습니다. 궁금해 하시는 경우, 어, 이 과에 속하는 다른 동물들로는 돼지, 양, 염소, 기린, 그리고 소 등이 있습니다. 낙타는 전형적으로 아프리카와 아라비아의 사막 지역, 그리고 인도, 중국, 몽골, 및 호주의 일부 지역에서 볼 수 있습니다. 이들 대부분은 길들여져 있습니다. 주요한 예외는 약, 오, 백만 마리 정도의 낙타 무리인데, 이들은 호주의 오지에서 야생으로 살아가고 있습니다.

남학생: 호주요? 낙타들이 어떻게 거기까지 갔나요?

교수: 아, 그에 대해서는 재미있는 비하인드 스토리가 있습니다. 19세기에 짐을 운반할 목적으로 소규모 무리의 낙타들이 호주로 보내졌죠. 결국 사람들이 이들을 기르는데 싫증이 나서 야생에 풀어놓았습니다. 이 낙타들은, 어, 그 이후로 번식을 해서 그 수가 많아졌습니다. 다른 대규모 낙타 무리에 대해 말씀을 드리면, 그들은 아프리카의 소말리아, 에티오피아, 수단 및 아라비아 반도에서도 서식합니다.

모든 낙타들이 다 똑같지는 않다는 점에 주의하세요. 똑같다고 생각하는 것은 낙타에 대한 흔한 오해입니다. 실제로 낙타는 두 개의 주요 그룹으로 존재합니다. 단봉 낙타와 쌍봉 낙타가 그것입니다. 단봉 낙타는 하나의 혹을 가지고 있는 반면 쌍봉 낙타는 두 개의 혹을 가지고 있기 때문에 이들을 구별하는 일은 꽤 쉽습니다. 게다가 쌍봉 낙타는 때때로 색깔이 더 어둡고 단봉 낙타보다 털이 더 긴 경향이 있습니다. 이 둘에 대한 여기 사진을 봐 주세요… 나란히 놓여 있기 때문에 둘 사이의 차이점을 알아보기가 쉽습니다, 그렇지 않나요? 또한 쌍봉 낙타는, 여러분도 알 수 있듯이, 둘 중에 보다 몸집이 큽니다. 그건 그렇고 쌍봉 낙타는 주로 중앙 아시아에서 발견되며, 모든 쌍봉 낙타들은 사실상 길들여져 있습니다. 자, 낙타에서 대부분의 사람들이 처음 주목하게 되는 것이 혹입니다. 혹은…

여학생: Collins 교수님, 끼어들어서 죄송하지만 질문이 하나 있습니다.

교수: 괜찮으니 말씀해 보세요.

여학생: 감사합니다. 혹은 물로 채워져 있나요? 낙타가 사막에서 그처럼 멀리까지 갈 수 있는 이유가 그것 때문인가요?

교수: 아, 마침 그에 대해 다루려고 하던 참이었어요. 혹은 물이 아니라 사실 지방으로 이루어져 있습니다. 하지만 한 가지에 대해서는 학생 말이 맞아요. 혹은 낙타가 사막의 극심한 열기와 극한 건조함 속에서도 생존할 수 있도록 만들어 줍니다. 혹에 있는 지방은 대사 작용으로 물이 되기 때문에 낙타는 물을 섭취하지 않고서도 장시간 여행할 수 있습니다.

낙타를 사막에서 번성할 수 있게 해 주는 또 다른 특징들이 있습니다. 포유 동물 중에서 낙타는 타원형 형태의 적혈구를 가지고 있는 유일한 동물입니다. 이러한 형태의 적혈구는 파충류와 어류가 가지고 있습니다. 이것이 왜 중요할까요? 음, 낙타의 신체가 탈수 증상을 겪게 되면 타원형 모양의 세포는 원형 모양의 세포보다 혈액의 흐름에 더 큰 도움이 됩니다. 따라서 낙타가 탈수 증상을 겪을 수는 있지만 혈액이 신체 내 생존에 필수적인 곳으로 계속해서 흘러 들어갈 수 있기 때문에 낙타는 다른 어떤 포유류보다도 더 오래 생존할 수 있습니다.

낙타는 또한 다른 대부분의 포유류들보다 땀을 적게 흘리며, 매우 높은 온도가 되어서야 땀을 흘리기 시작합니다. 아시다시피 온도가 섭씨 40도 이상이 되어야 낙타는 땀을 흘리기 시작합니다. 반면에 인간은 훨씬 더 낮은 온도에서 땀을 흘립니다. 봅시다. 낙타들이 또 어떤 장점들을 가지고 있을까요…? 아, 추운 사막의 밤과, 사막의 낮과 밤 사이의 급격한 온도 변화를 견뎌낼 수 있습니다. 특이한 코 때문에 낙타는 많은 양의 수분을 보유할 수가 있는데, 이들의 코는 호흡 시 수증기를 가두어 놓기 때문에, 수분이 다시 체내로 들어오게 됩니다. 낙타의 생존에 도움을 주는 또 다른 점은 물을 마실 때 많은 양의 물을 마시는 낙타의 능력입니다. 너무나 많은 양의 물을 마시기 때문에 만약 다른 포유 동물이 같은 양의 물을 마신다면 그들은 죽게 될 것입니다. 마지막으로 낙타는, 식물을 더 좋아하긴 하지만, 거의 모든 것을 — 식물이던 동물이던 간에 — 먹을 수 있습니다. 그리고 믿을 수 없을 정도로 강력한 소화 시스템 덕분에, 먹을 수 있는 무엇이던 사막에서 찾기만 하면, 낙타의 신체는 기능을 할 수가 있습니다. 간단히 말해서 낙타는 진화를 통해 사막에서 완벽히 살 수 있게 된 것이죠.

그리고 이러한 점이 낙타가 사막에서 짐을 운반하는데 사용되는 이유입니다. 이들은 사람을 태우고 하루에 거의 200킬로미터를 이동하며, 200킬로그램까지의 짐을 싣고 하루에 60킬로미터를 이동한다고 알려져 있습니다. 이러한 점은, 낙타가 걸을 때 옆으로 움직인다는 사실과 함께, 낙타에게 "사막의 배"라는 별명을 가져다 주었습니다.

WORD REMINDER

versatile 다재다능한, 다용도의 physiologically 생리학적으로 ungulate 유제 동물 outback (미개척의) 오지 dromedary camel 단봉 낙타 Bactrian camel 쌍봉 낙타 tell A from B A와 B를 구별하다 by all means 좋고말고, 물론 metabolize 물질대사로 변화시키다, 신진대사시키다 replenish 보충하다, 채우다 red blood cell 적혈구 dehydrate 수분이 빠지다, 탈수시키다 vital 생명의, 극히 중대한 retain 보유하다 water vapor 수증기 imbibe 물을 마시다 hearty 원기 왕성한, 강력한 moniker 이름, 별명

Lecture • Psychology p.87

교수: 다양한 분야의 과학에서, 특히 살아 있는 생명체에 대한 연구와 관련이 있는 생물학이나 동물학에서, 연구자들은 관찰을 통해 연구 중인 대상을 훨씬 더 잘 이해할 수 있습니다. 이는 자명한 이치로 보일 수 있습니다. 하지만 연구자들의 관찰 유형에 따라 학자들이 수집하는 자료와 그들이 도달하게 되는 결론이 영향을 받을 수도 있습니다. 관찰에는 세 가지 주요한 유형이 존재합니다. 자연 관찰… 참여 관찰… 그리고 실험 관찰이 그것입니다… 각각의 방법의 장단점들에 대해 간략히 검토하도록 하겠습니다.

자연 관찰 방법이 아마도 가장 일반적인 방법일 것입니다. 이는 또한 현장 관찰 및 현장 연구도로 불린다는 점을 기억해 주세요. 이러한 유형의 관찰에서는 연구자들이 아무것도 하지 않고 자연 환경에 놓인 대상을 관찰합니다. 야생 생물을 관찰할 때 매우 흔히 사용되는 방법입니다. 연구자들은 일정한 거리를 두고 떨어져 대상에 너무 가까이 가지 않고서도 기록을 남길 수가 있기 때문에 가장 안전한 방법이라고도 할 수 있을 것 같군요. 안전성 외에도 몇 가지 장점들이 더 있습니다. 주로, 음, 이때 관찰자들은 대상이 자연과 상호 작용을 할 때 이들을 지켜볼 수 있습니다. 관찰 대상은, 관찰자를 알아채지 못한다는 기대 하에, 평상시와 같은 행동을 합니다. 이는 관찰 대상의 행동을 이해하는데 있어서 특히 중요한 점입니다.

하지만 자연 관찰법은 수많은 문제점 또한 가지고 있습니다. 우선 야생에 있는 대상에 접근하는 일이 항상 쉽지만은 않습니다. 심지어 현대 기술로 연구자들에게 온갖 종류의 카메라 및 음향 탐지기뿐만 아니라 목표 동물들을 추적하는 인공 위성 추적 장치가 제공되는 오늘날조차, 온종일 대상을 관찰하는 것은 불가능한 일입니다. 동물들은 몸을 숨길 수도 있고, 새로운 영토로 이동할 수도 있으며, 혹은 죽을 수도 있습니다. 예를 들면 한 무리의 침팬지들이 어떻게 다른 무리를 공격하는지 연구했던, 아프리카의 한 현장 연구원에 대한 글을 읽은 것이 기억나는군요. 패배한 침팬지들은 다른 지역으로 가게 될 것이었기 때문에 실제로 침팬지들이 다른 침팬지들을 죽이지는 않았습니다. 하지만, 한번은, 어, 연구원이 패배한 무리의 침팬지 한 마리를 찾을 수가 없었습니다. 그는 그 침팬지가 — 아마도 상처로 인해 — 죽었다는 결론을 내렸지만, 이에 대해 확신할 수는 없었습니다. 네, 앞 줄인가요? 손을 든 것이죠?

학생: 네, 교수님. 궁금한 것이 있는데, 어… 그러한 동물들을 그냥 동물원이나 실험실에서 연구하는 것은 어떤가요? 야생에 있는 동물을 연구하는 것 보다 훨씬 더 쉬울 것 같은데요.

교수: 맞는 말입니다. 더 쉽겠죠… 하지만 그 방법은, 우리가 실험 관찰이라고 부르는 것인데, 자체적인 문제들을 가지고 있습니다. 먼저 장점은… 통제된 환경에서 대상을 면밀히 관찰함으로써 연구자들은, 어, 현장 연구를 한다면 불가능할 수 있는 여러 가지 실험을 할 수가 있습니다. 실험실에서는 안전한 환경에서, 보다 많은 통제 수단을 가진 채, 현장에서 이용이 불가능한 시설과 장비를 사용하여 실험을 할 수 있습니다. 이제, 문제점들은… 우리에 갇힌 동물들은 자연적인 습성을 잃으며 포획된 상태에서는 종종 예전과 같은 행동을 하지 않습니다. 야생에 있지 않을 때에는 또 다른 습성이 길러집니다. 다른 음식을 먹고, 수명이 달라지며, 심지어는 야생에 있을 때와 다른 방식의 짝짓기와 번식을 합니다. 간단히 말해서 실험 관찰로는 실제 환경에서의 동물들에 대해 알 수가 없는 것이죠.

자, 세 번째 주요 관찰 방법은 참여 관찰입니다. 여기에서는 연구자가 연구 대상과 적극적으로 상호 작용을 합니다. 이는 원시 부족 사람들을 연구하는 일류학자들이 주로 사용하는 관찰 방법입니다. 틀림없이 여러분들도 짐작할 수 있으리라고 생각하는데, 여기에는 좋은 점과 나쁜 점이 모두 있습니다. 먼저 연구자는 사람들의 신뢰를 얻고, 그들의 생활 속으로 들어가야 하며, 장시간 동안 그들과 함께 지내야 하고, 그들의 언어를 익히고, 그리고 마지막으로 그들의 삶을 관찰해야 합니다. 이 일은 모두 높은 위험성과 가파른 학습 곡선을 수반합니다. 사람들이 매우 원시적이고, 외진 곳에서 살며, 혹은 잘 알려지지 않은 언어를 사용할 때 특히 그렇습니다. 예를 들어, 가령, 아마존 우림 지대 깊숙한 곳에서 살고 있는 한 부족에 대해 참여 관찰을 한다고 생각해 보세요. 결코 쉬운 일은 아닐 것입니다. 하지만 장점이 무수히 많습니다. 연구자는 직접적인 체험을 통해 사람들의 사회, 문화, 그리고 이상에 대해 알 수 있습니다. 마찬가지로 부족의 역사를 배울 수도 있고, 운이 좋다면, 일부 의식에 참여할 수 있는 허락을 받을 수도 있죠.

단점으로서 일부 관찰자들과 관찰 대상인 사람들의 관계가 너무 깊어질 수 있습니다. 이는 판단을 흐리게 만들고 편견을 갖게 하여 공정한 관찰을 불가능하게 만들 수도 있습니다. 게다가 연구자들은 자신의 문화 프리즘으로 원시 부족 사람들을 바라보는 경향이 있습니다. 제 말은 연구자들이 자신의 문화 척도로 원시 부족 사람들을 판단할 수도 있다는 뜻입니다. 마지막으로, 외부인의 존재 자체가 원시 부족 사람들로 하여금 행동을 바꾸게 만들 수도 있습니다. 평소와 다른 행동을 할 수도 있으며, 외부인에게 알려지기를 원치 않는 문화적 측면은 감출 수도 있습니다.

WORD REMINDER

most notably 특히 subject 피실험자, 실험 대상 truism 자명한 이치 aside from ~ 이외에도 hopefully 바라건대, 아마 troop 무리, 떼 life span 수명 authentic 진짜의 entail 수반하다 obscure 불명확한, 알려지지 않은 firsthand 직접, 바로 on the downside 내림세로, 하락세로 biased 편견이 있는 impartial 공정한, 공평한 presence 존재

PART 2

Conversation p.92

학생: 안녕하세요, Fried 교수님. 어제 수업을 빠질 수 있도록 허락해 주셔서 정말 감사합니다. 정말 죄송하고, 다시는 그런 일이 없을 것이라고 약속드릴게요.

교수: 괜찮아요, Stephanie. 하지만 인턴쉽 프로그램의 상사에게 학생의 수업 시간표를 알려 줘서 더 이상 수업에 빠지는 일이 없도록 해 주세요. 어제 강의는 매우 중요한 것이었고, 우리가 다루었던 내용은 곧 있을 기말 시험에 나올 거예요.

학생: 걱정 마세요, 교수님. 제가 일찍 도착해야 했던 유일한 이유는 회사 대표 이사가 점검 차 방문을 해서 모든 인턴 사원들을 만나고 싶어했기 때문이었어요. 그런 일은 분명히 다시는 일어나지 않을 거예요.

교수: 그런 말을 들으니 기쁘군요.

학생: 하지만, 음, 교수님께 제 질문에 답해 주실 수 있는 시간이 있는지 궁금해요. 그게, 어, 어제 강의와 관련된 것이에요.

교수: 오? 벌써 다른 학생의 필기 노트를 구했나요? 빠르군요.

학생: 아, 네, 그랬죠. Eric Anderson이 제게 필기한 노트를 빌려 주었어요. Harper 홀의 같은 층에서 살고 있기 때문에 노트를 구하는 일은 문제가 없었어요.

교수: 잘 되었군요. 그러면… 질문이 무엇인가요?

학생: 태양계의 거대 가스 행성이 각각 가지고 있는 달의 개수와 관련된 것이에요. Eric은 노트에 토성이 53개의 달만 가지고 있다고 적었는데, 제가 읽은 바에 따르면 그 수가 훨씬 더 많았거든요. 제가 읽은 글에는 토성에 80개 이상의 달이 있다고 적혀 있었어요. 또한 그가 목성의 달 개수라고 적은 것도 제가 전에 봤던 것보다 약간 적었어요. 그래서, 어, 그가 필기를 잘못한 것인가요?

교수: 전혀 그렇지 않아요. 제가 수업 시간에 말한 것을 정확히 받아 적었군요.

학생: 어… 그러면 토성에 실제로 53개의 달만 있는 건가요? 분명 그 수가 더 많았던 것 같은데요.

교수: 53개의 확인된 달이 있죠.

학생: 확인된 달이요? 그게 어떤 의미인가요?

교수: 토성의 확인된 달은 모두 이름을 가지고 있다는 의미에요. 궤도가 알려져 있죠. 그리고 분명, 어, 예컨대 운석이 아니라 달이고요. 이들은 타이탄, 엔셀라두스, 그리고 포이베와 같은 달이에요.

학생: 그러면 토성 주위를 도는 달이 더 있지만, 아직 확인된 것은 아니라는 말씀이신가요?

교수: 맞아요. 기본적으로, 확실히 달이라고 말하기에 앞서 이러한 달에 대한 정보가 더 필요하죠.

학생: 궤도, 크기, 그리고 성분과 같은 정보들 말인가요?

교수: 네, 맞아요. 그래서 현재로서는 토성에 확인되지 않는 29개의 달이 있기 때문에 잠재적으로 총 82개의 달이 있는 것이죠.

학생: 아하! 그러면 80개 이상의 달이 있다는 제 말도 맞는 것이었군요.

교수: 네, 그래요. 망원경과 우주 탐사선으로부터 정보를 더 많이 얻게 되면 아마도 이들 천체 중 다수가 달로 확인될 수 있을 거예요. 그러면 이름이 붙여지고 토성의 확인된 달이 되겠죠. 다른 거대 가스 행성의 경우도 마찬가지에요. 알겠지만, 목성, 천왕성, 해왕성이요. 실제 달로서 간주하기에 앞서 이들 주위를 돌고 있는 몇몇 천체에 대해 더 많이 알아야 해요. 모든 것이 이해가 가나요?

학생: 이해가 가는군요. 자세히 설명해 주셔서 정말 감사합니다. 고맙습니다.

WORD REMINDER

inspection 사찰, 점검 pertain to ~와 관련되다 gas giant 거대 가스 행성 asteroid 운석 composition 성분 potential 잠재적인 space probe 우주 탐사선

Lecture • History

p.94

교수: 금입니다… 그래요. 모든 학생들이 집중할 줄 알았어요. 사실 모든 사람들이 금을 좋아합니다. 그래서 19세기 말 알래스카 근처의 유콘에서 금이 발견되었다는 소식이 외부로 알려지자 그곳은 부자가 되기 위해 금광에 몰려드는 사람들로 붐비게 되었습니다. 이 사건은 종종 알래스카 골드 러쉬, 때로는 클론다이크 골드 러쉬로 불립니다. 하지만 크게 보면, 실제로는 두 번의 골드 러쉬가 있었습니다. 첫 번째는 캐나다 유콘에서 일어났고, 규모가 더 작았던 두 번째는 알래스카의 여러 지역에서 일어났습니다.

1896년 몇몇 탐광자들이, 아, 즉, 광부들이 알래스카 국경 근처인 캐나다 유콘의 클론다이크 시내에서 사금을 채취하고 있었습니다. 이들은 1896년 8월 그곳에서 대규모 금광을 발견하고서는 곧 그에 대해 떠벌리고 다녔습니다. 인근 지방의 많은 광부들이 그 지역으로 몰려들었고, 겨울쯤에는, 그들 역시 부자가 되었기 때문에 본인들에게는 어리석은 행동이었습니다. 하지만 겨울이 되자 땅이 얼었고, 날씨가 좋아질 때까지는 누구도 그곳에서 나올 수가 없었습니다. 1897년 7월 한 선박이 워싱턴 시애틀에 입항했습니다. 이 배는 수십 명의 광부들과 몇 톤에 이르는 금을 싣고 있었습니다. 여러분들이 잘 모르고 있는 경우를 대비해 말씀을 드리면, 이는 어마어마한 양의 금입니다. 또한 유콘의 금에 관한 최초의 뉴스가 미 본토에 전해지게 되었습니다. 며칠 후 시애틀에서는 수천 명의 사람들이 기존 일자리를 버리고 알래스카의 스캐그웨이로 가는 항행권을 예약하고 있었는데, 이곳은 유콘의 금광 지대로 가는 입구였습니다.

학생: 그래서 때때로 알래스카 골드 러쉬라고 불리게 된 것인가요, Gorey 교수님?

교수: 네, 부분적으로 대부분의 탐광자들이 알래스카에 도착하여 내륙과 상류 지대로 이동을 해야만 금광 지대에 도착할 수 있었기 때문입니다. 하지만 알래스카에서도 금이 발견되었기 때문에 알래스카 골드 러쉬는 잘못된 명칭이 아닙니다.

어쨌든, 몇 년 내에 전 세계로부터 — 하지만 주로 미국과 캐나다로부터 — 오, 십만 명 이상의 사람들이 유콘의 금광 지대로 가기 위해 알래스카에 왔습니다. 그처럼 숫자가 많았던 이유가 궁금하시면 당시 미국에서는 경제 공황이 일어나고 있었다는 점을 알고 계세요. 그 결과 많은 사람들이 돈을 벌기 위해 북쪽으로 가서 위험을 무릅쓰더라도 잃을 것이 없다고 생각했습니다.

하지만 극복해야 할 수많은 장애들이 있었습니다. 첫째, 탐광자들은 물품이 필요했는데, 그곳 상인들은 모든 물품에 터무니없는 가격을 책정했습니다. 알래스카의 상인들에 의한 몇 차례의 가격 사기가 이루어지고 있었습니다. 둘째, 탐광자들은 유콘의 산악 지대를 횡단해야 했습니다. 도로가 없었기 때문에 도보와 개썰매로 이동을 하거나 배를 타고 여러 강을 거슬러 올라갔습니다. 그리고 극한의 기후로 인해 일 년에 몇 개월만 이동을 할 수 있었습니다.

또 다른 문제는 알래스카와 캐나다 국경에서 경찰이 모든 사람들을 제지하고 있었다는 점이었습니다. 북서 기마 순찰대… 어, 이들은 RCMP, 즉 캐나다 기마 경찰대의 전신이었는데… NMP들이 사람들을 멈춰 세웠습니다. 그들은 두 가지 이유로 탐광자들을 제지했습니다. 첫째, 알려진 범죄자들 중 누구도 그 지역에 들어가지 않기를 바랐습니다. 둘째, 그들은 탐광자들이 소지하고 있는 모든 총기를 압수했습니다. 일부 탐광자들이 금을 찾고 다른 이들은 그렇지 못한 경우에 발생할 수 있는 잠재적인 폭력 사태를 예방하기 위해 그렇게 했죠. 몇 번의 산발적인 다툼이 있기는 했지만 성공적인 편이었습니다. 아, 세 번째 이유도 있습니다. 경찰들은 모든 이들이 충분한 물품, 특히 식량을 갖고 있는지 확인했습니다. 골드 러쉬의 첫 해에 식량이 충분하지 않아서 아사에 직면한 사람들이 많았기 때문에 그렇게 했던 것이죠.

이러한 인간적인 그리고 자연적인 장애에도 불구하고, 꽤 많은 사람들이… 흠, 즉 수만 명의 사람들이… 금광 지대에 도착했습니다. 1849년 캘리포니아 골드 러쉬 때와 마찬가지로 알래스카 골드 러쉬에서도 성공 사례들이 나왔지만, 보다 많은 실패로 인하여 성공 사례는 종종 무색해졌습니다. 어

떤 사람들은 스캐그웨이에 머물면서 탐광자들에게 필요한 음식과 장비들을 공급함으로써 부자가 되었습니다. 알래스카의 금광 지대로 이동한 사람들도 있었습니다. 마침내 1880년 알래스카의 주노 근처에서 금이 발견되었습니다. 분명 1896년 유콘에서 금이 발견된 때처럼 많은 사람들의 이목을 끈 것은 아니었지만, 몇몇 사람들은 보다 위험한 유콘에 가는 대신 그곳으로 향했습니다. 또한 1898년에 알래스카 놈의 북쪽 끝에서 금이 발견되었습니다. 이로써 곧 두 번째 탐광자들의 물결이 그 지역으로 향하게 되었습니다. 하지만 놈은 너무나 멀리 떨어져 있는 곳이어서 그곳에 간 사람들은 보다 적었습니다. 어쨌든, 몇 년이 지난 후, 유콘에서 손쉽게 얻을 수 있었던 금은 대부분 채굴되었고, 골드 러쉬는 끝이 났습니다. 대다수의 탐광자들은 파산한 상태로, 혹은 부유해져서 고향으로 돌아갔지만, 일부는 유콘과 알래스카에 남아 그곳에 정착했습니다.

WORD REMINDER

gold field 금광지 put ~ into perspective ~을 넓게 보면 prospector 탐광자, 시굴자 creek 시내, 샛강 pan (사금을) 가려내다 deposit 침전물, 매장물 brag 자랑하다, 허풍떨다 dock 독에 넣다 phenomenal 놀라운, 경이적인 book 예약하다 misnomer 틀린 이름, 오칭 exorbitant 터무니없는, 과대한 price gauging 가격 부풀리기, 바가지 요금 traverse 횡단하다, 가로지르다 frigid 추운, 극한의 overshadow 그늘지게 하다; 무색하게 하다 perilous 위험한

Actual Test 05

PART 1

Conversation

p.100

교수: 좋아요, 그러면 그 사소한 문제는 처리될 것이고… 그 일은 끝났으니, 어, 학생을 제 사무실로 부른 진짜 이유에 대해서 얘기해야 할 것 같군요, Matt.

학생: 네, Jacobson 교수님.

교수: 학생은 이미 제 수업을 세 개나 들었어요, 그렇지 않나요? 제 말이 맞는 것 같은데요.

학생: 네, 교수님. 맞습니다. 신입생일 때 수업을 하나 수강했고, 2학년 때에 두 개를 수강했죠. 이번 주에 시작된 수업으로 교수님 수업은 4번째가 되는 것 같아요. 왜 물으시는 건가요?

교수: 음, 학생에게 제안할 것이 하나 있어서요.

학생: 오? 어떤 제안이신가요?

교수: 먼저 이번 수업에 대해 잠깐 이야기를 할게요. 알겠지만 이번 수업은 고급 물리학 수업이에요. 첫 등록에 60명의 학생들이 수강 신청을 했죠. 하지만 저는 이 수업을 지난 십 년 동안 가끔씩 맡아 왔어요. 제 경험상 이번 학기가 끝날 때쯤에는 처음 수강 신청을 한 학생 중 절반 이상이 수강 신청을 철회해 있을 거예요. 예를 들면 이 수업을 맡았던 마지막 때에는 처음 60명이었던 학생 중에서 27명의 학생만이 끝까지 남아 있었죠.

학생: 그렇게 많이 수강 신청을 철회했다고요? 어, 이런. 음, 이번 수업이 그렇게 어려운가요?

교수: 학생에게는 그렇지 않으리라 믿지만, 대부분의 수강생들이 많은 양의 공부를 하게 될 거예요. 그리고 이번 학기에는 그에 대한 조치를 취하려고 해요. 학생이 제게 큰 도움이 될 수 있으리라고 생각하는 부분이죠.

학생: 어, 어떻게요?

교수: 음, 안타깝게도 이번 수업에는 수업 조교가 없어요. 하지만 학과에 요청을 해서 이번 수업을 위한 약간의 자금을 제공받게 되었죠. 제가 제안한 것은 두 명의 학생으로 하여금 매주 스터디 모임을 진행시키도록 하는 것이에요. 알겠지만 스터디 모임은, 오, 가령, 일주일에 한 번씩 매번 한 시간 반 정도 모이게 될 거예요. 그렇게 해서 수업을 따라오지 못하는 학생들이 보충 학습을 할 수 있는 것이죠.

학생: 그리고 제가 그 스터디 모임 중 하나를 이끌기를 원하시는 건가요?

교수: 제가 학생을 좋아하는 이유가 바로 그거예요. 알아듣는 것이 빠르거든요.

학생: 감사합니다, 교수님.

교수: 그래서 제 제안에 대해 어떻게 생각하나요? 학생과 제가 고용할 다른 학생에게는 시간에 따른 보수를 지급할 수가 있어요. 많지는 않겠지만요. 시간당 15달러 정도 받게 될 거예요. 하지만 학생이 제 제안을 받아드리기를 정말로 바라고 있어요. 이번 학기에는 가능한 많은 학생들이 수업에 남으면 좋을 것 같아요.

학생: 좋아요. 해 볼 만할 것 같군요. 하겠습니다.

교수: 잘 되었군요. 스터디 모임은 밤에 하려고 생각 중인데, 주중에 — 주말은 아니고 — 학생이 편한 이틀의 날짜와 시간대를 알려 줄래요? 제가 모든 준비를 마친 후 다음 주 월요일 수업에서 새 스터디 모임에 대해 학생들에게 말을 할 수 있을 거예요.

학생: 문제 없어요. 언제 하면 좋을지 생각해 볼게요. 오늘 오후 늦게 제가 원하는 시간을 이메일로 보내 드릴 수 있을 거예요.

WORD REMINDER

get ~ out of the way (방해가 되지 않게) 치우다; 제거하다 proposition 제안 off and on 때때로, 불규칙하게 catch on 깨닫다, 알아듣다 retain 보유하다 challenge 해 볼 만한 일

Lecture • Physiology

p.102

교수: 골격은 인체의 틀이며, 근육은 인체의 힘입니다. 우리는 여러 가지 이유로 근육을 사용합니다. 봅시다… 우리는 근육 덕분에, 몇 가지 기능만 이야기하자면, 움직일 수 있고, 식사를 할 수 있고, 음식물을 소화할 수 있으며, 심장이 뛰도록 할 수 있고, 호흡을 할 수 있습니다. 신체에는 두 가지 주요한 유형의 근육이 있습니다. 수의근과 불수의근입니다. 일부는 횡문근인 반면, 평활근도 있습니다. 그리고 세 번째 유형의 근육도 있는데 — 심근입니다 — 이는 심장에서 찾아볼 수 있습니다.

신체 내 대부분의 근육은 횡문근입니다. 이들은 골격의 뼈에 붙어 있기 때문에 종종 골격근이라고도 불립니다. 또한 의지에 따라 움직일 수 있기 때문에 일부 사람들은 이를 수의근이라고도 부릅니다. 예를 들면 제가 여러분 모두에게 손을 들라고 해서 여러분들이 그렇게 한다면 여러분들은 뇌로 결정한 자발적인 움직임을 하고 있는 것입니다. 다른 말로 하면 여러분들은 의식적인 선택을 통해 몸을 움직인 것이죠.

이 근육들은 주로 근절이라고 불리는, 수천 개의 보다 작은 부분으로 이루어진 근육 세포의 묶음으로 이루어져 있습니다. 이들 근절은… 어, 단수형으로 S-A-R-C-O-M-E-R-E입니다… 그래서, 어, 이 근절들은 근원섬유라고 불리는 보다 작은 형태의 다발로 이루어져 있습니다. 근원섬유는

액틴과 미오신이라고 불리는 두 개의 단백질로 구성되어 있죠. 어, 이 단어들의 철자는 말씀드리지 않겠습니다. 책에서 철자를 찾아볼 수 있을 거예요. 알겠죠?

그래서, 어, 계속하면… 이 단백질들은, 아, 액틴과 미오신은 근육을 수축하는 능력에 있어서 중요한 역할을 합니다. 골격근에서 근육들은 기다랗고 줄이 있는 형태를 띕니다. 마치, 흠, 마치 근육에 선들이 조각되어 있는 것처럼 보입니다. 여러분 교재의 94페이지에 있는 신체의 그림을 확인해 주세요… 근섬유와 줄로 이루어진 긴 다발 형태에 주목해 주시고요. 또한 신체 내의 가장 큰 근육들, 예컨대 허벅지에 있는 근육이 골격근이라는 점에도 주목해 주세요.

골격근들이 크기뿐만 아니라 기능 및 작동 방식에 있어서도 서로 다르다는 점은 분명해 보일 것입니다. 일부는 지구력을 위해 설계되었기 때문에 피로에 잘 견딜 수 있지만 다른 근육들은 보다 쉽게 지칩니다. 이러한 능력은 근섬유 내의 미토콘드리아 수에 달려 있습니다. 기억하시겠지만… 적어도 기억하셨으면 좋겠는데… 지난 강의에서 배운 대로 미토콘드리아는 각 세포 내에서 공장과 같은 역할을 하며 산소와 영양분을 얻어 신체 에너지의 주된 원천인 ATP를 만들어냅니다. 서로 다른 근육들은 또한 혈류의 특성과 산화 작용에 있어서도 서로 다릅니다. 예를 들면 지구력을 위해 설계된 유형의 근육들은 다른 근육 보다 혈류와 산화에 필요한 모세 혈관을 더 많이 가지고 있으며, 에너지 생성에 필요한 미토콘드리아 역시 더 많이 가지고 있습니다.

다음은 평활근입니다. 이들은 비자발적인 기능을 통제하는 근육들입니다. 비자발적인 기능은 소화, 신체의 노폐물 이동, 혈류, 그리고, 음, 안구의 홍체의 개폐와 같은 활동을 담당합니다. 이러한 것들은 모두 신체의 평활근의 비자발적인 움직임에 의해 통제됩니다. 따라서, 당연하게도, 이러한 근육들은 눈, 음식을 통과시켜 위로 보내는 식도, 위, 장과 창자, 그리고 방광에서 발견됩니다. 또한 평활근은 혈관에 위치해 있는데, 이들은 혈액을 신체 곳곳으로 보내는데 도움을 줍니다. 횡문근과 마찬가지로, 평활근을 구성하고 이들이 기능할 수 있게 해 주는 두 개의 주된 활성 단백질도 액틴과 미오신입니다. 평활근은, 그 이름이 암시하듯, 줄무늬가 없이 매끄러운 형태를 띱니다. 그리고 평활근은 주로 사람이 통제하지 못하는 근육이라는 점을 기억해 주세요.

학생: 하지만 호흡은 어떤가요, Newton 교수님? 평활근이 호흡을 통제하나요? 제 말은 우리가 호흡을 통제할 수는 있지만, 보통 우리가 생각해서 그런 것은 아니잖아요.

교수: 좋은 질문이에요, Kimberly. 대부분의 경우, 우리는 우리가 호흡한다는 사실을 깨닫지 못합니다. 하지만 원한다면 숨을 멈추거나 혹은 보다 빨리 숨을 쉴 수가 있죠. 호흡을 통제하는 근육은 횡경막과 흉곽에 있는 골격근입니다. 따라서 이들은 골격근의 일부입니다. 아마도 우리가 항상 하고 있는 행동이기 때문에 호흡은 특히나 불수의근의 움직임처럼 보이게 됩니다. 하지만 그렇지가 않죠.

마지막으로 심근에 대해 이야기하면, 이들은 심장의 박동을 통제합니다. 심근은 횡문근이라는 점에서 골격근과 같습니다. 하지만 심근이 골격근처럼 길지는 않습니다. 대신 보다 짧고 조밀합니다. 또한 수의근이라는 점에서 골격근과 다릅니다. 이러한 두 가지 사실 때문에 — 횡문근이면서 불수의근이라는 점 때문에 — 심근은 별도의 카테고리로 분류됩니다. 자, 심근은, 아마 신체 전체에서 가장 중요한 근육일 것인데, 피로에 매우 잘 견딥니다. 또한 미토콘드리아로 산소를 섭취해서 에너지를 만들어 내는 능력이 탁월합니다.

WORD REMINDER

voluntarily 자발적으로 involuntarily 비자발적으로 striated 줄이 있는, 줄무늬가 있는 cardiac 심장의 voluntary muscle 수의근 conscious 의식하고 있는 muscle fiber 근섬유 sarcomere 근절 myofibril 근원섬유 thigh 넓적다리, 허벅다리 oxidation 산화 capillary 모세 혈관 smooth muscle 평활근 iris 홍체 esophagus 식도 intestine 장 bowel 창자 bladder 방광 blood vessel 혈관 diaphragm 횡경막 ribcage 흉곽 compact 빽빽한, 조밀한

Lecture • Art History p.105

교수: 모두들 리포트를 제출했나요…? 그래요, 좋아요. 빨리 읽어 보고 싶군요. 최선을 다해서 다음 주 목요일까지는 돌려 드릴게요. 좋아요. 그 얘기는 끝났으니까 수업을 시작해 볼까요…? 오늘 수업에서는 초현실주의를 살펴보도록 하겠습니다. 초현실주의라고 할 때 가장 먼저 머리 속에 떠오른 것이 무엇인가요? 누구 없나요…? Andy, 학생의 손이 가장 먼저 올라간 것 같군요.

학생: 감사합니다, Dodd 교수님. 저는 초현실주의라는 단어를 들으면 녹아내리는 시계와 살바도르 달리가 생각납니다.

교수: 실제로 제가 듣고 싶었던 두 개의 대답이군요. 여러분, 대부분의 사람들이 초현실주의에 대해 생각할 때 떠올리는 것이 바로 그러한 특정 이미지와 그 화가입니다. 그리고, 특히 살바도로 달리의 경우, 달리는 가장 유명한 초현실주의 화가이기 때문에 이는 당연한 일입니다. 하지만 이 운동의 역사에 대해 논의하기 전에 초현실주의의 기원에 대해 살펴봄으로써 이야기를 시작하고 싶군요.

일반적으로 초현실주의는, 1916년 시작되어 약 10년 동안 지속된, 다다이즘으로부터 비롯된 것으로 인정되고 있습니다. 다다는 저항 운동이었습니다. 그 멤버들은 폭력성, 어, 세계 1차 대전의 폭력성에 저항하고 있었습니다. 다다이즘은 스위스에서 몇몇 지성인들이 모여 전쟁과 전쟁에 대한 자신들의 감정을 논의하면서 시작되었습니다. 이들은 사회를 자극하는 무언가를 함으로써 전쟁의 잔인함에 대한 혐오감과 분노를 나타내고자 했습니다. 다다이스트들이 만들어 낸 글, 그림, 그리고 조각들은 미쳐 버린 세상을 반영했고, 예술계의 전통에 상당히 반하는 것이었습니다. 개인적으로 저는 다다이즘의 미술이 다소 기괴해 보입니다. 많은 사람들 역시 같은 느낌을 받고 있죠. 어쨌든 이들 예술가들이 결코 다다이즘을 하나의 실제 예술 운동으로 만들려고 한 것은 아니었지만, 실제로는 그렇게 되었습니다. 전쟁이 끝난 후 다다이즘은 서서히 사라졌습니다. 1925년경이 되자 완전히 사라졌죠. 음, 다다이즘은, 어, 일종의 초현실주의로 변형되었다고 말하는 것이 보다 정확할 것 같군요. 그러한 한 가지 이유는 다다이즘에 이끌렸던 사람들이 초현실주의에도 이끌렸기 때문이었습니다.

초현실주의의 탄생에 가장 큰 영향을 끼친 인물은 프랑스인인 앙드레 브르통이었습니다. 그는 프랑스 군인들이 전장에서 겪었던 트라우마에서 벗어나는데 도움을 준 정신과 의사였습니다. 전쟁 당시 브르통은 자크 바쉐라는 젊은 군인을 만났는데, 자크 바쉐도 작가였습니다. 전쟁 경험에 관한 바쉐의 글은, 흠… 비전통적인 방식으로, 그렇게 말해야 할 것 같은데, 쓰여졌습니다. 브르통은 바쉐의 글에서 영감을 얻어 1919년 파리에서 몇몇 다다이스트들과 모임을 갖기 시작했습니다. 그들과 함께 바쉐는, 그들이 자동 기술이라고 부른 것을 가지고 실험을 하기 시작했습니다. 자동 기술이란, 음, 도덕이나 이성의 제약 없이 생각나는 대로 글을 쓰는 방법이었습니다. 기본적으로 어떠한 제약으로부터도 벗어나 마음을 자유롭게 한 후 글을 쓰는 방법이었죠. 일부 다다이스트들 또한 자동 묘사를 하기도 했는데, 이 방법은 어떠한

계획이나 구조 없이 종이에다가 펜을 자유롭게 놀리는 것이었습니다. 심지어 어떤 다다이스트들은 생각의 자유를 표현하는 하나의 방, 방법으로서 꿈 분석을 이용하기도 했습니다. 본질적으로 브르통 및 그의 다다이스트 동료들은 무의식적인 마음을 열려고 노력하고 있었습니다.

초기 몇 년 동안 초현실주의는 다른 어떤 형태의 예술보다 자동 글쓰기에 초점을 맞추었습니다. 하지만 초현실주의는 예술의 모든 측면을 수용했는데, 여기에는 영화, 그리고, 물론, 회화가 포함되어 있었습니다. 시간이 지나면서 보다 많은 시각 예술가들이 이 운동에 참여했습니다. 1920년대 중반에 시작된 자동 묘사에 대한 초현실주의의 실험으로 이 운동의 참여자들은 미술의 시각적인 측면을 보다 강조하게 되었습니다. 그래서, 음, 다다이스트였던 많은 시각 예술가들이, 특히 파리에 있는 예술가들이 초현실주의의 모임에 들어오기 시작했습니다. 파리는 초현실주의에 있어서 매우 중요한 도시가 되었기 때문에, 1925년 최초의 초현실주의 미술의 전시회가 그곳에서 개최되었습니다.

하지만 초현실주의가 프랑스에만 국한된 것은 아니었습니다. 그 중심은 여전히 파리였지만, 그 영향력은 유럽 전역으로 퍼져 나갔습니다. 어쨌든 1930년대는 초현실주의 운동의 형성에 가장 중요한 시기였습니다. 주로 살바도르의 작품 때문이었는데, 살바도르 달리는 1929년 초현실주의 운동에 참여한 스페인 사람이었습니다. 1930년대 초 그는 초현실주의 미술 중 가장 유명해진 몇몇 작품들을 그렸습니다. 녹아 내리는 시계의 이미지와 상상력이 풍부한 꿈 장면에 대한 이미지는 대부분의 사람들이 초현실주의와 연결시키는 그림입니다.

초현실주의는 수십 년 동안 하나의 운동으로서 계속되었습니다. 브르통 자신이 1966년에 사망하자 많은 사람들은 초현실주의가 끝났다고 생각했습니다. 물론 일부 예술사가들은 그러한 사건이 일어나기 오래 전에 초현실주의가 끝났다고 주장합니다. 당연하게도 초현실주의의 정신이, 팝 아트와 포스트모더니즘과 같은 수많은 운동에서 계속되었다고 주장하는 사람들도 있습니다. 저는 이러한 쪽에 동의합니다. 또한 비트 세대로 불리는 1950년대와 1960년대의 미국 작가 세대들은 초현실주의의 영향을, 특히 자동 글쓰기의 영향을 받았습니다. 음, 이 운동에 대한 개관은 이 정도면 충분하다고 생각합니다. 이제 초현실주의 미술의 사례에 대해 살펴보고, 그렇게 하면서, 이 운동의 한 가지 측면을 더 알려 드리겠습니다.

WORD REMINDER

mention 언급하다 disgust 메스꺼움, 혐오감 outrage 격분시키다 bizarre 기괴한 morph 변형시키다 psychiatrist 정신과 의사 trauma 외상성 장애, 트라우마 constraint 제약 unconscious 무의식적인 embrace 껴안다, 기꺼이 받아들이다 circle 집단, 사회

PART 2

Conversation

p.110

학생: 안녕하세요. Laura Redding 선생님이신가요?

학생 활동 사무실 직원: 네, 저예요. 제가 도와 드릴 일이라도 있나요?

학생: 그런 것 같아요. 다가오는 동아리의 날의 책임을 맡고 계시죠, 그렇지 않나요? 여기에서 일하는 친구 중 한 명이 제가 선생님과 이야기를 해야 한다고 말해 주더군요.

학생 활동 사무실 직원: 아, 네. 동아리의 날에 대해 알고 싶다면 제대로 찾아왔어요. 제가 전체 행사를 책임지고 있죠. 프로그램에 대해 정확히 무엇을 알고 싶은가요?

학생: 음, 어, 행사에서 어떻게 하면 테이블을 얻을 수 있는지 알고 싶어요. 저는 연극반 회장인데, 저희는 신입 회원을 더 모집하려고 해요. 지난 2년 동안 가입 회원이 줄어들고 있지만, 저희가, 어, 이번 행사에서 광고를 해서 모집을 하면 많은 이들을 가입시킬 수 있을 것이라고 생각해요.

학생 활동 사무실 직원: 테이블이 필요하다고요? 신청이 조금 늦지 않았나요? 제 말은, 행사가 이틀 후면 시작되는데요.

학생: 어… 예, 제가 늦은 것 같군요. 그 점에 대해서는 유감이지만, 실은 어젯밤까지 동아리의 날 행사가 있을 것이라는 점을 몰랐어요.

학생 활동 사무실 직원: 몰랐다고요? 하지만 저희는 지난 2주 동안 매일 학생 신문에 광고를 냈는걸요. 어떻게 못 볼 수가 있죠?

학생: 정말 솔직하게 말씀을 드리면 저는 학생 신문을 거의 읽지 않아요. 이번 학기에는 그럴 시간이 없어요. 게다가, 어, 신문 기사의 수준에 흥미를 느껴본 적이 전혀 없었죠. 그래서 보통은 읽지 않아요.

학생 활동 사무실 직원: 무슨 말인지 이해할 수는 있지만, 동아리 회장으로서 이러한 종류의 행사들은 알고 있어야 해요. 리더가 해야 할 일 중 하나죠.

학생: 네, 이제 알 수 있을 것 같아요. 알려 줘서 고맙습니다.

학생 활동 사무실 직원: 어쨌든… 들어 보세요. 학생은 동아리에 대해 신경을 쓰고 있는 것으로 보여요. 동아리 회장들이 항상 그러는 것은 아니죠. 그래서 한 가지 방법을 알려 드릴게요. 마지막 신청자가 오는 경우를 대비해서 마지막 자리 하나를 따로 마련해 두고 있었는데, 학생에게 안성맞춤일 것 같네요.

학생: 사실인가요? 멋진 소식이군요. 정말 고맙습니다.

학생 활동 사무실 직원: 자, 단 하나 좋지 않은 점은 그곳이 학생 회관에서 사람들이 많이 다니는 곳은 아니라는 점이에요. 하지만 없는 것보다는 나을 것이라고 생각해요.

학생: 물론이에요. 그러면, 어, 제가 어떻게 해야 테이블을 얻을 수 있나요?

학생 활동 사무실 직원: 여기 이 서류를 작성해 주세요… 그리고 30달러의 요금을 내야 하고요.

학생: 30달러요?

학생 활동 사무실 직원: 네. 오, 걱정하지 마세요. 학생의 돈으로 내야 할 필요는 없어요.

학생: 안심이 되는군요.

학생 활동 사무실 직원: 음, 제 말은 지금 돈을 내야 하지만, 이곳 사무실에 신청을 하면 그 돈을 돌려받을 수가 있어요. 그래요, 약간 관료주의적으로 보일 수도 있겠지만, 그것이 이곳에서 일을 처리하는 방식이죠.

학생: 좋아요. 그렇게 말씀하신다면요. 여기 30달러요. 이 서류를 작성할게요. 그리고 또한 어떻게 돈을 돌려받을 수 있는지도 알려 주시면 좋을 것 같아요.

학생 활동 사무실 직원: 물론 그렇게 할게요. 제가 지금 여기 서류를 받았어요. 하지만 학생의 신청이 승인을 받기 위해서는 1주일이나 2주일 정도 걸릴 거예요. 그러면 그 후에 환불을 받게 될 거예요.

WORD REMINDER

in charge of ~을 책임지는 upcoming 다가오는 recruit 신입 회원을 모집하다 last minute 최후의 순간의, 막판의 fit the bill 만족시키다, 딱 필요한 것을 공급하다 reimburse 갚다, 상환하다

Lecture • Marine Biology p.112

교수: 아시다시피 천연 암초는 여러 형태의 수중 생명체들의 서식지입니다. 이러한 암초에는 많은 먹이가 있고 사나운 해양 포식자들로부터 몸을 피할 수 있는 장소가 제공되기 때문에 이곳은 종종 많은 생물들로 가득합니다. 하지만 전 세계에 있는 천연 암초의 수는 제한되어있으며, 일부 암초들은 자연적인 그리고 인간에 의한 이유들로 파괴되고 있습니다. 이 때문에 사람들은 인공 어초를 건설하기 시작했습니다. 인공 어초는 바다 속에 설치되어 시간이 지나면서 암초로 변하는 구조물입니다. 미국의 동부 해안뿐만 아니라 멕시코 만의 해안을 따라 수백 개의 인공 어초들이 있습니다. 이들은 많은 기능을 수행합니다.

우선, 인공 어초의 건설로 낡은 선박과 기타 인공 구조물들이 처분될 수 있는 장소가 마련됩니다. 많은 인공 어초들은, 아시는 바와 같이, 선박, 전철 차량, 석유 굴착 장치, 그리고 심지어 인공 어초를 만들기 위해 특별히 제작된 산호 구슬이라고 불리는 것들로 만들어지죠. 네? 덧붙이고 싶은 말이 있나요?

학생: Rand 교수님, 어떻게 그럴 수가 있죠? 제 말은, 그러한 물체들을 바다 속에 가라앉히면 환경에 해가 되지 않나요?

교수: 그렇게 생각할 수도 있겠지만, 해양이 겪게 되는 환경적 피해라는 것은 사실상 제로입니다. 왜 그런지 설명해 드리죠… 환경이 확실히 보호될 수 있도록 인공 어초의 건설은 신중하게 통제되고 감시됩니다. 선박을 예로 들어 보죠. 인공 어초를 만들기 위해 선정된 모든 배에서, 먼저 유해한 모든 요인들은 반드시 제거되어야 합니다. 석유 및 선박에 들어 있는 기타 액체들을 펌프로 빼내고, 모든 금속들을 — 물론 배의 선체와 구조는 제외됩니다 — 제거하고, 그리고 환경에 조그만 손상이라도 끼칠 수 있는 모든 것들을 배가 가라 앉기 전에 제거합니다. 하지만 인공 어초와 관련해서 몇 가지 좋지 않은 경우가 있었다는 점은 인정해야겠군요. 과거 1970년대 플로리다에서 어떤 사람이 수백만 개의 낡은 고무 타이어를 이용해 인공 어초를 만들겠다는, 다소 현명하지 못한 아이디어를 가지고 있었습니다. 결코 좋은 생각이 아니었죠. 산호와 기타 해양 생물들은 타이어에서 성장할 수가 없기 때문에 여기에는 생물들이 거의 달라붙지 못했습니다. 이후 타이어 다발이 서로 떨어져 플로리다 해변으로 타이어들이 밀려오기 시작했습니다. 소규모의 재난과 같은 것이었죠.

다행히도 인공 어초의 재료로 무엇이 좋고 무엇이 좋지 않은지는 알려져 있습니다. 따라서 타이어 사건과 같은 일이 되풀이되는 일은 없을 것입니다. 이제 다양한 재료에 관해 말씀을 드리겠습니다. 선체가 흔히 사용되는데, 여기에는 충분한 이유가 있습니다. 선체는 따로 떨어져 나가기 전까지 수십 년 동안 수중에 머물러 있을 수 있습니다. 전철 차량과 석유 굴착 장치들 또한 여러 해 동안 지속될 수 있고, 산호 구슬 역시 꽤 성능이 좋습니다. 오, 어, 여러분 중 산호 구슬을 본 사람이 없을 것 같아, 이들이 어떻게 생겼는지 설명해 드리도록 하죠. 산호 구슬은 벌집과 비슷하게 생겼습니다. 동그랗고, 수많은 구멍을 가지고 있으며, 콘크리트로 만들어져 있습니다. 산호 구슬의 크기는 다양한데, 하지만 대부분이, 오, 2미터 정도의 폭과 높이를 갖습니다. 인공 어초를 만들기 위해 사용될 때 이들은 해저 클러스터 내에 설치됩니다. 이러한 산호 구슬들과 기타 구조물들은 부착성을 지닌 산호 및 기타 생물들에게 강력한 정박점이 됩니다. 이러한 생물들이 어초에 붙으면, 또 다시, 다른 여러 동물들이, 특히 어류들이 어초로 오게 됩니다.

하지만 제가 약간 앞서 나가고 있군요. 다시 돌아와야 할 것 같습니다. 먼저, 질문을 하나 드리겠습니다. 왜 처음부터 생물체들이 인공 어초 주위에서 살까요? 정확히는 모르지만 인공 어초가 해류의 흐름을 차단하기 때문인 것으로 보입니다. 해류가 암초에 닿으면 물이 위로 이동하는데, 여기에는 플랑크톤과 기타 미세한 생명체들이 들어 있습니다. 이로써 영양분이 풍부한 물기둥이 올라가게 됩니다. 따라서 이 물 기둥은 많은 어류들을 유인합니다. 먼저, 정어리와 피라미 같은 작은 물고기들이 다가옵니다. 점차 다랑어 및 몇몇 상어와 같은, 보다 큰 물고기들이 유인됩니다. 그 다음에는 몸을 숨기기 좋아하는 해양 생물들이 찾아옵니다. 이들 중에는 그루퍼, 도미, 장어, 그리고 게와 새우, 바닷가재 등의 다양한 갑각류들이 있습니다. 그러면 수개월, 심지어 수년이 지나면, 산호와 기타 생물들이 인공 어초에 달라붙습니다. 곧 어초는 이러한 생명체들로 뒤덮여서 어초의 어떤 부분이 최초의 구조물이었는지 구분하는 일이 힘들어지죠.

여러분들도 틀림없이 짐작할 수 있으리라고 생각하는데, 인공 어초를 둘러싸고 있는 온갖 종류의 생물들로 인하여 이곳은 레저를 위해 다이빙을 하는 사람들에게 멋진 다이빙 장소가 됩니다. 인공 어초의 또 다른 장점이죠. 여러분이 다이빙을 한다면 — 혹은 미래에 다이빙을 하게 된다면 — 반드시 인공 어초에서 잠수를 해 보세요. 저도 몇 번 해 보았는데, 멋진 광경이었습니다. 물론, 인공 어초를 찾는 수많은 낚시용 대형 모터 보트는 피하셔야 할 것입니다. 일반적으로 다른 어떤 곳보다도 인공 어초 주위에서의 낚시가 훨씬 더 수월하다고 알려져 있습니다.

WORD REMINDER

teem with ~으로 가득 차다 sanctuary 피신처, 은신처 fierce 사나운, 흉포한 artificial reef 인공 어초 dispose of ~을 처분하다 oil rig 석유 굴착 장치, 석유 정제 시설 designate 지명하다 hull 선체 anchoring point 정박점 get ahead of oneself 앞서가다 in the first place 처음부터, 애당초 sardine 정어리 minnow 피라미 grouper 그루퍼(농엇과의 식용어) snapper 도미 encrust 외피로 덮다 sport fishermen 낚시용 대형 모터 보트

PART 3

Conversation p.116

학생: 안녕하세요, Anderson 선생님. 근무 시간이라 왔어요.

사서: 안녕하세요, Sheila. 오늘이 공휴일이라 그다지 바쁠 것 같지는 않군요. 오늘 아침에는 도서를 대출할 이용객들이 많지 않을 것 같으니 Robert를 도와서 반납된 도서들을 저쪽 책장에 정리하면 좋을 것 같아요.

학생: 문제 없어요. 하지만, 어, 제가 없는 동안 누가 대출대에서 근무할 건가요?

사서: 이곳으로 오는 사람은 제가 상대할게요. 잠시 데스크에 앉아 있는 건 상관없어요. 앞으로 30분 정도 책을 책장에 정리하고 다시 이곳으로 와서 나머지 근무 시간을 채우는 것이 어떨까요?

학생: 그럴게요.

사서: 오, 잠시만요. 가기 전에 학생과 이야기해야 할 것이 있어요.

학생: 네?

사서: 이틀 전에 제가 보낸 이메일을 받았나요?

학생: 이메일이요?

사서: 못 받은 것 같군요. 어쨌든, 어, 겨울 방학 동안 이곳에서 일하는 것에 관심이 있는지 물어보려고 이메일을 보냈어요. 알다시피 도서관은 방학 기간에도 문을 닫지 않기 때문에 대출대를 맡아 줄 사람이 필요하거든요.

학생: 아, 예, 사실 그 이메일은 받았어요. 답장을 하지 못해서 정말 죄송해요. 인류학 수업의 보고서를 쓰느라 너무 바빠서 답장할 시간이 없었어요.

사서: 어떻게 생각하나요? 제 기억으로는 학생이 이번 겨울 방학에 집에 갈 계획이 없다고 말한 것 같아서요.

학생: 네, 맞아요. 겨울 방학이 2주밖에 되지 않기 때문에 그처럼 짧은 기간 동안 집에 가기 위해 비행기 티켓 값을 낼 필요는 정말 없죠. 그래서, 어, 네, 일하는 것이 분명 관심이 있어요. 어찌되었든 여기에 있을 예정이라면 돈을 버는 것이 좋을 테니까요. 아무것도 하지 않는 것보다는 낫잖아요.

사서: 좋아요. 좋은 소식이군요. 방학 동안 일하는 것에 대해서 여기에 근무하는 거의 모든 사람들에게 이미 물어보았거든요. 학생이 할 수 있다니 매우 기쁘네요. 몇 시간 동안 일하고 싶은가요?

학생: 몇 시간 동안 일하는 것이 가능한가요?

사서: 음, 원한다면 하루에 8시간 일할 수 있어요. 학교측은 학생들이 일주일에 40시간까지 일하는 것을 허용하고 있죠. 그리고 방학 동안 도서관은 단축 근무를 하게 될 거예요. 9시부터 6시까지 문을 열 예정이라서, 1시간의 점심 시간을 포함해 하루 종일 일할 수 있어요.

학생: 오··· 제가 알아보고 다시 말씀을 드려도 될까요?

사서: 하루 종일 근무하는 것에는 관심이 없나요?

학생: 아니요, 그렇지 않아요. 사실, 음, 꽤 매력적으로 들려요. 전혀 예상치 못했던 일이라서요. 일주일에 40시간 대신 아마도 20시간 정도 일하게 될 것으로 생각하고 있었거든요. 하지만, 흠··· 생각해 보니 하루 종일 일하는 것도 그다지 나쁘게 들리지는 않아요. 방학 때 여기가 얼마나 바쁜가요?

사서: 전혀 바쁘지 않아요. 그 기간에는 주로 교수님들과 대학원생들이 이곳으로 와요. 하지만 대체적으로 조용해요. 바쁘지 않으면 일하는 동안 공부를 하거나 책을 읽을 수 있을 거예요.

학생: 아시겠지만··· 꽤 좋게 들리는군요. 밀린 독서를 할 생각이었는데, 이제 그러면서도 돈을 벌 수 있겠어요. 저를 설득시키셨네요. 종일 근무를 할 수 있게 해 주세요.

사서: 잘 되었군요. 정말 고마워요, Sheila.

WORD REMINDER

patron 후원자; 도서관 이용객 check out 대출하다 circulation desk (도서관의) 대출대, 대출 데스크 might as well ~하는 편이 낫다 graduate student 대학원생 catch up with ~을 따라잡다

Lecture • Psychology

p.118

교수: 여러분 모두들 몇 가지 긍정적인 기억을 가지고 있기를 바랍니다. 아시겠지만, 어, 여러분을 행복하게 만드는, 과거에 일어났던 일이요··· 좋아요. 자, 여러분에게 일어났던 좋지 않은 일들을, 어, 부정적인 기억에 대해 생각해 보세요··· 기억이 나나요···? 좋아요. 긍정적인 기억에 대해 보다 상세한 내용을 기억하고 있으면 손을 들어 주세요··· 그리고 부정적인 기억을 더 잘 떠올릴 수 있으면 손을 들어 주시고요··· 아, 정확히 제가 예상했던 바대로, 어, 대다수의 학생들이 부정적인 경험을 보다 자세히 기억하고 있군요. 좋아요, 질문이 하나 더 있습니다··· 여러분들 중 몇 명이나 어젯밤에, 가령 7시 30분에 자신이 무엇을 하고 있었는지 기억할 수 있나요···? 그렇게 많지는 않군요, 그렇죠? 음, 십중팔구 그 시간에는 특별한 일이 일어나지 않았기 때문에 무엇을 하고 있었는지 기억할 수 없을 것입니다.

제가 드리려고 말씀은 감정과 기억이 서로 연관되어 있다는 점입니다. 제가 여러분에게 생각해 보라고 했던 두 개의 기억은 — 긍정적인 기억과 부정적인 기억은 — 감정이 고조된 상태에서 이루어졌던 것입니다. 여러분들은 행복하거나 아니면 슬펐을 것입니다. 아마도 그 당시에 희열이나 공포를 느꼈을 수도 있습니다. 보다 중요한 것은 여러분들이 이러한 사건들에 대해 꽤 명확한 기억을 가지고 있다는 점입니다. 하지만 저녁 식사를 하거나, TV를 시청하거나, 혹은 공부를 하는 것과 같은 다소 평범한 일상 생활들에 대해서는 어떨까요? 그러한 기억 중 어느 것과 관련해서도 감정이 고조된 바가 없기 때문에 세부적인 내용들이 약간 불명확하게 느껴질 것입니다. 여러분들 중 어젯밤 7시 30분에 무엇을 하고 있는지가 기억나는 사람들 조차도··· 다음 주에 제가 똑같은 질문을 드린다면 그때 무엇을 하고 있었는지는 분명 깨끗이 잊고 있을 것입니다. 그러한 이유는 뇌가 감정적인 기억을 저장하는 것과는 달리, 무미건조한 기억들은 저장하지 않기 때문입니다.

긍정적인 기억과 부정적인 기억 간의 한 가지 주요한 차이는 사람들이 이들을 어떻게 인식하는지와 관련되어 있습니다. 감정적으로 긍정적인 경험을 한 대부분의 사람들은 이를 보다 상세히 기억하지만, 일부 사소한 측면들은 잊는 경향이 있습니다. 반대로 부정적인 기억을 가진 사람들은 종종 사소한 세부적인 내용들을 기억하는 반면, 보다 큰 문제들은 기억하지 못합니다. 이러한 일이 발생하는 것에는 이유가 있습니다. 일부 연구에 따르면 이것은 부정적인 기억과 연관된, 보다 강력한 감정의 결과입니다. 기본적으로 부정적인 감정에 대해 생각해 보세요··· 슬픔, 우울함, 부끄러움, 그리고 당혹감, 이 네 가지가 있습니다. 여러분들은 가족의 장례식에 대해 자세히 기억할 수도 있는데, 이는 여러분의 인생에서 그러한 일이 슬픈 사건이었기 때문입니다. 그리고 수업 발표 직전 옷에 음료를 쏟으면 매우 당황스럽기 때문에 이에 대해서는 생생한 기억을 할 수 있을 것입니다. 심지어 보다 강력한 부정적인 감정들, 예컨대 두려움이나 공포 등은 강력한 기억을 떠올릴 수 있게 해 줍니다. 여러분이 자동차 사고, 주택 화재, 혹은 주먹다짐을 겪은 적이 있거나 강도를 당하고, 혹은 성난 개에게 쫓긴 적이 있다면, 그와 관련된 두려움이나 공포의 상태가 고조되었기 때문에 그 사건을 매우 상세히 기억하고 있을 것입니다.

감정 이외에도 기억의 유지 및 회상과 관련이 있는 또 다른 요인들이 있습니다. 일반적으로 기억의 유지 및 회상에 있어서 여성들이 남성들보다 더 뛰어납니다. 일부 연구에 의하면 그러한 이유가 감정적인 사건들이 발생할 때 남성들 보다 여성들이 감정적으로 더 고조되기 때문이라고 합니다. 따라서 더 잘 기억하고, 보다 쉽게 기억을 떠올릴 수가 있는 것이죠. 게다가 젊은 사람들은 나이든 사람보다 감정을 잘 통제하지 못하는 경향이 있기 때문에 나이든 사람보다 부정적인 일을 더 잘 기억하는 경향이 있습니다. 왜 그런지는 알려져 있지 않습니다. 오, 사람의 기분 역시 기억 회상과 관련이 있습니다. 기분이 좋을 때에는 긍정적인 기억을 떠올리는 경우가 많지만, 기분이 좋지 않을 때에는 부정적인 기억을 떠올립니다.

학생: Bean 교수님, 뇌는 어떻게 기억을 저장하나요?

교수: 좋은 질문입니다. 흠··· 그에 대해서는 다루지 않으려고 했지만, 이제는 그럴 수 있을 것 같군요. 아시다시피, 음, 이 주제에 대해서는 많은 연구가 진행되고 있습니다. 그 중 다수는 그룹 연구로 진행되고 있는데, 이 연구에서는 피실험자들이 뇌주사 사진을 찍는 장치와 연결되어 있습니다. 전문가들이 이끌어 낸 거의 공통적인 결론은 뇌의 두 부분이 기억을 통제한다는 것입니다. 바로 편도선과 해마입니다. 이 둘 모두는 뇌에 있는 작은 부분입니다. 사람이 감정적인 상태에 도달하면 신체는 스트레스 호르몬을 분비합니다. 하나의 호르몬이, 이는 코티솔이라고 불리는데, 편도선과 상호 작용하고 이는 또 다시 해마에 영향을 끼쳐 기억이 유지되도록 합니다. 이를 나타내기 위해 심리학자들이 사용하는 용어는 기억 강화입니다. 안타깝게도 이러한 뇌의 영역은 알츠하이머 병으로 통상 손상되는 부분인데, 이러한 손상은 알츠하이머 병환자들이 병이 진행됨에 따라 기억을 잃어버리기 시작하는 이유일 수 있습니다.

자, Erika, 학생이 질문을 했으므로 여러분 모두에게 뇌의 그림을 보여 드려야겠네요. 여기 위쪽의 스크린을 봐 주세요. 기억 유지와 관련된 여러 센터들이 뇌의 어디에 위치해 있는지 알려 드리고자 합니다. 모두들 자세히 봐 주세요.

WORD REMINDER

in all likelihood 아마, 십중팔구 ecstatic 희열에 넘친, 황홀한 mundane 세속적인, 평범한 fuzzy 불분명한, 흐릿한 neutral 중립의, 특성이 없는 retain 보유하다 fistfight 주먹다짐 chase 쫓다, 추격하다 retrieval 복구, 회복 brain scan 뇌주사 사진 amygdala 편도선 hippocampus 해마 schematic 개요의; 도식의

Actual Test 06

PART 1

Conversation

p.124

재정 지원 사무실 직원: 안녕하세요. 혹시 Susan Sanders 아닌가요, 맞나요?

학생: 음, 아니에요. 죄송해요. 제 이름은 Emily Jenkins예요. 3시 20분 약속을 했죠.

재정 지원 사무실 직원: 아, 그렇군요. 음, 벌써 3시 15분이고, Susan과의 약속은 3시 정각이었네요. 그녀가 오늘 모습을 보이지 않을 것 같은데, 우리가 이야기를 조금 일찍 시작하는 것이 어떨까요?

학생: 저는 괜찮아요.

재정 지원 사무실 직원: 좋아요… 어떤 일 때문에 이곳 재정 지원 사무실로 오게 되었나요?

학생: 다음 학기의 등록금 때문이에요. 10% 가량 오르고 있는데, 부모님과 제가 감당하기에는 인상폭이 너무 크거든요.

재정 지원 사무실 직원: 알겠어요. 현재 재정 지원을 받고 있나요?

학생: 네, 받고 있어요.

재정 지원 사무실 직원: 약간 더 자세히 말씀해 주실래요?

학생: 아, 네. 물론이요. 학교로부터 5천 달러의 보조금을 받고 있어요. 그리고 또 각기 다른 대출을 두 번 받았는데, 총… 음, 3천 5백 달러 정도 되는 것 같아요. 나머지 수업료와 주거비 및 식비에 대해 말씀을 드리면, 부모님과 제가 각각 수천 달러씩 부담하고 있어요.

재정 지원 사무실 직원: 그렇군요… 지금 제 컴퓨터에 학생의 정보가 나와 있어요. 여기에서 공부를 시작한 후로 재정 지원을 받아 왔군요, 맞나요?

학생: 맞아요. 추가적인 지원이 없었다면 이곳보다 훨씬 저렴한 학교로 전학을 가야만 했을 거예요. 그렇게 하거나, 아니면, 어, 학교를 그만두고 일자리를 얻었겠죠.

재정 지원 사무실 직원: 그런 일이 일어나지 않기를 바라보죠.

학생: 학교에서 제 재정 지원금을 인상시켜 주는 것이, 어, 약 천 달러 정도요, 적절하다고 생각한다면 저는 분명 여기에 남아 있을 수 있을 거예요. 그런 일이 가능할 거라고 생각하시나요?

재정 지원 사무실 직원: 학점이 어떻게 되죠?

학생: 지난 학기에 평점 3.92를 받았어요. A가 4개이고 A-가 하나였죠. 성적이 가장 좋았던 학기였어요. 4학기 연속으로 장학생 명단에 올랐고, 제 평점이 충분히 높기 때문에 우수한 성적으로 졸업을 할 수 있을 거예요.

재정 지원 사무실 직원: 훌륭하군요. 현재의 평점이 어떻게 되는지 물어봐도 될까요?

학생: 그게… 3.51이에요. 학기를 마치기 전에 3.60까지 끌어올릴 수 있기를 바라고 있어요. 가능할지는 잘 모르겠지만 최선을 다할 거예요.

재정 지원 사무실 직원: 좋아요… 학점이 꽤 높기 때문에 특별 장학금을 받을 수 있는 자격이 될 것 같군요.

학생: 특별 장학금이요?

재정 지원 사무실 직원: 네. 아시겠지만, 많은 사람들이 ― 특히 졸업생들이 ― 이곳에 장학금을 기부하고 있어요. 통상 1년에, 오, 수백 달러 정도 되죠. 천 달러나 그 이상이 될 수도 있고요. 개인적으로는 신청할 수가 없어요. 하지만 학교가 그럴 자격이 있는 ― 그리고 재정적으로 어려운 ― 학생들을 학기 마다 검토해서 장학금을 지급해 주죠. 각기 다른 두 개의 장학금에 학생을 추천할게요. 사실 성적에 따른 장학금이지만, 지원이 필요한 학생들에게만 지급되고 있어요.

학생: 와. 잘 되었군요. 제가 해야 할 일이 있나요?

재정 지원 사무실 직원: 여기에 온 것만으로 충분해요. 절차는 이미 시작되었어요. 자, 약속할 수 있는 것은 아무것도 없어요. 그 점은 이해해 주세요. 학생이 어떤 종류의 장학금도 받지 못할 가능성도 있어요. 하지만 학생이 최소한 몇 백 달러의 장학금을 받을 수 있는 확률은 평균보다 높다고 해야 할 것 같군요. 장학금을 받게 되는 경우, 다음 주말 전까지 통보가 이루어질 거예요.

학생: 좋아요. 시간을 내 주셔서 감사합니다.

WORD REMINDER

show up 모습을 나타내다 grant 보조금, 지원금 loan 대출(금), 융자 room and board 방세와 식비 see fit to ~하는 것이 적당하다고 생각하다 GPA 평점 graduate with honors 우등으로 졸업하다, 우수한 성적으로 졸업하다 do one's hardest 전력을 다하다 alumnus 졸업생 endow 기부하다, 부여하다 odds 가능성, 확률 notify 통지하다, 통보하다

Lecture • Anthropology

p.126

교수: 일반적으로 인간과 다른 영장류들은 같은 조상으로부터 비롯되었다고 여겨집니다. 모든 영장류 중 인간과 신체적으로 가장 유사한 것은 유인원입니다. 그리고 제가 말한 유인원에는, 음, 고릴라, 오랑우탄, 침팬지, 그리고 주머니긴팔원숭이가 포함됩니다. 그건 그렇고, 침팬지에는 두 가지 유형이 ― 보통 침팬지와 피그미침팬지가 ― 존재하며, 긴팔원숭이도 두 가지 유형으로 존재합니다. 어, 보통 긴팔원숭이와 주머니긴팔원숭이입니다. 인간과 이들 유인원 모두를 비교해 보면, 우리는 피그미침팬지와 고릴라와 가장 밀접히 연관되어 있습니다. 실제 몇 퍼센트의 DNA 차이로 이 둘 유인원들과 분리되어 있을 뿐입니다. 흥미롭게도 DNA 및 신체적 외모가 모두 비슷하다는 점 때문에, 우리는 오래 전 공통의 조상을 가지고 있었다고 알고 있습니다. 하지만 문제는 그러한 일이 얼마나 오래 전에 일어났는지에 관한 것입니다. 흠… 그 미스터리에 관한 몇 가지 단서를 알려 드리죠. 약 천만 년 전에 고릴라가 공통의 조상으로부터 분리되었고, 약 7백 만년 전에는 우리가 분리되었으며, 그리고 약 3백만 년 전에 피그미침팬지와 보통 침팬지가 분리되어

나왔습니다.

이러한 사실을 알 수 있는 이유는 DNA 분석 때문입니다. 모든 종의 DNA에는 특정한 용해점이 존재하는 것으로 밝혀졌습니다. 그리고 서로 다른 두 개의 종의 DNA를 섞으면 용해점이 낮아져 각각의 종의 DNA 용해점보다 낮은 수준이 됩니다. 여러분이 기억해야 할 점이 있습니다. 용해점은 종의 DNA 구조에 1%의 차이가 있을 때마다 섭씨 1도씩 감소합니다. 예를 들면 인간의 DNA와 고릴라의 DNA가 섞이면 2.3도에서 녹는데, 이는 인간의 DNA 용해점 보다 더 낮은 온도입니다. 이는 인간과 고릴라가 DNA에 있어서 2.3%만 다르다는 점을 의미합니다. 여러분도 알 수 있듯이 우리는 고릴라와 97.7%의 DNA를 공유하고 있습니다. 지금까지의 내용들을 모두 이해했나요…? 좋습니다. 좋아요. 많은 수업에서 그러한 점을 이해하는데 어려움을 겪고 있습니다. 이야기를 계속해 보죠.

자, DNA의 용해점과 관련해서 유용한 점을 또 하나 알려 드리겠습니다. 우리는 이를 하나의 시계로서 활용할 수 있습니다. 하지만 이 방법에 대한 확고한 지지를 얻기 위해서는 유인원들과 원숭이들의 화석 기록을 검사해야 합니다. 약 3천만 년 전의 어느 시점에 결국 원숭이, 유인원, 그리고 인간이 될 공통 조상이 살고 있었습니다. 화석 기록을 연구함으로써 우리는 원숭이와 오랑우탄이 대략 언제 분리되었는지 알게 되었습니다. 원숭이들은 약 3천만 년 전에 존재했습니다. 그건 그렇고, 원숭이들은 DNA에 있어서 인간과 7.3%의 차이를 보입니다. 오랑우탄은 약 천 5백만 년 전에 분리되었고, 이들은 DNA에 있어서 인간과 3.6%의 차이를 보입니다. 이는 DNA의 차이가 2배 가까이 되면, 각 종이 분리된 시기 간에도 거의 2배의 차이가 존재한다는 점을 의미합니다. 좋아요. 복잡한 문제라는 것은 알고 있지만, 이러한 모든 정보가 일목요연하게 정리되어 있는 유인물을 잠시 후에 나누어 드리도록 하겠습니다. 그러니 너무 스트레스 받지 마시기 바랍니다. 그리고 이러한 내용을 필기하는 것에 대해 걱정하지 마세요. 유인물에 나와 있습니다.

이 공통 조상이 실제로 무엇이었는가는 아직까지 우리가 알지 못하는 점입니다. 하지만 공통의 조상이 현대 인류와 유사하고도 다른 특성을 지니고 있었다는 점은 확실합니다. 그러나 이 점을 명심하세요… 원래의 조상으로부터 분리되어 나온 종에서 또 다시 유사한 방식으로 새로운 종이 분리되어 나타났습니다. 다시 한번 원숭이가 약 3천만 년 전에 나타났다는 점을 기억해 주세요. 그 기간 동안 몇몇 새로운 종의 원숭이들 또한 진화를 했습니다. 또 다른 사례가 있습니다. 긴팔원숭이는 약 2천만 년 전에 분리되었고, 이후 약 8백만 년 전 이들은 다시 보통 긴팔원숭이와 주머니긴팔원숭이로 나누어졌습니다. 그런 다음, 제가 언급한 대로, 오랑우탄의 분리가 천 5백만 년 전에, 고릴라는 천만년 전에, 인간은 7백만 년 전에, 그리고 피그미침팬지 및 보통 침팬지들은 3백만 년 전에 분리가 되었습니다.

그래서 고릴라는 인간에 앞서 별개의 종으로 진화되었고, 반면 인간은 침팬지보다 먼저 나타났습니다. 고릴라, 인간, 그리고 침팬지들 모두 7백만 년이라는 시차 내에서 차례대로 진화했습니다. 따라서 동물계에서 인간과 가장 가까운 친척은 고릴라와 침팬지입니다. 하지만 DNA 상의 차이가 중요합니다. 결국 우리의 DNA 때문에 인간은 현대 문명을 만들어낸 반면, 고릴라와 침팬지는 계속해서 야생에서 살고 있습니다. 우리는 복잡한 도구를 사용할 수 있고, 언어로 의사소통을 할 수 있으며, 유일하게 직립보행을 할 수 있습니다. 다른 영장류들은 그렇게 하지 못하죠.

우리의 공통 조상에 대해 짧게 언급하도록 하겠습니다. 그러한 조상이 무엇이었는가는 아무도 정확히 알지 못합니다. 현대 인류의 조상인 몇몇 원인들이 발굴되어 화석 기록으로 남아 있습니다. 그 중 일부는 — 혹은 하나는 — 인간, 원숭이, 그리고 유인원 간의 고리가 될 수도 있을 것입니다. 하지만 확실한 것은 모릅니다. 아마도 미래의 누군가가 우리의 조상이 누구였는지 혹은 무엇이었는지를 알려 줄 새로운 종을 아프리카에서 발굴해 낼 것입니다. 하지만 그런 일이 일어나기 전까지, 우리는 추측만 하고 있을 뿐입니다.

WORD REMINDER

descend from ~의 자손이다, ~의 계통을 잇다 gibbon 긴팔원숭이 siamang gibbon 주머니긴팔원숭이 diverge from ~으로부터 갈라지다 melting point 용해점 handout 유인물, 배포용 인쇄물 subdivide 다시 나누다, 세분하다 emerge 나타나다 kingdom 계(界) exclusively 배타적으로, 독점적으로 upright 직립의 hominid 사람과의 동물, 원인 dig up 파내다, 발굴하다 guesswork 억측

PART 2

Conversation

p.130

교수: 아, Martha, 기다리게 해서 정말 미안해요. 약속이 2시라는 점은 알고 있지만 교수 회의가 약간 많이 길어졌어요. 몇몇 교수님들께서 이야기하는 것을 얼마나 좋아하는지 모를 거예요. 어쨌든, 여기에서 오래 기다리고 있었나요?

학생: 몇 분 동안만요, 교수님. 괜찮습니다. 사무실 밖에서 기다리면서 책을 읽고 있었어요.

교수: 좋아요, 좋아요. 음, 안으로 들어와서 앉으세요. 재킷을 좀 벗을게요… 좋아요. 자, 오늘 이야기해야 할 것이 무엇인가요?

학생: 다음 학기 제 시간표예요, 교수님. 시간표를 작성하고 있었는데, 두 수업에서 완전히 막혀 버렸어요. 제가 어떤 수업을 수강해야 할지 도와 주실 수 있으신가요?

교수: 전혀 문제 없죠. 학생의 지도 교수로서 제가 해야 할 일인걸요.

학생: 잘 되었군요. 저기, 제가 다음의 세 수업은 등록을 하기로 결심했는데… 미술사 104를 수강할 거예요. 현대 미술에 관한 개론 수업이죠. 수학 102도 수강하려고 해요. 대수학 수업이죠. 첫 번째 필수 수학 과목을 끝내고 싶어서 그 수업에 등록할 거예요. 그리고 세 번째 수업은 이탈리아어 101이고요.

교수: 이탈리아어요?

학생: 항상 그 수업이 듣고 싶었는데, 어, 제가 미술사 전공이라서, 이탈리아어를 알고 있으면 좋을 것 같아요. 어쨌거나 많은 위대한 미술이 이탈리아 사람들에 의해 만들어졌기 때문에, 그래서…

교수: 좋은 지적이군요. 논리적이에요. 좋아요. 이 세 수업들은 모두 꽤 괜찮아 보여요. 결정하려고 하는 다른 두 개의 수업은 무엇인가요?

학생: 좋아요. 저는 정말로 역사학과 수업을 하나 듣고 싶어요. 현대 미국에 관한 수업과 중세 유럽에 관한 수업 중에서 고르려고 하고 있어요. 교수님께서 생각하시기에 제가 어떤 것을 선택하면 좋을까요?

교수: 왜 역사를 들으려고 하죠? 역사를 전공하려고 하는 것인가요, 어, 아니면 단지 역사에 흥미가 있는 건가요?

학생: 실은 둘 다예요. 복수 전공을 할 수도 있기 때문에 1학년이 끝나기 전에 최소한 역사 수업 하나는 수강해 두어야 할 것 같아요.

교수: 현명한 결정이군요. 그런 경우라면 어떤 수업에 더 관심이 가나요?

학생: 중세 역사 수업이요. 확실히요.

교수: 그러면 그 수업을 들으세요. 수업을 맡을 교수님을 알고 있는데, 뛰어나신 분이죠. 그분의 수업을 많이 좋아하게 될 거예요. 자, 두 번째 수업은

요?

학생: 화학 개론 수업이나 철학 수업 중 하나를 들으려고 생각 중이에요. 철학 수업이 재미있어 보이기는 하지만, 어, 화학 수업을 듣는다면 필수 과학 과목을 끝낼 수 있죠.

교수: 대부분의 화학 수업에는 실험이 있다는 것을 알고 있죠, 그렇지 않나요? 특히 교양 과목으로 듣는 학생들에게는 쉽지 않을 거예요.

학생: 아, 그 점에 대해서는 확인해 봤어요. 제가 등록하려고 생각 중인 수업은… 화학 110 수업인데… 어, 실험이 없어요.

교수: 정말인가요? 그러면 그 수업을 듣고 과학 필수 과목을 끝내는 것이 어떨까요? 그렇게 하면 이후의 학기에서 더 많은 선택 과목을 수강할 수 있는 시간이 생길 거예요.

학생: 멋진 계획으로 들리는군요. 도움을 주셔서 정말 감사합니다, 교수님.

WORD REMINDER

faculty meeting 교직원 회의, 교수 회의 introductory 입문의, 개론의 algebra 대수학 double major 복수 전공 prudent 신중한, 현명한 get rid of ~을 제거하다 liberal arts 교양 과목 polish off 재빨리 끝내다, 해치우다 elective 선택 과목

Lecture • Physics

p.132

교수: 방사선으로 주의를 돌려야 할 시간이군요. 우선, 그것이 무엇일까요…? 간단히 말해서 방사선은 우리 주변의 모든 곳에 존재하는 에너지의 한 형태입니다. 방사선에는 두 개의 주요한 유형이 있습니다. 바로 전리 방사선과 비전리 방사선이죠.

전리 방사선은 원자를 이온화시킬 수 있다는 점에서 그 명칭이 유래되었습니다. 원자가 이온화되면 양전위를 갖게 됩니다. 이러한 일은 원자 내의 전자가 궤도를 벗어날 수 있을 정도로 충분한 에너지를 얻게 될 때 일어납니다. 그 결과 전자가 손실되면 원자는 양극을 띱니다. 기초 화학 수업의 내용으로부터 기억해 낼 수 있어야 하는데, 중성 원자 내에서는 음극을 띠는 전자와 양극을 띠는 양성자의 수가 동일합니다. 하지만 전자를 잃으면, 어, 양성자의 수가 더 많아져서 원자는 양극을 띠게 됩니다. 이것이 바로 전리 방사선에서 일어나는 일입니다. 전리 방사선에는 몇 가지 유형이 존재하는데, 여기에는 알파 입자, 베타 입자, 중성자, 중성 미자, 뮤온, 감마선, 그리고 X선이 포함됩니다. 각각은 서로 다른 특성을 가지고 있으며, 다양한 방식으로 생물체에게 잠재적인 피해를 끼칠 수 있습니다. 이들 입자 간의 차이가 표시되어 있는 표가 수업 홈페이지에 있습니다. 여러분의 기말 시험 점수가 달려 있기 때문에 확인해 보실 것을 강력히 추천합니다. 아시겠죠…?

두 번째 유형은 비전리 방사선입니다. 이것은 무엇일까요? 음, 비전리 방사선은 주로 전자기 스펙트럼상 보다 긴 파장을 가지고 있는 것들로 이루어집니다. 이번 학기 초에 배운 것처럼, 전자기 스펙트럼은 에너지 파동으로 구성되어 있습니다. 가시 광선 및 전파를 포함한, 보다 긴 파장을 가지고 있는 부분들은 보통 무해합니다. 파동의 길이가 증가하면, 어, 자외선과 마이크로파를 시작으로 생물체에게 미치는 위험성이 증대됩니다. 마지막으로, 스펙트럼의 끝에는 X선과 감마선이 존재하며, 이들은 매우 짧은 파장을 지니고 있습니다. 이들은 생물체에 심각한 위험을 초래할 수 있습니다.

음, 우리 주변에 다양한 유형의 방사선이 존재한다는 점은 것은 확실합니다. 하지만 어디에서 나오는 것일까요…? 방사원으로 자연적인 것과 인공적인 것 모두가 있습니다. 우리 주위에 항상 존재하는 한 가지 유형이 있는데, 음, 적은 수준입니다. 우리는 이를 배경 복사라고 부릅니다. 흥미롭게도 이 중 상당 부분은 우주로부터 나오는 것입니다. 이것이 우주선입니다. 우주선은 태양 및 기타 항성에서 비롯됩니다. 다른 방사원으로 토양, 암석, 그리고 심지어 식물과 물을 들 수 있습니다. 이들 방사선은, 붕괴함으로써 방사선을 방출하는 우라늄 같은 원소로부터 비롯됩니다. 이러한 방사선의 수준은 장소에 따라 다르며, 일정 지역 내에 우라늄과 같은 원소가 얼만큼 붕괴되는지에 따라 다릅니다. 마지막으로 우리의 신체 내에서 매우 낮은 수준의 방사선이, 음, 칼륨, 탄소, 그리고 납 동위 원소로부터 만들어집니다. 이러한 것들은 자연적으로 존재하는 주요한 방사원들입니다.

그러면 인간이 만들어 낸 방사원들은 어떨까요…? 봅시다… 사람들이 피는 담배에는 방사선이 들어 있습니다. 또한 TV 및 화재 경보기와 같은 전자기기에도 들어 있습니다. 병원에서 X레이 촬영을 받는다면 일정량의 방사선을 쬐게 됩니다. 위험할 정도의 양은 아니지만, X레이 기술자로 일을 한다면 방사선에 과도하게 노출되지 않도록 안전 조치들을 취해야 할 것입니다. 핵 발전소는 원자로 누출이 일어나는 경우 명백한 방사원이 됩니다. 또한, 음, 라디오 타워, 전자레인지, 마이크로웨이브 송신기, 그리고 전자기 스펙트럼상의 파장을 사용하는 통신 기기로부터 방출되는 방사선이 있습니다. 여러분도 알 수 있듯이, 우리는 방사선에 둘러싸여 있습니다.

학생: 그러한 유형의 방사선들은 모두 위험하지 않나요?

교수: 솔직히 말하면, 그렇습니다만, 상당한 양을 받을 때만 그렇습니다. 그리고 지금쯤이면 아실 수 있을 텐데, 사람에게 해를 끼칠 수 있는 양은 노출된 방사선의 유형에 따라 달라집니다. 알파 입자가 가장 위험하기 때문에, 이는 적은 양이라도 매우 해로울 수 있습니다. 반대로 X선은 훨씬 덜 위험해서 보다 많은 양이 있어야 합니다. 마지막으로 전파는, 상당히 긴 파장을 갖고 있는데, 거의 피해를 주지 않습니다. 흠… 약간 더 자세히 말씀드릴까요? X선은… 1년에 1,000번을 쬔다면 위험할 정도의 방사능 양에 노출될 수 있습니다. 아시다시피 많은 양의 X선입니다. 여러분은 평생 동안 몇 차례나 접해 보았나요? 많지 않을 것으로 확신합니다.

방사능 노출 정도는 라드라고 불리는 단위로 측정됩니다. 철자는 R-A-D-S입니다. radioactively absorbed dose의 첫 글자를 따서 만든 단어죠. 라드가 클수록 더 많은 위험에 처해 있는 것입니다. 또 다른, 음, 보다 작은 측정 단위는 그레이입니다. 1라드는 100그레이와 같습니다.

방사선이 생물에게 미치는 가장 큰 영향은 세포를 파괴시키는 것으로, 이는 암의 발병으로 이어질 수 있습니다. 단기간 많은 양에 노출되는, 예컨대 일본의 히로시마와 나가사키에서 이루어진 원자 폭탄의 폭발과 당시 소련에 속해 있던 체르노빌의 원자력 발전소 사고와 같은 극단적인 경우, 사람들은 방사능에 노출된지 수일 혹은 수주 내에 목숨을 잃을 수 있습니다. 하지만 장기간 적은 양에 노출된 사람들은 수십 년 동안 암에 걸리지 않을 수도 있습니다. 그리고 많은 사람들이 어떠한 피해도 입지 않습니다.

WORD REMINDER

ionizing radiation 전리 방사선 non-ionizing radiation 비전리 방사선 neutral atom 중성원자 proton 양성자 highlight 강조하다 electromagnetic spectrum 전자기 스펙트럼 visible light 가시 광선 background radiation 배경 복사 cosmic radiation 우주선 potassium 칼륨 isotope 동위 원소 smoke detector 연기 감지기, 화재 경보기 run a risk of ~의 위험을 무릅쓰다 leak 누수, 누출 wager (돈 등을) 걸다, 내기하다 onset 시작, 발단

Lecture • History

p.135

교수: 오늘날 네덜란드는 작지만 부유한 국가입니다. 이러한 점은 17세기 이후 네덜란드 대부분의 역사에서도 마찬가지였죠. 17세기는, 역사가들이 지칭하는 바와 같이, 네덜란드의 황금 시대가 진행되던 시기였습니다. 이 기

간 동안 네덜란드 사람들은 무역, 과학, 그리고 예술에 있어서 글로벌 리더였습니다. 네덜란드인들이 그러한 성공을 거둘 수 있었던 몇 가지 이유가 있었습니다. 그 중에는 숙련된 노동력, 풍부하고 저렴한 에너지, 그리고 원활한 국내 커뮤니케이션 시스템 및 도로와 운하의 운송 시스템이 포함되어 있었습니다. 네덜란드인들은 더 나아가 거대한 함대를 보유했고, 능숙한 해군 사령관들을 두고 있었으며, 그리고 해외 식민지 제국을 건설하기 시작했습니다. 이러한 요인들이 모두 합쳐져 막대한 양의 부가 만들어졌는데, 이러한 부는 다시 그곳의 과학과 예술을 발전시키는데 도움을 주었습니다.

제가 과거의 네덜란드에 대해 이야기할 때에는 현재의 벨기에와 네덜란드에 걸쳐 있는 지역을 언급한다는 점을 알아 두세요. 이들은 한때 단일 국가였습니다. 이 국가는 17개의 주로 구성되어 있었습니다. 16세기 네덜란드 역사에서 두 번의 중요한 사건이 있었습니다. 첫 번째 사건은 찰스 5세의 지배 하에 있던 스페인 국민들이 스페인 영토를 장악했을 때 일어났습니다. 두 번째는 종교 개혁이 일어나서 북쪽 끝에 있던 7개 주의 대부분의 주민들이 개종에 성공한 것이었습니다. 가톨릭 국가였던 스페인은, 찰스 왕의 아들인 필립 2세의 통치를 받고 있었는데, 무력에 의존하여 그러한 주에서 가톨릭을 복원시키려고 했습니다. 이 7개의 개신교 주들은 반란을 일으켰고, 통합을 통해 네덜란드 연합주를 형성했습니다.

10개의 남부 주들은 가톨릭으로 남아 있었습니다. 그래서 1568년에 전쟁이 시작되었죠. 전쟁은 80년 동안 계속되었습니다. 그래요, 80년입니다. 물론 많은 전투가 불규칙적으로 일어났지만, 그래도 긴 전쟁이었습니다. 전쟁 당시 10개의 남부 주들은 스페인의 속국으로 남아 있었습니다. 하지만 그곳에 있던 많은 사람들이 개신교로 개종하여 남부 주를 떠났습니다. 이러한 사람들은 종종 숙련된 노동자, 선원, 군인, 그리고 상인들이었습니다. 많은 이들이 1648년 스페인으로부터의 독립을 얻어내는데 기여했습니다. 오래 지속되기는 했지만, 전쟁은 네덜란드 사람들을 단결시켰고 그들의 전성기의 시작을 알려 주었습니다.

언급한 대로 17세기에 네덜란드 사람들이 그러한 번영을 누릴 수 있었던 한 가지 이유는 그들의 전력원 때문이었습니다. 산업 혁명 이전, 전력은 인간, 동물, 그리고 몇몇 천연 자원들, 예컨대 바람이나 낙수로부터 얻었습니다. 네덜란드 사람들은 상당량의 에너지를 풍력으로부터 얻었습니다. 바다를 간척하기 위해 바닷물을 펌프로 빼내는데 필요한 양의 에너지를 풍차를 이용해 얻었습니다. 어, 네덜란드의 많은 부분이 해수면 보다 낮은 곳에 있다는 점을 기억하세요. 한때 북해에 가라앉아 있던 지역이, 물을 없애고 물이 다시 들어오는 것을 막아 준, 네덜란드의 뛰어난 펌프 및 제방 시스템 덕분에 육지가 되었습니다. 또한 이 풍차들은 제재소뿐만 아니라 제분소의 곡식을 빻는 기계에도 전력을 공급해 주었습니다.

네덜란드인들은 또한 상대적으로 작은 영토와 높은 인구 밀도를 장점으로 승화시켰습니다. 국토가 매우 작았기 때문에 효율적인 도로 및 운하 시스템을 발전시킬 수 있었습니다. 이로써 사람들과 물품들이 쉽고 빠르게 이동할 수 있었습니다.

네덜란드 사람들은 항해에 능숙했고 거대한 상단을 가지고 있었기 때문에, 그들의 선박이 네덜란드의 수출품들을 유럽의 각지로 운송해 주었습니다. 게다가 이 선박들은 네덜란드 사람들에게 필요했던 수입품들을 싣고 돌아왔습니다. 여기에는 방직 산업에 필요한 양모와, 조선 산업에 필요한 목재, 피치, 그리고 로프와 같은 원자재들이 포함되어 있었습니다.

해외에서 네덜란드 탐험가들은 — 부분적으로 그들의 강력한 해군 덕분에 — 북아메리카, 아프리카, 인도, 일본, 그리고, 어, 인도네시아에 식민지를 건설했습니다. 암스테르담과 기타 네덜란드의 주요 항구들은 유럽의 무역 중심지가 되었고, 이러한 도시의 많은 사람들이 믿을 수 없을 정도로 부유해졌습니다. 1602년 네덜란드인들은 세계 최초의 대규모 주식 회사인 네덜란드 동인도 회사를 설립했습니다. 또한 암스테르담에 세계 최초의 주식 시장을 설립하기도 했습니다. 네덜란드 동인도 회사는 거의 두 세기 동안 세계에서 가장 큰 무역 회사로 남아 있었습니다. 이 회사기 이룬 부의 양은, 음, 어, 경이로운 것이었죠.

이러한 부는 또한 네덜란드의 다양한 과학 및 예술의 발전에도 기여했습니다. 예를 들어 세계 최초의 망원경은 세 명의 네덜란드인이 발명했습니다. 광학, 수학, 물리학, 그리고 생물학 분야의 발전에 기여한 네덜란드인들도 있었습니다. 렘브란트 및 베르메르와 같은 위대한 화가들도 세계 일류의 화가로서 자리매김을 했습니다.

학생: 대단한 시기였던 것처럼 들리는군요. 그런데 왜 지속되지 못했나요?

교수: 몇 가지 측면에서 네덜란드인들은 자신들의 성공에 대한 희생자가 되었습니다. 부유해지고 권력이 커지자 그들은 유럽의 거대한 파워 게임 속으로 들어가게 되었습니다. 스페인이 끊임없이 문제를 일으켰습니다. 프랑스도 마찬가지였는데, 프랑스는 네덜란드의 바로 옆에 위치해 있었죠. 당시 프랑스는 유럽에서 가장 강력한 국가였고, 프랑스 지도자들은 영토를 확장시키려는 야망을 가지고 있었습니다. 여기에는 네덜란드와의 합병도 포함되어 있었습니다. 영국인들 또한 때때로 네덜란드인들과 갈등을 빚었습니다. 영국과 네덜란드는 실제로 17세기에 세 차례의 전쟁을 치렀습니다.

WORD REMINDER

internal 내부의, 국내의 fleet 함대 commander 지휘관, 사령관 entity 실체 province 지역, 주 convert 전환하다, 개종하다 resort to ~에 의지하다, ~에 호소하다 gain control of ~을 통제하다, ~을 장악하다 off and on 때때로, 불규칙하게 windmill 풍차 reclaim 개간하다, 간척하다 levee 둑, 제방 grind 갈다, 빻다 sawmill 제재소 fabulously 믿을 수 없게 shareholding corporation 주식 회사 phenomenal 놀랄 만한, 경이적인

Actual Test 07

PART 1

Conversation

p.142

교수: 안녕하세요, Jodie. 오늘 저를 만나고 싶다는 학생의 이메일을 받았어요. 어떻게 하면 될까요?

학생: 음, 교수님, 괜찮으시면 어제 수업에서 돌려 주신 보고서를 확인해 보고 싶어요.

교수: 그래요. 미안하지만, Jodie, 학생의 보고서를 정확히 기억을 할 수가 없군요. 그랬으면 좋겠지만 제가 개개인의 보고서를 기억하기에는 수업의 학생수가 너무나 많아요. 혹시 가지고 오지는 않았나요, 그런가요?

학생: 실은, 교수님, 지금 가지고 있어요. 보시겠어요?

교수: 그래요. 큰 도움이 될 것 같군요.

학생: 여기 있어요…

교수: 아, 네… 이 보고서가 기억나는군요.

학생: 그러신가요? 그러면 왜 제가 보고서에서 C학점을 받았는지 말씀해 주시겠어요? 제 말은, 어, 이 보고서를 쓰는데 많은 노력을 기울였거든요. 최

소한 A-나 B+를 받게 될 것으로 생각했지만, 교수님께서 이와 같은 학점을 주셨죠.

교수: 무엇보다도, Jodie, 제가 학생에게 학점을 준 것이 아니에요. 학생이 학점을 얻은 것이죠. 알겠지만 여기에는 차이가 있어요. 또한, 학생이 보고서를 쓰는데 몇 시간을 보냈는지는 사실 중요하지 않아요. 중요한 것은 최종 결과물이죠. 솔직히 말하면, 학생이 보고서에 30분을 쓰는지 혹은 30시간을 쓰는지는 제게 중요하지 않아요. 학생이 제출한 보고서에 적혀 있는 것에만 관심이 있을 뿐이에요.

학생: 하지만 제가 제출한 내용이 좋지 않다고 생각하신 것이잖아요?

교수: 그런 편이었죠. 그랬어요. 기분이 나빴다면 미안해요.

학생: 음, 어, 더 자세히 말씀해 주시겠어요? 제가 무엇을 잘못했는지 알고 싶기도 하고, 음, 교수님께서 이번 보고서에 많은 주석들을 달아 주지는 않으셨거든요.

교수: 그래요. 함께 보고서를 검토하면 되겠군요.

학생: 감사합니다.

교수: 무엇보다… 학생은 서론을 쓰지 않았어요. 몇몇 통계를 언급하고 그에 대해 설명하면서 보고서를 시작했죠. 그래서, 어, 학생의 보고서가 무엇을 다룰 것인지를 전혀 알 수가 없었어요. 서론을 써서 독자들로 하여금 보고서의 주제가 무엇인지, 그리고 보고서에서 무엇을 주장할 것인지를 알 수 있도록 해야 해요.

학생: 알겠습니다. 그 밖에는요?

교수: 봅시다… 아, 맞아요. 많은 사실들이 잘못되어 있었어요. 제가 빨간 색으로 동그라미 표시를 한 이 지문들을 보세요. 여기에 하나가 있고… 여기에 또 하나가 있군요… 이렇게 동그라미로 표시된 지문들은 모두 사실 관계가 잘못되어 있어요. 사실들은 훨씬 더 잘 확인해 봐야 해요.

학생: 그 밖의 것이 또 있나요?

교수: 결론도 잘 써야 해요. 보고서가, 어, 너무 갑작스럽게 끝이 났어요. 결론에서는 무엇을 입증해 냈는지 설명해야 해요. 어떤 보고서에서도 필수적인 부분이죠.

학생: 알겠습니다. 좋아요. 어, 감사합니다.

교수: 알겠지만… 제 수업에서는 리라이트를 허용하고 있어요. 보고서를 다시 제출하고자 한다면, 오, 지금부터 3일 내로요, 기꺼이 다시 한 번 검토해 줄게요. 아마 학점이 바뀌게 될 거예요.

학생: 그런가요? 제가 몰랐네요. 좋은 소식 알려 주셔서 감사합니다, 교수님. 반드시 보고서를 수정할 건데, 그러면 그때까지 훨씬 더 좋은 보고서가 나올 거예요.

WORD REMINDER

go over 검토하다 recall 회상하다, 기억하다 tremendous 막대한 at worst 아무리 나빠도 distinction 차이 comment 주석, 논평 cite 언급하다

Lecture • Economics

p.144

교수: 선물 시장으로도 알려져 있는 상품 시장으로 주의를 돌려보죠 여러분 모두가 전에 이러한 용어들을 들어본 적이 있으리라고 확신합니다, 그렇죠? 하지만 상품 시장에서 어떤 일이 일어나는지 아시나요…? 흠… 아마도 모르실 것입니다. 좋아요, 제가 말씀해 드리죠. 선물, 어, 상품 시장에서 거래를 하면 무엇을 실제로 구입하거나 판매를 하는 것이 아닙니다. 여기에서 하는 일은 미래에 특정 상품의 가격이 어떠한 방향으로 나아갈 것인지 추측하는 것입니다. 따라서 가격이 상승할 것이라고 생각하면 구입을 합니다. 당연히, 가격이 떨어질 것으로 생각되면 매각을 하죠. 이러한 점에서 상품 시장은 주식 시장과 같습니다. 하지만 상품 시장의 중요한 한 가지 측면은, 모든 거래에 구매자와 판매자가 있기는 하지만, 어느 쪽도 거래하는 품목을 실제 소유하고 있지는 않다는 점입니다.

약간 이상하게 들릴 수도 있다고 생각합니다. 저도 처음 들었을 때 혼란스러웠어요. 하지만 여러분들이 인내심을 갖는다면, 이해가 되는 방식으로 제가 이를 설명할 수 있으리라 생각합니다. 그렇게 하기 위해서는 과거로 거슬러 올라가 상품 시장의 기원에 대한 역사를 짧게 알려 드려야 할 것 같군요. 1840년대 일리노이 주의 시카고는 미국의 상업 중심지로 번성했습니다. 중서부 지방 및 서부의 여러 지역들을 동부 해안가 지역과 연결시켜 준 철도로 인해, 시카고는 중요한 교통 중심지였습니다. 당시 중서부 지방의 농부들은 환금 작물로서 종종 밀을 재배했습니다. 밀을 수확한 후 농부들은 시카고로 가서 그것을 구매할 중개인들을 찾았습니다. 그런 다음 중개인들은 시카고의 철도를 이용하여 밀을 미 전역으로 보냈습니다. 이해하기 쉽죠, 그렇죠?

하지만 농부들이 직면했던 한 가지 문제는 빨리 팔 수 있기를 바라면서 시카고에 왔을 때 중개인들이 우위를 점하고 있다는 사실이었습니다. 아시겠지만 시카고에는 밀을 보관할 수 있는 저장 시설이 거의 없었습니다. 또한 농부들이 밀을 팔고자 할 때 농부들을 상대하고 밀을 처리하는 절차도 확립되어 있지 않았습니다. 마지막으로 농부들은 주로 밀을 팔아 농장으로 돌아오기를 원했는데, 농장에는 항상 해야 할 일들이 있었습니다. 이러한 모든 요인들로 인해 농부들은 중개인들의 손아귀에 놓여 있었고, 중개인들은 자신들이 제안한, 보다 낮은 가격을 농부들이 받아드릴 때까지 가만히 버티고 있을 수 있었습니다.

그 후 1848년에 농부들과 중개인들이 서로 만날 수 있고, 중개인들이 즉시 현금을 주고 밀을 인수할 수 있는 중심지가 생겼습니다. 이러한 경미한 시작으로부터 선물 계약이 탄생했는데, 어, 선물 계약에서는 — 판매자와 구매자로 행동하는 — 농부와 중개인들이 미래에 밀과 기타 곡물들을 돈과 교환하자는 약속을 할 수 있었습니다. 농부들은 자신의 곡식에 대해 얼마를 받게 될 것인지 확실하게 알 수 있었고, 중개인들 또한 자신의 구매 비용이 얼마가 될 것인지 알 수 있었기 때문에, 이는 모두를 만족시켰습니다.

이러한 유형의 거래는 곧 일반적인 것이 되었습니다. 계약서가 작성되면, 선물 계약서는 은행 대출에서 담보로까지 인정을 받았습니다. 곧 이러한 계약은 기한이 끝나기 전에 당사자가 바뀌기 시작했습니다. 예를 들어 한 농부가 자신의 곡물을 팔고 싶지 않다는 결정을 내리면 또 다른 농부를 찾아 자신의 인도 의무를 그에게 넘길 수 있었습니다. 중개인들도 마찬가지였습니다. 중개인들은 또한 다른 농부들과 맺은 계약을 사고 팔았습니다. 마침내 이로 인해 투기꾼이 생겨났습니다. 투기꾼은 상품을 사거나 팔려는 의도 없이, 낮은 가격에 사고 높은 가격에 팔려는 목적으로 계약상의 거래만을 하는 사람입니다.

방금 전 제가 주식 시장의 이야기를 꺼내면서 주식 시장과 상품 시장 간의 유사성을 언급했습니다. 하지만 이 둘이 차이를 보이는 한 가지 중요한 측면이 있습니다. 상품 시장에서 구매되고 판매되는 상품에는 수명이 있습니다. 밀, 옥수수, 혹은 기타 상품들이 시장에 들어오면 그에 대한 계약은 종료됩니다. 그래서, 음, 투기꾼들은 이윤을 빨리 얻으려 할 때 가까운 장래에 대해 면밀한 조사를 합니다. 상품 시장에서는, 어, 주식 시장에서와 반대로, 장기적인 고려가 이루어지지 않습니다.

상품 시장의 특성 때문에 몇 가지 중요한 일들이 일어났습니다. 먼저 판매

되는 상품이 표준화되었습니다. 그럼으로써 구매자와 판매자들이 무엇을 거래하는지에 대해 혼란이 없었습니다. 다음으로 부패할 수 있는 모든 거래 물품들은, 그에 대한 판매가 차후로 미루어지기 때문에, 충분한 저장 수명을 가지고 있어야 했습니다. 마지막으로 상품의 가격은 고정되지 않았습니다. 가격이 충분히 오르내릴 수 있어서 불확실성이 생겼습니다. 이로써 사람들은 모든 거래에서 수익을 얻거나 아니면 손해를 볼 기회를 얻게 되었습니다. 그것도, 제가 생각하기에, 상품 시장의 매력 중 하나입니다. 막대한 수익을 거둘 수 있는 가능성도 존재하지만, 동시에, 재산을 잃을 위험도 감수해야 합니다. 매일 조금씩 가격이 바뀌는 일은 일상적인 것으로, 이는 상품 투자가에게 막대한 영향을 끼칩니다.

WORD REMINDER

futures market 선물 시장 speculate 생각하다, 추측하다 party 당사자 hub 중심(지) cash crop 환금 작물 ship 보내다, 수송하다 encounter (우연히) 만나다 upper hand 우위, 우세 at the mercy of ~에 좌우되어, ~의 마음대로 settle for ~을 감수하다, (마지못해) ~을 받아들이다 hold out 버티다, 저항을 계속하다 in return for ~에 대한 답례로, ~에 대한 보수로 upfront 솔직한 transaction 거래 contractual 계약상의, 계약에 보장된 collateral 담보(물) change hands 주인이 바뀌다 give birth to ~을 낳다 speculator 투자가, 투기꾼 scrutinize 세밀히 조사하다 perishable 썩기 쉬운 shelf life 저장 수명 fluctuate 변동하다, 오르내리다 allure 매력, 매혹

PART 2

Conversation

p.148

교수: Jim, 찾고 있었어요. 잠깐 안으로 들어오세요. 학생과 이야기를 하고 싶어요.

학생: 오, 안녕하세요, Samson 교수님. 물론 그럴게요. 교수님과 잠깐 이야기할 시간은 있어요. 다음 수업은 30분 후에 있거든요. 필요하신 것이 무엇인가요?

교수: 아직도 아르바이트 자리를 찾고 있나요?

학생: 네? 그걸 어떻게 아셨죠?

교수: 아, 오늘 오후에 Douglas 교수님과 점심을 같이 먹었는데, 그분께서 학생이 교내 아르바이트 자리를 찾고 있다고 말씀해 주셨어요. 학생에 대해 그와 같은 이야기를 했다고 해서 기분 나빠하지는 않았으면 좋겠어요.

학생: 전혀 나쁘지 않습니다. 제가 두 분 교수님 사이의 대화 주제가 되다니 사실 어깨가 으쓱해지는걸요. 그에 대해 생각하니 기분이 좋네요.

교수: 음, 훨씬 더 좋은 것은, 제 생각에, 학생을 위한 기회를 제가 갖고 있다는 점이죠. 제가 4층 화학 실험실을 담당하고 있다는 것을 알고 있죠, 그렇죠?

학생: 네, 누군가로부터 들은 것 같아요. 실험실에 가 본 적은 없지만 몇 차례 지나친 적은 있어요. 1학년과 2학년 학생들을 위한 실험실이죠, 아닌가요?

교수: 맞아요. 그리고 그곳에 가 본 적이 없다고 하더라도 최소한 어디에 있는지는 알고 있겠군요. 어쨌든, 제 실험실 조교 중 한 명이 지난 주에 학교를 그만두었어요. 개인적인 문제가 있었는데… 음, 왜 그가 학교를 떠났는지는 중요하지 않아요. 중요한 것은 그가 떠났고, 저는 실험실 일을 도울 새로운 사람을 찾고 있다는 점이죠.

학생: 좋아요. 제가 정확히 무엇을 하면 되나요?

교수: 대부분의 일이 꽤 평범한 것들이에요. 주로 실험실을 청소하고 물품들이 — 화학 물품 같은 것들이 충분히 있는지를 확인하게 될 거예요.

학생: 알겠어요. 학생들이 수강하는 실험 수업을 이끌 기회가 있을까요?

교수: 음… 이번 학기에는 없어요. 없네요. 유감이군요. 학생에게 그럴 자격이 충분히 있다는 점은 알지만, 그 자리는 모두 채워져 있어요. 제가 학생을 우선시해서 다른 누군가를 밀어내는 것은 공정하지 않은 일이죠.

학생: 네, 무슨 말씀인지 알겠어요. 괜찮아요.

교수: 하지만…

학생: 하지만 무엇인가요?

교수: 학생들이 수업을 받는 동안 실험에 참여할 기회는 있을 거예요. 그래서 다른 조교들이 학생들을 어떻게 가르치는지, 그리고 어떻게 학생들을 상대하는지 지켜볼 수 있을 거예요. 직접적인 경험을 많이 해 볼 수 있을 것이라고 생각하는데, 그러면 다음 학기 실험 수업에서 좋은 자리를 얻을 수 있을 거예요. 즉, 어, 학생이 그 일에 흥미가 있다면요.

학생: 정말로 흥미가 있어요. 저도 고려해 주세요.

교수: 잘 되었군요. 그렇게 말해 주기를 바라고 있었죠. 그러면 실험실에서 근무할 수 있는 시간이 언제인지 알려 줄게요. 오랜 시간 일하는데 관심이 있다면 일주일에 20시간을 근무해도 될 정도로 충분한 자금을 지원받았어요.

학생: 일주일에 20시간이요? 멋지군요. 제가 원했던 근무 시간과 정확히 맞아 떨어지네요.

교수: 오늘 Douglas 교수님과 함께 점심을 먹길 잘 한 것 같군요, 그렇지 않나요?

WORD REMINDER

flattered 우쭐한 sophomore (대학의) 2학년 학생 drop out of school 학교를 그만두다, 중퇴하다 bump 밀어내다 in favor of ~을 좋아해서, ~을 선호하여 hand-on experience 직접 경험 count in 계산에 넣다

Lecture • Literature

p.150

교수: 공상 과학 소설의 주요 소재 중 하나는 시간 여행입니다. 아시겠지만, 어, 시간상 앞뒤로 이동할 수 있는 능력입니다. 알버트 아인슈타인에 의하면 시간 여행에서는 개인이 빛의 속도보다 빠르게 이동해야 하므로 시간 여행은 불가능한 것입니다. 아인슈타인은 빛의 속도를 뛰어넘는 것이 불가능하다고 믿었기 때문에 시간 여행은 불가능한 것이라고 선언했죠. 하지만 아인슈타인은 시간이 상대적인 것이라고도 생각했습니다. 그의 견해를 따르면 사람이 얼마나 빨리 이동하느냐에 따라 시간은 더 빠르게 갈 수도, 혹은 더 느리게 갈 수도 있습니다. 예를 들어 어떤 사람의 이동 속도가 빛의 속도에 근접하면 그 사람에게 있어서 시간은 느려질 것입니다. 따라서, 어, 그 사람에게 하루가 지나갔을 때, 정상 속도로 움직이는 사람들은 며칠을 보냈을 수도 있습니다.

저는 그것을 일종의 시간 여행으로 간주할 수 있다고 생각하지만, 아인슈타인은 사람이, 어, 타임 머신이나 그와 비슷한 장치를 사용하여 시간상 앞뒤로 이동하는 것은 불가능하다고 생각했습니다. 반면에 대부분의 공상 과학 소설가들은 아인슈타인과 달리 물리학 법칙이라는 제약에 묶여 있지 않습니다. 사실 많은 공상 과학 소설에서 시간 여행은 중요한 문학적 구성 장치입니다. 오늘은 그러한 두 개의 소설을 간단히 언급하고, 소설 속 인물들이 시간 여행을 위해 사용하는 장치에 대해 설명하고자 합니다.

시간 여행에 관한 글을 쓴 대부분의 작가들은 두 개의 주요한 방법 중 하

나를 사용합니다. 첫 번째는 사람으로 하여금 시간 여행을 할 수 있도록 만드는 기계와 관련된 것입니다. 두 번째는, 흠… 자연적인 방법이라고 할 수 있는 것이죠. 다른 말로 하면 기계와 관련이 없는 것입니다.

먼저 기계와 관련이 있는 두 개의 이야기를 설명해 드리겠습니다… 음, 시간 여행과 관련된 최초의 — 그리고 아마도 가장 유명한 — 작품 중 하나는 H.G. 웰스의 걸작인 *타임 머신*이었습니다. 제 생각에는 여러분 대부분에게 이 소설이 친숙할 것 같습니다. 아니라면 곧 그렇게 될 텐데, 다음 주에 이 소설을 읽고 자세히 논의해 볼 것이기 때문입니다. 소설이 마음에 들 것이라고 생각합니다. 개인적으로 가장 좋아하는 소설 중 하나죠. 어쨌든, 줄거리에 대한 흥미를 뺏지 않는 선에서, 타임 트레블러라고만 알려진 주인공이 기본적으로 의자 형태를 띈 타임 머신을 만들어 냅니다. 타임 트레블러가 의자에 앉으면 그를 미래로 데려다 주는 타임 버블이 만들어집니다. 이야기가 진행되는 동안 타임 트레블러는 자신의 타임 머신을 이용해서 수만 년 앞으로 이동한 후 다시 자신의 시대로 돌아옵니다.

시간 여행을 활용한 또 다른 유명 소설은 *여름으로 가는 문*인데, 이는 공상 과학 소설의 거장인 로버트 하인라인에 의해 쓰여졌습니다. 주인공은 가사 상태에 들어간 후 나이를 먹지 않은 상태로 몇 년 후의 미래에 깨어나게 됩니다. 그 후 미래에 있는 동안 주인공은 사람이나 사물을 과거 혹은 미래로 보낼 수 있는 타임 머신을 발명한 과학자에 대해 알게 되죠. 주인공은 이 타임 머신을 이용해 과거로 돌아오고 자신의 미래가 좋아지도록 만듭니다.

*타임 머신*과 *여름으로 가는 문*은 기계를 이용해 극중 인물들의 시간 여행을 가능하게 만드는 전형적인 공상 과학 소설입니다. 작가가 타임 머신의 일부 측면들을 묘사할 수는 있지만, 기술적인 세부 사항들은 최소한으로 언급됩니다. 하지만 보통 타임 머신 자체는 소설에서 중요한 부분을 차지합니다.

다른 공상 과학 소설에서는 다양한 수단을 통해 시간 여행이 이루어집니다. 마크 트웨인의 소설 *아서 왕국의 커네티컷 양키*를 읽어 본 사람이 있나요…? 흠… 몇 명 되지 않는군요. 음, 그 책이 더 이상 학교 수업에서 다루어지지 않는다고 생각되네요. 트웨인의 소설에서는 행크 모건이라는 주인공이 머리에 충격을 받은 후 과거로 가게 됩니다. 그것이 다예요. 트웨인은 시간 여행의 실제 과정에 대해서는 관심을 갖지 않았습니다. 그리고 그것이, 어, 시간 여행의 자연적인 수단에 의존하는 소설에서 중요한 점입니다. 작가들은 어떻게 시간 여행이 이루어지는지에 대해 많은 관심을 기울이지 않습니다. 그냥 발생하는 것이죠.

또한 보다 현대의 소설도 있는데… 켄 그림우드의 *리플레이*라는 책입니다.

학생: 오, 그 책을 정말 좋아해요. 서너 번 정도 읽었어요.

교수: 아, *리플레이*의 팬이 최소한 한 명은 있다니 기쁘군요. 음, 아직 보지 못하신 분들을 위해 내용을 알려 드리죠. 소설에서 주인공은 심장 마비로 죽지만, 깨어나 수년 전 과거에 있게 됩니다. 그는 인생을 다시 한번 살게 되고 이전 생애에서와 정확히 똑같은 시간에 또 한번 심장 마비를 겪는데, 그런 다음 또 다시 깨어나서 과거로 돌아가지만, 어, 전과 다른 시대에 있게 됩니다. 주인공은 죽고, 깨어나고, 새로운 삶을 살며 자신의 인생을 — 책 제목처럼 — 되풀이합니다. 이 책이 친숙하지 않다면 대출하실 것을 추천합니다.

WORD REMINDER

staple 주요 산물; 요소 exceed 초과하다 elapse (시간이) 경과하다 contraption 고안물, 기묘한 장치 constrain 강요하다, 억제하다 plot device 플롯 장치, 문학적 (구성) 장치 suspended animation 생명 활동의 중단, 가사 상태 heart attack 심장 마비

PART 3

Conversation

p.154

학생: 안녕하세요. 기숙사 방에 문제가 있는데, 기숙사 사감 선생님께서 이곳 사무실을 방문해서 문제를 해결하라고 말씀하시더군요.

생활관 직원: 그래요. 방에 어떤 문제가 있나요?

학생: 문이 열리지가 않아요.

생활관 직원: 음… 문이 움직이지 않는다는 말인가요?

학생: 오, 그렇지 않아요. 그건 아니에요. 잠금 장치에 문제가 있다는 뜻이었어요. 키리스 잠금 장치에 학생증을 대고 PIN 번호를 입력했는데도 아무 일도 일어나지 않아요. 문이 열리지가 않아요. 그리고 제 룸메이트가 방으로 들어올 때에는 전혀 문제가 없기 때문에 잠금 장치가 제대로 작동한다는 점은 알고 있어요.

생활관 직원: 알겠어요. 흠… 학생증을 이용해서 기숙사나 교내 다른 건물들의 출입문을 통과해서 안으로 들어갈 수 있나요?

학생: 음… 솔직히 말씀을 드리면 잘 모르겠어요. 오늘 아침에 문제가 발생했거든요. 8시쯤 화장실에 간 후 방으로 되돌아왔을 때 안으로 들어갈 수가 없었죠. 룸메이트가 아침 식사를 하고 돌아올 때까지 기다린 후에야 들어 갈 수 있었어요. 여러 번 문을 열려고 시도했지만, 아무런 일도 일어나지 않았어요. 그리고, 어, 제가 기숙사를 나선 뒤에는… 음, 하루 종일 수업을 들었기 때문에 아직 그곳에 되돌아 가지는 못했고요. 그래서… 잠금 장치가 문제인지, 제 카드가 문제인지 모르겠어요.

생활관 직원: 제가 학생증을 볼 수 있을까요?

학생: 물론이죠… 여기 있어요.

생활관 직원: 좋아요. 학생의 이름을 컴퓨터 화면으로 불러 올게요… Jason Whitman. W-H-I-T-M-A-N이군요.

학생: 무언가를 찾으셨나요?

생활관 직원: 흠… 네, 문제를 찾은 것 같아요. 아직 등록금을 납부하지 않았군요.

학생: 네?

생활관 직원: 학생 파일에 메모가 달려 있어요. 보아 하니 이번 학기 등록금을 납부하지 않은 것 같은데, 등록금 납부 기간은 어제까지였어요. 매 학기마다 재무처에서 미납 청구서가 있는 학생 명단을 저희에게 보내는데, 어, 그러한 사람들은 등록금을 납부하기 전까지 기숙사 방에 들어가지 못하죠.

학생: 분명히 오류가 있는 것 같군요.

생활관 직원: 무슨 뜻인가요?

학생: 저는 이곳에서 전액 장학금을 받고 있어요. 학교 농구팀에 속해 있기 때문에 제 등록금과 숙식 비용은 모두 지불된 상태죠. 미납된 것은 있을 수가 없어요.

생활관 직원: 흠… 분명 착오가 있는 것처럼 들리는군요. 지금으로서는 제가 도울 수 있는 일이 없어요. 지금 바로 재무처로 가서 이번 문제를 해결할 것을 추천해요. 지금이 3시 정각이기 때문에 그곳에 가면 한 시간 이내로 문제를 해결할 수 있을 거예요. 해결을 해서 다시 이곳으로 오면 제가 기숙사 방으로 들어갈 수 있도록 해 줄 수 있어요. 저희가 5시 반에 문을 닫기 때문에 학생이 필요한 모든 조치를 취할 수 있는 시간이 어느 정도 있어요. 오, 코치 선생님께 연락을 해서 재무처의 사람과 이야기를 나누도록 할 수도 있겠

군요. 그것이 이번 문제를 해결할 수 있는 가장 빠른 방법일 거예요.

학생: 아, 좋은 충고군요. 전화를 한 다음에 바로 재무처로 갈게요. 도와 주셔서 감사합니다.

> **WORD REMINDER**
> keyless lock 키리스 락 (열쇠가 필요 없는 전자식 잠금 장치) Bursar's office (대학의) 재무처, 경리과 full scholarship 전액 장학금 room and board 숙식비 mix-up 혼동, 착오

Lecture • History of Science p.156

교수: 역사를 통해 몇몇 사람들이 다양한 우주의 모델을 제시했습니다. 현재에도 우주 내 지구의 위치에 관한 많은 이론들이 있습니다. 하지만 역사의 상당 기간 동안 두 개의 주된 이론이 존재했습니다. 첫 번째는 지구가 우주의 중심이라고 주장했습니다. 이는 약, 음, 약 16세기까지 가장 널리 인정받았던 우주 모델이었습니다. 16세기는 니콜라스 코페루니쿠스가 우주에 대한 자신의 모델을 제시한 때로, 이 모델에서 지구는 다른 행성과 마찬가지로 태양의 주위를 돌고 있었습니다.

천동설이라고 알려진 이론에 대해 설명함으로써 이야기를 시작하고 싶군요. *Geo*는 그리스어로 지구를 뜻하기 때문에 "geocentric"은 지구가 우주의 중심이라는 개념을 나타낸다는 점을 추측하실 수 있을 것입니다. 천동설은, 그리스와 로마를 포함하여, 고대 사회에서 제시되기 시작했습니다. 가장 유명한 가설 중 하나는 그리스인인 프톨레미의 이론으로, 그는 기원후 90년에서 168년까지 이집트에서 살았습니다. 당시 이집트는 로마 제국의 일부였기 때문에 프톨레미는 로마 시민이었습니다. 고대에 학식이 높았던 많은 사람들과 마찬가지로 프톨레미도 여러 과목에 대한 교육을 받았으며, 그 중 하나가 천문학이었습니다. 그의 유명한 작품 *알마게스트*는 프톨레미가 우주에 대해 알고 있었던 것을 — 혹은 그가 안다고 믿었던 것이라고 해야 할 것 같은데 — 다루었습니다.

*알마게스트*는 13개의 항으로 되어 있었고, 태양, 달, 행성, 그리고 항성의 움직임에 대한 다양한 측면을 다루었습니다. 프톨레미가 살았던 당시 알려진 행성은 목성, 토성, 화성, 금성, 그리고 수성뿐이었습니다. 음, *알마게스트*가 실제로 많은 양의 정보를 담고 있었지만, 그러한 정보의 상당 부분은, 음, 정확히 말하면, 잘못된 것이었습니다. 첫째, 프톨레미는 지구가 우주의 중심이라고 믿었습니다. 둘째, 그는 지구를 제외한 우주의 모든 것들이 지구 주위를 돌고 있다고 생각했습니다. 셋째, 그의 우주에서는 지구가 고정되어 있었고 전혀 움직이지 않았습니다. 넷째, 우주는 둥근 형태였습니다. 다섯째, 달, 태양, 행성, 그리고 항성 모두가 지구를 중심으로 원형을 그리면서 움직였습니다. 이들 원형 중에서 달의 천구가 지구와 가장 가까이에 있었습니다. 그 다음으로 수성, 금성, 태양, 목성, 토성, 그리고 항성들이 순서대로 있었죠. 약간 바뀐 부분도 있었지만, 프톨레미의 우주 모델은 거의 1,500년 동안 인정을 받았던 견해였습니다.

학생: 잘못된 것이 명백했는데 왜 그렇게 오래 지속되었나요?

교수: 음… 오늘날 저와 여러분에게는 명백할 수 있지만, 과거에는 명확하지가 않았습니다. 당시에는 지식이 천천히 전파되고 축적되었다는 점을 기억하세요. 책은 손으로 필사되었고, 이때 오랜 시간이 걸렸기 때문에, 책은 상당히 희귀한 것이었습니다. 프톨레미의 *알마게스트*는 꽤 자주 필사되던 몇 안 되는 책 중의 하나였기 때문에, 그 책에 있는 지식은 여러 지역으로 퍼져 나갈 수 있었습니다. 다른 많은 지역 사람들이 그러했던 것처럼 아랍 사람들도 그의 연구를 사실로 받아들였습니다. 유럽의 중세 시대 동안에도 프톨레미의 견해는 인정을 받았습니다.

하지만 시간이 지나고 사람들이 과학에 대해 더 많이 알게 되자 몇몇 사람들이 프톨레미 및 그의 우주 모델의 타당성에 대한 의문을 제기하기 시작했습니다. 프톨레미의 이론이 천체 움직임의 많은 부분을 논리적으로 설명하지 못한다는 점을 깨달았던 것이죠. 물론 우리는 현재 그 이유가, 프톨레미의 모델에서는, 지구가 실제 움직이는 것과 달리 지구가 움직이지 않는다고 했던 점 때문이라는 것을 알고 있지만, 과거에는 그에 대해 아무도 알지 못했습니다. 단지 프톨레미의 우주에서 무언가 잘못되어 있다는 것만을 알았을 뿐이죠.

하지만 니콜라스 코페루니쿠스가 천체에 대한 자신의 연구를 발표한 1543년이 되자 우주 모델에 대한 강력한 경쟁 모델이 등장했습니다. 코페루니쿠스는 천동의, 즉 태양 중심의 우주를 믿었습니다. 코페루니쿠스가 쓴 책은 *천구의 회전에 관하여*라고 불렸습니다. 이 책에서 코페루니쿠스는 지구가 아니라 태양이 우주의 중심이라고 주장했습니다. 코페루니쿠스의 우주에는 8개의 천구들이 포함되어 있었는데, 즉 항성들에 대한 것 하나, 태양에 관한 것 하나, 그리고 알려진 6개의 행성에 대한 것들이 각각 하나씩 있었습니다. 달은 태양이 아니라 지구를 돌고 있기 때문에 자체적인 천구를 가지고 있지 않았습니다. 코페루니쿠스는 태양이 이동하지 않는다고 믿었고, 행성과 항성 모두는 태양을 중심으로 완벽한 원을 그리면서 움직인다고 생각했습니다.

여기 스크린 위쪽을 봐 주세요. 프톨레미와 코페루니쿠스의 우주를 여기에서 볼 수 있습니다… 몇 가지 유사성이 있다는 점에 주목하시고요… 이 둘 모두에는 그 중심에 고정된 물체가 있습니다. 이 둘 모두 궤도들이, 실제로 행성들이 갖고 있는 것으로 알려진 타원형 형태의 궤도가 아니라, 완벽한 형태의 원형이라고 믿고 있습니다. 그리고 천체 움직임에서 모순되는 부분을 설명하기 위해 이 둘 모두 복잡한 이론과 공식에 의존하고 있습니다.

코페루니쿠스의 책은 널리 읽혀졌고, 그의 이론은 과학계에서 잘 알려지게 되었습니다. 교회를 비롯한 일부 세력들의 저항이 있기는 했지만, 갈릴레오 갈릴레이와 같은 여러 과학자들이 지동설의 발전에 기여를 했습니다. 갈릴레오가 최초로 밤하늘 관측에 사용했던 망원경 덕분에 과학자들은 프톨레미의 우주에 잘못된 측면이 있고 코페루니쿠스의 우주의 일부가 옳다는 점을 입증하기 시작했습니다. 자, 잠시 휴식을 취하기에 앞서, 갈릴레오가 기여한 바에 대해 알아보도록 하겠습니다.

> **WORD REMINDER**
> geocentric 지구를 중심으로 한, 천동설의 notion 개념, 명제 bear in mind 명심하다 veritable 실제의 delicately 섬세하게, 자세하게 cosmos 우주 stationary 고정된, 움직이지 않는 spherical 구형의, 둥근 apparent 명백한 validity 타당성, 유효성 heavenly body 천체 heliocentric 태양 중심의, 지동설의 elliptical 타원(형)의 account for ~을 설명하다 inconsistency 불일치, 모순 contribution 기여, 이바지

Lecture • Microbiology p.159

교수: 마지막 몇 분 동안, 수업을 끝내기에 앞서 한 가지 더 논의해 보도록 하겠습니다. 다양한 환경에서 생물막이 담당하는 역할에 대해 살펴보고자 합니다. 그리고 생물막이란, 어, 유명한 사람에 대한 전기 영화를 말하는 것이 아닙니다. 전기 영화에 대해 공부하고 싶다면, 이곳 건물 아래층에서 Ford 교수님의 영화 수업을 들을 수가 있죠. 우리가 학습하고 있는 생물막은 얇은 막으로 된 생물학적 물질로, 자연적인 혹은 인공적인 물체의 표면에 달라붙는 것입니다. 생물막은 사실상 어떤 자연 환경에서도 발견될 수 있지만, 생존하기 위해서는 습기, 어, 수분을 필요로 합니다. 인공적인 환경의 경우, 생물막은, 몇 가지 장소만 이야기해 보면, 파이프, 욕실 벽면, 유리창, 그리고 선박의 바닥에서 찾아볼 수 있습니다.

생물막은 생물학적인 물질로 형성됩니다. 때때로 균류 및 해조류와 같은 기타 미생물들도 있을 수 있지만, 주로 박테리아입니다. 처음에는 이러한 미생물들이 무작위로 표면에 달라붙습니다. 반데르발스의 힘이라고 알려진 것 때문에 표면에 달라붙을 수 있는 것이죠. 미생물들은 표면에 붙어 있는 동안 변하기 시작합니다. 구조물 표면에 달라붙는 자신만의 방법을 만들어 냅니다. 곧 다른 미생물들이 유인되고, 시간이 지나면, 하나의 층이 형성됩니다. 생물막은 끊임없이 새로운 층을 더해 갑니다. 이러한 모든 층은 매우 얇으며 실제로 육안으로는 볼 수가 없습니다.

층의 수가 증가하면서 EPS라는 물질이 분비됩니다. EPS는 외부 세포 고분자 물질을 의미합니다. EPS는 각각의 미생물들을 서로 연결시켜 주고, 미생물 간의, 일종의, 어, 의사소통을 가능하게 만듭니다. 물론 말을 하는 것은 아닙니다. 생물학적으로 의사소통을 하는 것이죠. 예를 들어 생물막의 바깥쪽 층은 보호 기능을 담당하기 때문에 다른 층보다 중요성이 더 큽니다. 새로운 층이 형성되기까지 마치 방어막과 같은 역할을 하는 것이죠. 그 후에는 새로운 층이 방어막 역할을 물려받게 됩니다.

대부분의 생물막이 해로우며 다양한 질병을 확산시킬 뿐 아니라 인간에게 여러 가지 감염증을 일으키는 원인이 될 수 있다는 점은 놀라운 일이 아닙니다. 보호 기능을 담당하는 바깥쪽 생물막 때문에 안쪽 층에 있는 미생물들은, 이들을 제거하기 위해 사람들이 가장 강력한 항균성 로션 및 살균 제품들을 바르더라도, 생존할 수 있습니다. 실제로 일부 연구에 의하면, 음, 일부 생물막은 시간이 지남에 따라 항균성 클렌징 제품에 대한 내성을 갖게 됩니다. 그 결과 몇몇 경우에 있어서 실제로 생물막이 살균 의료 장비, 식당 테이블, 가정용 파이프, 그리고 기타 중요 장소에 붙어 있을 수 있습니다. 따라서 병원의 수술실과 같은 장소에서도 생물막에 의해 사람이 감염될 수 있습니다.

학생: 생물막이 모든 곳에 존재한다는 말씀이신가요? 심지어 가장 깨끗한 집과 병원에서도요?

교수: 아니요, 전혀 아닙니다. 그런 의미를 나타내려고 한 것은 아니었어요. 생물막이 그러한 장소 중 일부에 존재한다는 점을 말씀드리는 것입니다. 그러나 생물막이 모든 표면에서 발견되는 것은 확실히 아닙니다. 또한 모든 생물막이 치명적인… 혹은 그로 인해 위험하다는 것도 아니라는 점에 주목해 주세요. 예로써, 음, 치태를 들어 봅시다. 치태는 생물막으로 분류됩니다. 하지만 만약 이것이 치명적인 것이라면 우리 모두는 살아 있지 못할 것입니다, 그렇겠죠? 그리고 인체는 감염으로부터 스스로를 보호하기 위한 수많은 수단을 가지고 있다는 점을 기억해 주세요.

좋아요. 그러면 생물막이 항상 치명적인 것은 아니라는 점을 알았습니다. 하지만 그 영향으로 인해 비싼 대가를 치를 수 있습니다. 해마다 생물막 때문에 전 세계적으로 수백만 달러가 낭비되고 있습니다. 일어나고 있는 몇 가지 일들을 알려 드리면… 생물막은 식물에서 자랄 수 있기 때문에 농작물의 밭 전체를 황폐화시킬 수 있는 질병을 일으킵니다. 파이프와 다른 종류의 설비에도 피해를 입힐 수 있습니다. 설비를 부식시켜, 이를 테면 파이프가 터져 버릴 수도 있습니다. 또한 선박의 바닥에도 생물막이 생길 수 있습니다. 이런 일이 발생하면 생물막이 따개비와 같은 생물들을 유인하게 됩니다. 따개비가 선체에 쌓이기 시작하면 선박의 속도가 크게 느려질 수 있습니다. 이로써 선박은 더 많은 연료를 소모하게 되고, 선주는 추가적인 비용을 부담해야 합니다. 생물막 때문에 때때로 선박을 건조한 독에 집에 넣고 바닥에 있는 이러한 생물들을 제거해야 합니다. 오, 생물막은 선박의 구조적 안전성에도 피해를 줄 수 있는데, 이로써 배의 수명이 줄어들게 됩니다.

흥미롭게도 모든 생물막이 나쁜 것은 아닙니다. 실제로 유용한 것들도 있습니다. 예를 들면 하수 처리장에서는 미처리 하수를 걸러내는 필터에 의도적으로 생물막을 기르고 있습니다. 생물막은 하수로부터 유기 물질들을 추출해 내며, 이는, 어, 유기 물질 분해에 도움이 됩니다. 또한 일부 생물막은 해양에 유출된 기름을 제거하는데도 사용됩니다. 일부 생물막의 박테리아는 석유에 있는 탄화수소 분자를 분해시킬 수 있는데, 이로써 물에서 탄화수소가 제거됩니다. 여러분도 짐작할 수 있듯이 과학자들은 생물막을 활용할 수 있는 또 다른 방법들을 찾기 위해 많은 노력을 기울이고 있습니다.

WORD REMINDER

call it a day 그만하기로 하다 biofilm 생물막 cling to ~에 달라붙다 initially 초기에, 처음에 at random 되는대로, 무작위로 naked eye 육안 excrete 배설하다, 분비하다 stand for ~을 상징하다, 나타내다 take over 인계받다, 떠맡다 antibacterial 항균성의 disinfectant 살균제 assuredly 확실하게 dental plaque 치태 wipe out 없애다 barnacle 삿갓조개, 따개비 accumulate 축적하다 hull 선체 dock 부두, 독 scrub 문질러 씻다 integrity 완전한 상태, 온전함 sewage treatment plant 하수 처리장 degrade 가치를 떨어뜨리다, 분해하다

TOEFL® MAP

ACTUAL TEST

New TOEFL® Edition

Listening 1